This book should be returned to any branch of the
Lancashire County Library on or before the date

5\13 Gree		EBU
− 4 FEB 2016 1 9 FEB 2018		

WILLIE WATSON

WILLIE WATSON

A biography of England's most successful double international

Frank Garrick

SPORTS
BOOKS

Published in Great Britain by
SportsBooks Limited
1 Evelyn Court
Malvern Road
Cheltenham
GL50 2JR

© Frank Garrick 2013
First Published February 2013

Cover designed by Alan Hunns.

A catalogue record for this book is available from
the British Library.

ISBN 9781907524349

Print and production managed by Jellyfish Solutions.

This book is dedicated to my wife of 50 years, Franca, and to our sons Robert and Andrew

ACKNOWLEDGEMENTS

From the outset I received the full support and encouragement of the late Mrs Barbara Watson, Willie Watson's widow, and also of their daughter, Val, both of whom were based in South Africa.

I greatly appreciated talking to the late Trevor Bailey, Dickie Bird, Peter Richardson and the late Fred Trueman. I also received help from Ken Taylor, Ted Lester, Doug Insole, Mike Turner and Richie Benaud. I was also encouraged by Neil Robinson of the MCC Library and by David Barber of the Football Association.

Further support came from Johnny Meynell of Halifax Town FC, from Dr Ali Bacher of the South African Cricket Board, from Lindsay Price, archivist of the Colwyn Bay Cricket Club, and from Alan Betts of Fenners of Hull. Last but not least I was advised by Elise Lombard, chief executive of Centurion Park, South Africa.

Contents

INTRODUCTION

THE GREATEST DOUBLE INTERNATIONAL

IT IS AN impossible task to compare sportsmen who played in different eras because so much changes over the years. For example, the role of the gentleman amateur has diminished while the quality of pitches has improved and the number of fixtures has multiplied, especially at Test match level. However, in comparing England's double internationals, it is possible to total the number of caps gained at cricket and football. It is not an infallible judgement but it is a helpful guide.

Only 12 English men have become double internationals over the past 120 years, a number that would almost certainly have reached 14 but for the intervention of two world wars. In either case, it is a remarkably exclusive club.

The first man to achieve this distinction was the Rt Hon Alfred Lyttelton, born in 1857 and capped for a second sport in 1884. He was a future Colonial Secretary in Arthur Balfour's government. The 12th, and almost certainly the last, to join this select band was Arthur Milton, born in 1928, who completed the double in 1958. Lyttelton was an amateur who played football for Old Etonians and cricket for Middlesex. He won four caps at cricket but only one at soccer. Milton was a professional footballer with Arsenal and for 27 years a professional cricketer for Gloucestershire. He gained six cricket caps and one surprise cap at football, when he was selected ahead of Stanley Matthews for a match with Austria in November 1951.

The task is to try to establish who was the greatest of the 12 players. First it is possible to identify two players who gained just a single cap at each game. They are Wally Hardinge, who opened the batting for Kent and scored 75 centuries and played football for Arsenal and Sheffield United. Secondly, John Arnold, an opener for Hampshire and a magnificent cover-point. He played football on the left wing for Southampton and Fulham.

Another double international was Leslie Gay, like Lyttelton a Victorian amateur, who also had a relatively short sporting career. He kept goal for England three times and kept wicket for England once. Four caps in all do not make him a strong candidate but he served Corinthians and Hampshire well.

A much stronger claim for best double international can be made for Reginald 'Tip' Foster. One of seven cricketing brothers, he came to his peak in the Edwardian period. He was a stalwart for the newly emerging Worcestershire club. His greatest claim to fame is that he is the only man to captain England at both games. He was selected for England at cricket eight times and in his first Test innings on tour in Australia he scored 287. He was also a brilliant amateur footballer with wonderful ball control and a powerful shot. He made five appearances for England between 1900 and 1902, all of which then were home internationals.

Of the first five double internationals only one, William Gunn, was a professional sportsman. A mainstay of Nottinghamshire for 24 years, he regularly represented England in the 1890s. He played his football in the same county, mainly for Notts County, and won two caps in 1884. He was chosen as one of *Wisden*'s Cricketers of the Year in 1890 and, in total, he gained 11 cricket caps.

Two dual-internationals had sporting careers which spanned the First World War. John Sharp and Harry Makepeace were linked by representing both Lancashire and Everton. They played together in Everton's FA Cup final success in 1906. Sharp was quick and clever and matured into a fine right winger who won two caps for England. Makepeace was an attacking midfielder who was awarded four England caps. A free-scoring batsman and a good medium-fast, left-arm bowler, John Sharp played in three Tests. Harry Makepeace was an opening batsman, very difficult to remove, and an excellent cover-point. He played in four Tests and became, at 40, the oldest player to score a maiden Test century.

The First World War also interrupted the career of Andrew Ducat, who played 422 times for Surrey. He was an attractive stroke-maker with 52 centuries. When he was informed that he had been chosen to play against Australia, he thought the message was a hoax by a team-mate. That Test at Headingley was his only cricket cap. However, his football career was more successful, as he won three caps in 1910 while playing for Arsenal and then gained three more in 1920 while at Aston Villa. He also captained Villa in their successful Cup final that year played at the newly completed Stamford Bridge.

The ten double internationals considered so far have been awarded between two and 13 caps. However, the final two contenders have gained more than twice the number of caps obtained by their main rivals. Together they stand on 27 each but there the similarity ceases.

From the Victorian era sprang CB Fry of Repton School and Oxford University, a brilliant scholar and multi-talented sportsman. Nearly 50 years later, out of elementary education and the mills and mines of Yorkshire, emerged Willie Watson. At Wadham College, Oxford, Fry won blues in three sports: cricket, football and athletics, while 14-year-old Watson became a trainee upholsterer who had been signed up for Huddersfield Town's 'A' team and who had joined Paddock cricket club in the Huddersfield and District league.

CB Fry's batting blossomed gloriously during the early years of the 20th century. In 1902 he scored six consecutive centuries for Sussex and went on to make 3,147 runs in the season. In 1912, he captained England in a triangular tournament against Australia and South Africa in which he did not lose a match. In total, he was awarded 26 cricket caps over a period of 16 years.

At football, Fry's career was not nearly so distinguished. After success at Repton School, he won a football blue at Oxford but his team was thrashed 5-1 by Cambridge. Later, at the age of 29, he joined a successful professional club, Southampton, in order to receive more press coverage and so impress the England selectors. As a fleet-footed full-back, he was welcomed at The Dell, and the team proceeded to win the Southern League. In March 1901, Fry was selected to play against Ireland but his performance was disappointing and he was not chosen again. However, in the following season, he reached the Cup final with Southampton, only to be beaten 2-1 by Sheffield United in a replay.

Willie Watson steadily worked his way through the A team and reserve team of Huddersfield Town and the second XI of Yorkshire Cricket Club so that, at the age of 19 in 1939, he was able to make his debut in the English First Division and in the County Cricket championship. Unfortunately at this point his career was halted for six years by the Second World War. From 1946, Watson had to rebuild his sporting career, now with Sunderland AFC but still with Yorkshire Cricket Club.

Watson's potential for international honours was recognised in a Wartime international against Wales when he played on the left wing. However, a full cap was not obtained until his Sunderland manager converted him from an attacking left winger into a right-sided midfielder. Aged 29, he won the first of his four soccer caps. He also made two appearances for England B, which earned him a place in England's first experience of the World Cup finals in Brazil in 1950. He was skilful, tireless and tenacious but always fair.

In 1951 he gained his first cricket cap against South Africa at Trent Bridge. He was to win 22 more, including Tests against India, Australia, West Indies and New Zealand. He batted in every position from number one to number six. His greatest Test innings came at Lord's in 1953 against the formidable Australian attack spearheaded by Ray Lindwall and Keith Miller. He and Trevor

Bailey held off their opponents for 257 minutes and the match was saved. Watson scored 109 in what was his first Ashes Test.

Willie Watson was a superb natural athlete, who shone as a fielder and as the judge of a quick single. He was a graceful and classical left-handed batsman who was adept on wet or damaged wickets. As he was a professional, he was not considered for the Yorkshire captaincy although he did occasionally stand in when the amateur captain was not available. However, when he moved to Leicestershire, he was captain for four seasons. He was also a soccer captain with Sunderland in 1949–50 when they came closest to winning the First Division title since the War. On his retirement from cricket, he was appointed a Test selector. In 1964, almost 60 years after CB Fry became a *Wisden* Cricketer of the Year, Willie Watson achieved the same distinction.

Therefore, in terms of caps, CB Fry and Willie Watson stand clear on 27 each. Any final selection between the two is largely subjective. My choice is Willie Watson because he was equally good at both games and would undoubtedly have won many more football caps had he not been a contemporary of the legendary Billy Wright. CB Fry was an outstanding cricketer but his football was not quite up to international standard.

Frank Garrick

CHAPTER 1

LATECOMERS

IN 1910 HUDDERSFIELD TOWN Football Club were elected to the Football League Second Division, replacing Grimsby Town. The Town's progress in the five seasons before the First World War was unremarkable. However, some important seeds were sown; one of which was the arrival in 1912 of a young man from Bolton Upon Dearne, a small village close to Barnsley, called Billy Watson, a former miner.

Billy Watson had made an unlikely debut for the first team in 1912 at right back. In fact, he was a natural left half and established himself in that position in the first team in the spring of 1915. Soon afterwards, League football came to a halt because of the First World War. Once the war was over, Billy Watson became the father of two sons, Albert (1919) and William (1920).

The first post-war season was a dramatic one for Huddersfield Town. On the pitch there was a sustained promotion challenge while in the boardroom there was a takeover bid from Leeds. The West Yorkshire rivals had lost their league status because of financial irregularities. However, Huddersfield preserved their independence and gained promotion to football's top flight.

Crucial to the club's future success was the appointment of Herbert Chapman, initially as assistant manager in January 1921 and subsequently as manager in April. His exceptional managerial talents were first revealed at Northampton Town. His successes were repeated at Leeds City during the wartime competitions.

Chapman was a shrewd businessman, a superb publicist and a powerful motivator. He was also a strict disciplinarian, which was soon apparent to Billy Watson. Chapman introduced a clause into the players' contract that they 'must reside in Huddersfield as soon as a suitable house can be found'. Consequently, the Watson family moved from Bolton Upon Dearne to Huddersfield when Albert was two-and-a-half and Willie 18 months. Another clause stated that Huddersfield players could not become publicans.

Above all, Chapman brought to his management style a requirement that he would control all team matters. He determined transfer deals and selected the team in an era when chairmen and directors dominated such decisions. Chapman was way ahead of his time, the forerunner of Busby and Cullis in the years after 1945. His impact was immediate. Experienced Aston Villa inside forward Clem Stephenson, aged 31, was acquired and the club again reached the Cup final. Billy Watson had played a crucial part in an earlier match when he scored a last-minute equaliser at Burnley. The final against Preston North End was a disappointing match decided by a disputed penalty scored by Billy Smith for Huddersfield.

In the League that cup-winning season, Huddersfield Town had managed to come only 14th, but in the following season, 1922–23, Chapman's blend of experience and shrewd signings, like Billy Watson's, began to produce results, as Huddersfield finished third behind champions Liverpool and Sunderland. However, this achievement was just a prelude to even greater success. They were on the threshold of greatness but this would be the closest league competition ever.

During the season, Billy Watson played in 42 matches at left half. He was a key member of a powerful halfback line with David Steele and Tom Wilson. Watson was seen by supporters as an essential part of the team. He was a tough, no-nonsense Yorkshireman with broad shoulders and thick legs. However, he was again frustrated by the manager's rules when his request to become the manager of a billiard hall in Huddersfield was refused.

During the season 1923–24, Cardiff City proved to be Huddersfield's closest rivals. At the end of October, the two clubs jointly headed the League on 17 points (only two points for a win). In the New Year, Billy Watson chose the fixture at Huddersfield's Leeds Road home against Cardiff as his benefit match. Unfortunately, a near blizzard cut the gate to 18,000, so his collection was reduced, but Cardiff were beaten. By Easter, Huddersfield Town were three points behind Cardiff, with a game in hand.

On the final day of the season, Huddersfield were one point behind but faced a home match against Nottingham Forest, while Cardiff were away to Birmingham City. At this point, supporters turned their attention to the system of goal average, which would determine the title if points were equal. Dividing the goals scored by the goals conceded produced very similar goal averages for the two clubs. All Cardiff needed to do was win but, at halftime, they were drawing 0-0 at Birmingham. At Huddersfield, the home team led 1-0. Communication between the two grounds was quite basic but telephone calls allowed Huddersfield fans to be informed about Cardiff's progress. During the second half, Cardiff were awarded a penalty but two of their senior players declined to take the vital kick. Len Davies stepped up to take responsibility only to see his shot comfortably saved by Dan Tremelling. The score remained 0-0. Meanwhile at Huddersfield, two goals were added by the home team to make the victory 3-0. After the final whistle there was a very tense wait for the Huddersfield supporters before the Cardiff result was confirmed as a goalless draw. This was to be the most desperate calculation most fans had ever experienced. The maths showed that Huddersfield were champions with a superior goal average of 0.024 of a goal. Huddersfield had scored 60 and conceded 33, while Cardiff had scored 61 and conceded 34. Today, using goal difference, the clubs would be equal, but Cardiff would be champions by scoring one more goal. The present system favours attacking teams while the 1920s system rewarded defensive tactics.

Under Herbert Chapman's inspired leadership, Huddersfield were in no mood to relinquish the title. From November 15 1924, when they were beaten 1-0 at Bolton Wanderers, until early May, Huddersfield lost only once in the league – at West Ham on January 17 – and took their second successive title by two points from West

Brom. It was the first time a title-winning side had gone through the season without conceding more than two goals in a match, which showed Chapman's inclination towards defensive excellence. The versatile Billy Watson even took over in goal during a game in which the 'keeper was injured and 'played as if to keep the jersey forever' (*Huddersfield Examiner*). Watson was also dropped after 90 consecutive appearances but was back after a week. He would miss only two more games in the next season and a half.

Much to everyone's shock and surprise, at the end of the season Herbert Chapman resigned. Perhaps as surprising was his choice of new employer – the Arsenal. By 1925, no London club had won the First Division title and the capital boasted only two FA Cup triumphs, both by Tottenham Hotspur.

On July 2 1925, Huddersfield Town's board appointed a new secretary-manager, Cecil Potter, formerly manager of Derby County. Before leaving, Chapman had advised the Huddersfield board that three positions needed strengthening. Surprisingly, one of these was left half, where Billy Watson had been such a regular choice. Perhaps Chapman still resented Billy Watson's attempt to become manager of the Adega billiard hall. For Cecil Potter, Chapman must have seemed like a hard act to follow, especially as a third consecutive title had never been achieved. But Potter had something else to cope with – the biggest change in laws since 1891, when the penalty kick was introduced. The new offside law reduced from three to two the number of players required to be between the opposing attacker and the goal when the ball was passed forward.

In spite of this, Cecil Potter coped well both with his legacy at Huddersfield and the new law. Huddersfield Town opened the new 1925–26 season with an unbeaten run of ten matches. By Christmas, they were third in the table, five points behind Herbert Chapman's Arsenal. In early February, Huddersfield took over the leadership and by the end of March a third league title was virtually assured. The triple title had been achieved and the local press hailed the outcome as 'monumental' (*Examiner*). The fact was that an unglamorous club from a modest West Yorkshire mill town had reached a goal that had proved to be beyond the reach of all the major clubs over the past 34 seasons. What is more, they might easily have won a fourth title the next season. Only one win in the last seven matches meant they finished second to Newcastle United. Billy Watson's contribution to Huddersfield's triple success was immense. With only four games missed over the title years, he made the most appearances for Huddersfield Town. In total he played in more than 400 matches for the club, including wartime games. In a career spanning 14 years, he was unlucky never to be selected for England or the Football League, or even for an England trial. He lost his first-team place during the 1926–27 season but continued on the playing staff for another 12 months. Then he joined the coaching staff but, in 1929, he left the club's employment. However, by then, Albert and Willie Watson, aged ten and nine, were waiting in the wings. They would not be long in following in their father's footsteps.

CHAPTER 2

GROWING UP IN THE PADDOCK

WHEN BILLY WATSON moved his family from Bolton Upon Dearne they settled in the Paddock district and later the boys attended the Paddock Council School. Both grew up to be accomplished sportsmen, particularly keen on cricket and football. Their keenness was rewarded with a great deal of talent in both games. Mr Shaw, the Paddock School sports master, went out of his way to encourage Willie in his interest in football, while for school cricket, Mr Whitwam was equally supportive.

The school had a one-hour-and-50 minute lunch break. The aim of the schoolboys was to maximise the amount of time which could be spent at football or cricket on the recreation ground. In order to speed up the process, Willie was often found to have 'borrowed' Albert's bike after bolting down his dinner.

At that time, Willie's sporting heroes were Yorkshire's Maurice Leyland, Duleepsinhji of Sussex and Somerset's Arthur Wellard at cricket, and Alf Young and Dave Magnall of Huddersfield Town at football. Willie only saw his father play once for Huddersfield Town, right at the end of his career, when a persistent ankle injury re-occurred.

Willie was soon challenging for a place in the school team. Once this was achieved, the next step was a trial for Huddersfield schoolboys. It was this ambition which caused young Willie one of the biggest dilemmas of his life. At the age of 12 he and the other pupils at Paddock School sat the scholarship exam for entrance to the grammar school already attended by brother Albert. When the results were published, Willie had also made the grade, so could follow in his brother's footsteps. But he refused. At that time grammar school boys were not eligible to play for the town's schools' team. Willie was determined to play for the Huddersfield Boys Football Team. Surprisingly, perhaps, he got his own way, and the possibility of secondary and higher education was rejected in order to play for Huddersfield Boys. It may seem like a juvenile decision but Willie Watson does not appear to have regretted it. In his autobiography he posed the question, 'If I had gone to the Grammar School, would I ever have become a double international? Remember, there have only ever been 12 of us.'

And, anyway, in 1931–32, he had set his heart on playing for Huddersfield Boys. In fact, Willie went one step further in his schoolboy football career by being selected for a trial for Yorkshire Schools. The match was played at Selby but he did not make the county team.

In cricket, similar progress was made and Willie was chosen for the school team. In a match against a rival school, the Paddock batsmen came up against an aggressive fast bowler who Willie thought more intimidating than he later found Ray Lindwall, Keith Miller or Frank Tyson. Nevertheless, Willie defended well and was the only player to be praised at Mr Whitwam's team talk. It was not long before he was captaining the school cricket team. From there, he progressed to the town's schools cricket XI and eventually he made an appearance for Yorkshire schools against Lancashire at Nelson. Unfortunately he only made a few runs and was not selected again.

Just after his 14th birthday in Easter 1934, Willie left school. Now he faced the cold, hard world of employment in the recessionary pre-war years. He attended an interview at Rippon Brothers, the local motor coach building company, for the post of an upholsterer. The interview was intimidating but he was offered the job, which he accepted without knowing the wage. It turned out to be seven shillings (35p) per week, less than half what he had hoped for. But nobody turned down a job in Huddersfield in the 1930s. Before any upholstering was undertaken, the younger workers were required to sweep out the workshop and remove the rubbish to the yard and burn it. This job caused Willie one of the most serious injuries of his life. The mixture of rubbish, oil and unsupervised teenagers led to Willie's trouser leg catching fire. He fled back into the works where one of the men beat out the fire. Willie's first thought was whether he would be fit for the local league cup final, due to be played that evening. His leg was burned from ankle to knee and he was not fit for 32 weeks while the local infirmary treated the wound. Fortunately, a full recovery was made and the injury never interfered with his sporting career.

As soon as Willie Watson reached the age of 15, Huddersfield Town signed him as an amateur. He played several games for the A team, which must have been well received, because he was invited to play for the mid-week league team. This was the usual route for promotion to the club's second team, which played in the Central League. The match was away against Leeds United; Willie asked his firm for time off, but they refused on the grounds that they had indulged him too much already. So Willie made the bold decision to end his short career as an upholsterer.

Although Billy Watson had moved into the hotel business, he continued to be involved with Huddersfield Town, in charge of their A team. While he showed his son no favours, it did mean that Willie would get every chance to show his potential. Billy Watson is remembered as a modest, unassuming man who shied away from the limelight. But for young Willie, there was no great praise or plaudits, just an examination of any mistakes and how to put them right. Quite hard for the youngster at the time, but much appreciated in the longer term. Elder brother, Albert, was also a promising footballer, and making progress at Huddersfield Town.

Eventually, Willie joined the club's ground staff. This involved a mixture of football experience and hard work. His duties included helping to clean up the ground after matches; assisting the groundsmen to replace the divots kicked out of the pitch and acting as an odd-job man. More to his taste, there were regular training sessions and lots of contact with the club's star players. This meant he became fully involved in all aspects of the club.

During this period, Willie Watson did not neglect his cricket. He joined the Paddock Cricket Club, which played in the powerful Huddersfield League. His progress was noted as he established himself in the second XI. It was over a Whitsun weekend that his breakthrough came. The match for the second XI was against Primrose Hill, played in the morning. Willie was a success with the bat and took a hat-trick so the club decided to plunge him into the first XI by driving him to a match in the afternoon. At this stage, Willie still considered himself an all-rounder, bowling right arm and mixing spin and swing. As a schoolboy, he had even kept wicket if the opportunity arose.

Willie Watson was soon making a good impression with the Paddock first team. His progress was noted beyond the district, as cricketing talent could never be hidden for long in Yorkshire. This was exemplified at an important cup match against Lascelles Hall. The match was spread over several evenings and Willie made an impressive 122 not out in the first innings. On the second evening, when Willie was padding up for the second innings, he was told that Mr Cross of the Yorkshire committee was in attendance. Willie's reaction was to wish Mr Cross had been there for his century. Perhaps not unsurprisingly, Willie's second innings was less impressive, but Mr Cross must have seen something he liked because shortly afterwards there was an invitation to Willie to attend the nets at Headingley. This was the goal of every young cricketer in Yorkshire. It was the first step on the road to county cricket.

There was also progress in Willie Watson's football career because on his 17th birthday he signed professional terms for Huddersfield Town. By this time, Aussie Campbell was his great hero, but there were many other fine professionals at the club, like Ken Willingham, Alf Young, George Mountford and Eddie Boot. Also important was the influence of coach Ted Magner, who insisted his players 'mastered the ball'. Willie was starting to make regular appearances for the second team; however, brother Albert was beginning to break into the first team.

In fact, Albert would become linked to one of the most extraordinary changes in fortune ever experienced in the top division of the Football League. In the season 1936–37, the First Division title was won by Manchester City, three points clear of Charlton Athletic, while Huddersfield Town only managed 15th. In the following season, when Albert was beginning to get into the Huddersfield team, Manchester City were struggling in the regulation zone. In fact, their survival depended on the result of their final fixture, at home to Huddersfield Town. At left half for Huddersfield was Albert Watson, and the result was a 1-0 defeat for Manchester City. Had Manchester City won, they would have survived because they would have equalled Grimsby's points but would have had a better goal average. One year champions; the next relegated.

The summer of 1938 was an important one for Willie Watson when he was tested in the Yorkshire second XI. It proved to be a traumatic debut – a duck against Cheshire in a Minor Counties match at Barnsley. By contrast, Harry Halliday, also making his first appearance for the second XI, made an impressive century. The game was won by an innings, so there was no second chance for Willie Watson. However, Yorkshire did not discard him; instead he was thrown into a Roses match against Lancashire Seconds at Old Trafford. This was the ideal venue at which to redeem himself but he was quickly dismissed lbw for nought. The second innings was a repeat performance, making three ducks in a row for Willie Watson and 'a pair' against Lancashire. Happily, the Yorkshire committee had faith in him and John Nash, the secretary, wished him 'Good luck' on the printed card which notified him that he had been selected again. This sympathetic gesture must have worked because Willie made 63 and his career was salvaged. He had also resisted the offer from his captain to bat lower down the order because he thought such a move would be an admission of defeat, something which was never acceptable in sport. So he had opened as usual.

It was soon time for Watson to resume his football career at the start of the 1938–39 season. Huddersfield Town remained a major power in English football. In the previous season, they had again reached the FA Cup final (for the fifth time between the wars) only to lose to Preston North End through a disputed last-minute penalty. In the new season, Willie Watson's progress was swift. He was chosen for the first team at inside left at Portsmouth on September 10. His left-wing partner was Pat Beasley, who would be capped by England that season. It was not a promising debut for the 18-year-old. The large crowd was intimidating and his inexperience was evident. He never stopped running but rarely touched the ball, while Portsmouth sailed to a 4-0 victory. Nevertheless, the *Huddersfield Examiner* expressed satisfaction with his progress thus far, and compared his impact with that made by Albert the previous season.

Between December 1938 and February 1939, Albert Watson featured in seven Huddersfield games while Willie had to wait until March 18 for his recall. His home debut was against Middlesbrough, who included the precociously talented Wilf Mannion. Willie was on the left wing with another reserve as his partner. Although a George Camsell goal gave the visitors a 1-0 victory, Willie Watson's performance was a big improvement on his first game, even though he had to go off for treatment to an injury. By this time Huddersfield had reached the FA Cup semi-final against Portsmouth at Highbury. The main question for Willie Watson was: would he keep his place for the semi-final or would Pat Beasley recover from injury in time to play? Willie was in the party which travelled to London but unfortunately for him Beasley played and Huddersfield lost. Even more serious news had arrived from Europe, which announced that the Germans had occupied Prague and that the Czech State had come to an end.

As soon as the semi-final was over, Huddersfield had to turn their attention to a difficult relegation battle involving Leicester City, Birmingham City and Chelsea. Willie Watson played in the last ten League fixtures on the left wing and Huddersfield survived with 36 points, fourth from bottom, their lowest place in the First Division. While battling to remain in the top division, Huddersfield contested the semi-final of the West Riding Cup against Halifax on April 27 1939. Willie Watson was one of only two first-team players chosen but at left half was Albert. The Watsons helped secure a 1-0 victory. During the season, Willie Watson had played for the Huddersfield Town A team, the reserve team and the first team. He was still only 19.

As the summer of 1939 approached, storm clouds were gathering over Europe. There was a state of nervousness in Britain which meant there was little enthusiasm for the new cricket season. Willie began the season in the second XI and it was not until August that his chance of promotion came. He was playing at Old Trafford against Lancashire's second team when a message was received that he was needed at Leicester because some of the senior professionals were injured. This was the great opportunity which all Yorkshire cricketers dreamed of, a debut in the first XI. The nearness of war was evident in Leicester where they were holding a blackout test. Willie Watson had walked a girl home after a dance when at midnight all the lights went out. Locating his hotel was difficult enough but when he finally found it inevitably it was locked. Willie was anxious not to reveal his nocturnal activities to senior players in the lounge, so, with the cooperation of the night porter, he was smuggled back to his room. Obviously not the recommended activity the night before your county baptism!

Next day, things were still not working to plan – the wicket was wet (left uncovered in those days). Yorkshire had soon lost three wickets including Len Hutton, and Leicestershire's Jack Walsh was turning the ball both ways. It was an alarming start for Watson as his first ball unexpectedly turned out to be an off-break, beat him and shaved the stumps. Nevertheless, Watson survived long enough to score 30 and impress JM Kilburn, who wrote in the *Yorkshire Post*, 'His bat was notably straight. He played a most useful and encouraging innings.'

There were only a couple more opportunities for Willie Watson that summer before the situation in Europe put a stop to his emerging sporting career. However, Yorkshire managed to win the County cricket championship for the 21st time.

CHAPTER 3

A CAREER ON HOLD

ON SEPTEMBER 1, the German government in Berlin announced that Poland had rejected Hitler's terms. The following day the British government delivered an ultimatum to Berlin and ordered the mobilisation of the Armed forces. The day after that Prime Minster Neville Chamberlain broadcast that Britain was now at war with Germany. Over these three days, Huddersfield Town played at Brentford, their third fixture of the season, while for Yorkshire Hedley Verity took seven Sussex wickets for nine runs in a nine-wicket victory. Huddersfield's match in London coincided with the mass evacuation of children from the capital. At Fulham and Arsenal, kick-off times were delayed to allow the evacuation to proceed efficiently.

Within a week of Chamberlain's broadcast, the Football Association announced that all football under its jurisdiction would be suspended until further notice. All contracts between clubs and players were suspended, although the clubs retained the players' registrations. The result was that all professional footballers, including Willie Watson, were out of work. Those players who had joined the Territorial Army or other national service organisations in the season 1938–39 were liable to swift call-up to the forces while others had to wait for the call-up. Most Huddersfield players found work in the area or close to their homes.

The total blackout of civilian football lasted only a few days as approval for friendlies in areas specified as safe could be granted by the local police. On September 15 1939, Huddersfield Town played a friendly against Barnsley, whom they had not met in the League since 1919–20. Huddersfield were able to field practically a full team, except that Willie Watson filled a vacancy at centre forward. He scored in a 2-1 defeat. The players received no payment and the crowds were limited to 8,000 or half the ground capacity, whichever was smaller.

Huddersfield's first friendly at home was against Sheffield United on September 22, just about the time when the Football Association announced that they supported friendly and competitive matches confined to localities and played on Saturdays or Bank Holidays. For this game, Watson was moved to the more familiar position of inside left, but it did not affect the outcome which was another 2-1 defeat. At Crewe, on October 2, the Football League finalised their plans for regional competitions to begin on October 21. The menu of friendly games arranged thus far had not inspired much enthusiasm. Even what Willie Watson described as 'phony regional leagues' would prove more entertaining to the public.

Six clubs, including Aston Villa, Derby County and Sunderland, decided not to participate in the regional leagues. There were ten leagues in 1939–40, each with between nine and 12 clubs. Huddersfield Town were allocated the north east League, which had 11 clubs drawn from Yorkshire, Durham and Northumberland.

An early sign of how wartime football would survive was the announcement, in the *Huddersfield Examiner* for October 6, that among the 12 chosen to play against Blackburn Rovers was a mysterious 'AN Other.' This turned out to be the Sunderland and England forward, Raich Carter. His club was not participating, so he was able to play as a guest for Huddersfield (although many thought he was travelling unnecessarily far, as Newcastle and Hartlepool were so much closer). More important to the Huddersfield supporters was the way in which Carter and Watson combined to produce a 5-0 victory over Blackburn. The *Examiner* claimed that Raich Carter's presence '...helped us better to appreciate the natural football arts of Willie Watson, who followed his mentor's promptings in the most able manner and his own with great originality.'

Competitive football returned to Leeds Road on October 21 with a visit from Bradford Park Avenue. Huddersfield recorded their first win in wartime competition by four goals to one. Guest star Carter and homegrown Watson shared the goal scoring. In the period leading up to the end of 1939, Huddersfield lost only one game in eight and were a close contender with Newcastle for the title. A feature of the friendly game against Doncaster Rovers was the promotion of Albert Watson to join Willie in the first team. On this occasion the brothers were part of a well-beaten team. In the New Year of 1940, they were team-mates again in mid-January against Grimsby. Willie scored but the match was abandoned after 70 minutes because of the harsh weather.

In fact, the severe weather caused widespread postponements in January and February 1940, so that eventually the season had to be extended. On many occasions, Willie Watson was selected to play at centre forward, but the *Examiner* believed his creative powers had more scope when he played at inside forward.

Late in January it was announced that Len Hutton had joined the Army. He hoped to become a Physical Training Instructor. Yorkshire cricketers Sutcliffe, Sellers, Verity, Bowes, Leyland and Smailes had already enlisted and it would not be long before Willie Watson joined them.

A key match in the north east Regional League came on March 8 1940 when Huddersfield visited Newcastle United. These clubs led the table and Huddersfield's 5-3 victory was crucial to their challenge. Willie Watson had registered for military service in the morning, having reached his 20th birthday, and then contributed to several of the five goals. But the greatest satisfaction must have gone to Raich Carter, scoring three times against his old club's greatest rivals. However, Carter's successful spell at Huddersfield Town was about to end because he was appointed a permanent member of the Sunderland Fire Brigade, which would involve shifts and weekend duties. By early April, Huddersfield were clear leaders of the north east regional league, a position they would hold until the end of the season. Meanwhile, the news from Europe worsened as Hitler invaded Norway and Denmark. Denmark was soon in

German hands while the Allies pledged full support to Norwegian resistance.

On April 18 1940, Willie Watson joined the army but, a week later, he was back to lead the Huddersfield Town forward line in a cup tie with Chesterfield, '...where he frequently showed how good his command of the ball is' (*Examiner*). Eventually, Huddersfield were defeated in the third round by West Ham. Clearly, by early May 1940, restrictions on teams' travel had been eased and Huddersfield were champions in the north east region.

The Second World War, like the first, disrupted cricket. The Yorkshire County Cricket Club remained in being, without attempting any of its usual functions. No county games were organised and the game survived in the Leagues, the most powerful of which was the Bradford League. For four seasons there was no first-class cricket in England.

For Willie Watson, the summer of 1940 was dominated by army training, so cricket became irrelevant. This was particularly disappointing for him because he had been close to establishing himself in the Yorkshire team. The same regrets were felt about his football career, where he had just become a first-team regular at Huddersfield, although without identifying his best position. During the first season of regional football, he had played in four of the five forward positions, but not inside right. Like all other professionals in the armed services, Willie attempted to reach his official club but when this was not possible the aim was to guest for a team within reach. In the season 1940–41, Willie Watson only managed four games for Huddersfield, which now played in the Northern region. This proved to be one of the most arduous seasons in the whole war.

Winston Churchill was the Prime Minster and the 'Phoney War' was over. The Battle of Britain was fought in the skies over southern England. Close to the action was Willie Watson, in the sense that he guested 15 times for Bournemouth and Boscombe. The club struggled in the League, winning only nine of their 27 matches. Clubs played as many southern fixtures as they could arrange and Luton and Watford managed 35 each, while Swansea played only ten. League positions were calculated on goal average, not points. Bournemouth on 0.641 came 29th out of 34 teams. The winners on 1.95 goal average were Crystal Palace. In the Cup, Bournemouth lost in the first round to Spurs over two legs on aggregate 10-2.

Again, in the season 1941–42, Willie Watson was able to make only four appearances for Huddersfield. Even his games for Bournemouth were restricted to ten matches, but the club managed only 18 games that season and failed to qualify for the first round of the cup. In total, Watson would make 25 guest appearances for Bournemouth during the war, scoring only once in a 5-2 defeat against Southampton.

The season 1942–43 coincided with a new posting further north, not far from Manchester airport, which allowed Willie Watson to turn out regularly for Huddersfield Town. He was able to get home for 28 of the club's 37 North League fixtures. The season was divided into two League competitions either side of Christmas and Huddersfield were prominent in both league tables. Unfortunately, they were eliminated in the first round of the cup by Bradford Park Avenue on aggregate by three goals to two.

While servicemen needed to get accustomed to guesting in strange surroundings and to unreliable wartime rail services, there was plenty of military football. Company teams, regimental teams and divisional teams turned out regularly. In the army there were lots of talented footballers, former full-time professionals, non-league professionals and those from senior amateur clubs. Many were well-established First Division players in their mid and late twenties, sometimes with pre-war full caps, like Stan Cullis, Cliff Britton and Frank Swift. Also, from the start of the war, there was a proliferation of representative matches where new talent could be tested. One of the earliest examples was a match between a Football League XI and an All British team in November 1939 at Goodison Park. Most of these games were played for charities such as the Red Cross.

Through these service games and regional competitions, those professionals like Albert and Willie Watson, who were just establishing themselves in the game, had the chance to progress their careers. However, if like Albert, who had joined the RAF, they were posted abroad, then their development would be put on hold. For Willie Watson, in the season 1943–44, Army football must have dominated because he managed only seven games for Huddersfield, scoring three goals, plus one lone appearance for Nottingham Forest.

A new posting for Watson at Kimmel Camp, St Asaph, near Rhyl, meant that, in the season 1944–45, he did most of his guesting for Wrexham. He played 13 times in North Wales and the same number for Huddersfield. His debut for Wrexham was at Anfield in October 1944, where the visitors won 3-0. By this time, he had also represented the Army's Western Command, plus two guest appearances for Burnley. With the Western Command team, he met for the first time Billy Wright, Bert Sproston (Manchester City) and Jack Rowley (Manchester United).

When on leave in Huddersfield in 1943, Willie Watson met Barbara Smith at a dance at the Huddersfield Town Hall. Barbara was 18 while he was 23. Barbara's parents were members of the Huddersfield Town Football Club and she can remember when she could be brought in to matches at three-quarters' time for free. So Barbara knew who Willie Watson was when she met him, although she was not from the Paddock area and she had not gone to the same school. In September 1944 they were married at Barbara's parish church, St Andrew's in Huddersfield. After the marriage, she continued to live in her parents' house while Willie went back to camp. But it was not Willie who returned to the Army but Bill, because that was what he asked her to call him. In fact, many of his closest sporting colleagues, especially those in the north, always called him Bill. Nevertheless, to the wider public and press, he was usually 'Willie'. At the time the couple were courting, Barbara's future father-in-law, Billy Watson, was running the Walpole Hotel on the outskirts of Huddersfield. She remembers him as a 'lovely guy, unassuming and modest who shied away from the limelight'. The new Mr and Mrs W Watson did not move into their first home together in Huddersfield until August 31 1945.

CHAPTER 4

THE ITALIAN JOB AND SWISS CAPS

IN THE SPRING of 1945, the FA was sufficiently aware of Willie Watson's progress to select him for the party to tour Italy in May. The war in Europe was virtually over and the FA party was being sent to entertain the troops after the tough Italian campaign. An 18-strong group was ordered to report to Paddington's Great Western Hotel on May 5. Willie felt overawed in the company of such famous internationals as Tommy Lawton, Joe Mercer, Frank Swift and Matt Busby. The hotel manager had received news from the radio that the German forces in north-west Europe had surrendered to Field Marshal Montgomery, so he ordered the hotel's floodlights to be switched on.

The tour was to last from May 6 to June 2, except for those chosen to play in the international at Wembley (Lawton and Mercer) against France on May 26. The party left England from Swindon by a Warwick aircraft. To avoid any lingering danger zones, the plane flew across the Bay of Biscay down to Corsica and across to the Bay of Naples, landing at Pomigliano airfield after five-and-a-half hours.

Tuesday May 8 was spent being fitted out with khaki drill uniforms and sightseeing around the remains of Pompeii. It was not until the evening that they learned that it was 'Victory in Europe Day'. The King's speech was heard on the radio at the

Ensa Show they were attending. The first match, against the No 3 Army District, was won easily by the visitors 6-0 before the biggest crowd seen at the Vomero Stadium. Next day, they were on the road to Rome by lorry. The journey was hectic and alarming over hilly terrain recently fought over by large armies. En route they passed Cassino, scene of a vicious and destructive battle in which thousands had been killed only months before. The famous hill-top monastery and the town were devastated by the war. This was a depressing journey.

Once in Rome, they were shown round the Vatican and together with other servicemen were given an audience by the Pope. Next day, a large crowd of servicemen filled the stadium to see the visitors play a representative army team and triumph again, 10-2. The next stage of the tour involved crossing Italy from the Mediterranean coast to the Adriatic coast at the port of Ancona, a long, tortuous journey but ending with a warm welcome from the Italian citizens, who were out on a Sunday afternoon to watch the town's cross-country race. This time the local servicemen, led by Jesse Pye, future England international, were beaten 7-1.

Soon the party moved on up the coast to the resort of Rimini. Here, the opponents, including Bryn Jones, who had cost Arsenal a world record fee of £14,000 when he joined from Wolverhampton Wanderers in 1938, were expected to be the toughest. This proved to be the case as the FA team had a hard-won victory by 2-0. Tommy Lawton thought that Willie Watson, Billy Elliott and Joe Bacuzzi played extremely well in trying conditions. Refereeing the match was the former Huddersfield and Scottish winger, Alex Jackson, a contemporary of Willie's father and now an Army captain.

The next destination was Florence and again the journey was mountainous with the narrow roads frightening, the lorry wheels apparently only inches from steep precipices. On arrival, lunch was served at Forli, the Dorchester hotel of Italy, now taken over by the NAAFI to provide everything for troops on leave. Sightseeing included the famous 'Duomo' and the Piazza. The next fixture was played at the magnificent Florence stadium against the 5th Army. Unfortunately, it was at this game that a little unpleasantness crept into the proceedings. As the local Army team fell behind, there was some barracking for the visitors. 'Come on the real soldiers!' came the shouts, followed by the ironic 'Come on the D-Day dodgers', a reference to the visitors' home postings. This kind of welcome seemed to make the FA XI more determined because they won by 10-0 (Lawton 4). Both Watson and Lawton found this hard to take at the time but were quick to understand the spectators' frustration. They had fought through a bitter battle in Italy for the Allies and were anxious to get home.

The visitors had the magnificent half-back line of Matt Busby at centre-half, flanked by England internationals and Evertonians Cliff Britton and Joe Mercer. After the match, the two teams met up at the exclusive Riverside Club for a couple of hours and there were no hard feelings.

On Tuesday May 22, the tour moved on with a 14-hour return trip to Rome via Pisa and Leghorn. Once again, there were opportunities to visit the historic sites of the Eternal City. When the party arrived at the ruins of the Roman Coliseum, Willie Watson was heard to say, 'The RAF didn't half give this place a bashing.' Tom Lawton explained this as a dry-witted comment from the Yorkshire man. A less generous interpretation was that the visitor was not aware of the building's 2,000 years of history. The next day, the party was on the move again back to Naples and the conclusion of the tour.

The Football Association's War Emergency Committee met on May 3 and 4 1945, faced with a long agenda, but where item 140 stood out. It was an invitation from the Swiss Football Association to send an England team to play a Switzerland XI on July 21 1945 to celebrate the Swiss FA's Jubilee Anniversary. The Emergency Committee agreed, in principle, to send a team, military conditions permitting. The committee meeting on June 26 discussed the latest Swiss proposals, which were to play two matches in Switzerland. It was noted that the travel arrangements were not yet complete; nevertheless, it was decided to purchase a piece of Wedgwood 'in appropriate design' to be presented to the Swiss FA.

The Services Association Committee had reported transport difficulties by rail and sea and decided to recommend to the War Emergency Committee that the Tour be organised by the Services Association, who would request the RAF to arrange an airlift.

Once again, Willie Watson found himself in the company of a party of established star players like Tom Lawton, Joe Mercer and Frank Swift. The main difference from the party to Italy was that this time all the players were English. The two matches against Switzerland were arranged for July 21 and 24 and were included initially with the 'Victory Internationals' arranged in the season 1945–46.

One of the selected players, Tom Finney, was serving in Italy and was awoken in the middle of the night by the arrival of a telegraph from the FA requesting his release from the Army to play for England in the unofficial international.

This invitation came out of the blue and for a while Tom Finney thought he must be dreaming. He thought to himself that he was an inexperienced footballer, stationed in a foreign country miles from home, and he was being told that he was chosen to play for his country! Reality soon sank in with a long haul back to England via the Austrian border and Naples.

As the war in the Far East was not over, and because Switzerland was a neutral country, the tour party was instructed to wear civilian clothes. At short notice, the RAF had no suitable aircraft to transport the players and officials. The games were close to cancellation but the Swiss authorities rescued them by providing a Swiss air flight, the first to land in England since 1939. When the FA party landed in Zurich they were mobbed: the hospitality was overwhelming. Apart from the tremendous reception from the people, this was a country which was a total contrast to wartime Britain. The shops were full of goods and the food was plentiful. The visitors were taken by train to the capital, Berne, for the first match. Willie Watson was not chosen but the party was able to field a team of full internationals or wartime internationals: Frank Swift; Laurie Scott, George Hardwick; Frank Soo, Neil Franklin, Joe Mercer (captain); Tom Finney, Bert 'Sailor' Brown, Tommy Lawton, Doug Hunt, Leslie Smith. Only

Hunt out of these players failed to win a full cap or victory cap over the next 12 months. The only other serious contenders for a place in the team against the Swiss were Stanley Matthews and Raich Carter, both back in England. It was a very strong England XI.

Before the Berne match, the Swiss had been gathered together for fitness training and tactical planning for three weeks. They proved to be much too fresh and energetic for the jaded English servicemen, who came straight from their various Army and RAF camps. The small ground was packed to capacity (35,000) and, despite a magnificent display of goalkeeping by Swift, the Swiss won comfortably 3-1. One of their goals was scored by their captain, Lauro Amado, who had played as an amateur in England for Tufnell Park in the Isthmian League between 1933 and 1935. The Swiss also caused problems with a new tactical formation which involved a deep-lying centre-forward.

The next day the English party was taken to the Neufeld Athletic Stadium, where the top event was a race between the world's top milers, Gundar Hägg and Arne Andersson from Sweden. As a result of their keen competition, the Swiss all-comers 1500 metres record was beaten by three seconds. The party then moved on to Zurich for the second match against Swiss B, which had recently beaten the Swiss first team in a trial match. Willie Watson was one of four changes and this time the English players, having rested and dined well, were more than a match for their hosts. A Willie Watson cross laid on a headed goal for Tom Finney and later he scored a picture goal himself from outside the penalty area. Mick Fenton completed the scoing in a comfortable 3-0 win. This was the first time Willie Watson had seen floodlights or played with a white ball.

There is a lot of evidence to show that the Swiss matches were originally included in England's series of Victory internationals. Tom Lawton, Harry Kinsell and Willie Watson all confirmed later that they believed the games to be unofficial internationals. In fact, in the illuminated address awarded by the Football Association in April 1946 – instead of caps – wartime internationals included the match against Switzerland. At the dinner held by the Swiss FA after the first game, the menu card clearly indicates that this was a 'Schweiz V England' match. Also, an action photograph taken during the game shows Tom Lawton wearing an England badge on his football shirt. However, in a *History of the Football Association,* published in 1953, the teams for the Swiss tour are listed but annotated as being combined services teams and not therefore internationals.

Tom Finney's return journey was so convoluted that he was put on a charge of 'absent without leave'. Quite an anti-climax after, apparently, making his first appearance for England. However, he went on to win 76 full caps between September 1946 and October 1958.

CHAPTER 5

END OF THE WAR AND CRICKET

WILLIE WATSON WAS still based near Rhyl in the summer of 1945 when he was invited to take part in the Colwyn Bay Cricket Festival. He batted really well, scoring a century, but just as important for his career was the presence of Herbert Sutcliffe and Abe Waddington in the ground. They were impressed and were swiftly reminded that this was not only a Yorkshireman but a pre-war Yorkshire colt. What they had seen was soon forwarded to the Yorkshire headquarters in Leeds.

In September 1945 the Scarborough Festival began with a match between Yorkshire and the RAF, in which Herbert Sutcliffe, now 50, played his final game for Yorkshire, having decided to retire. Willie Watson first took the eye for Yorkshire by running 30 yards to make a brilliant catch. When batting, after a couple of excellent cover drives, he was out for 22. The cricket revival moved next to Lord's for a most unusual fixture. It was a match between players under and over 33 years of age, although this age grouping was not exactly adhered to. Harry Halliday, of Yorkshire, played for the over-33s although only 25 while Willie Watson, just four weeks younger, played for the under-33s. More important was that Watson's score was 80, part of a total of 421 which included a stand of 75 in 28 minutes with AW Mallett of Dulwich College. Rain ensured the match was drawn.

The County Cricket Championship resumed in 1946. Yorkshire held the title from 1939 but the war had taken the life of left-arm spinner Hedley Verity, weakened pace bowler Bill Bowes through three years of imprisonment and had significantly shortened opener Len Hutton's left arm.

Willie Watson had not established his first team place in 1939 but was now seen as a potential replacement for Maurice Leyland, now 45. Sutcliffe had retired and six others were in their final years. The only consolation was that all the other counties were in a similar state of reorganisation. In the meantime, Watson was still in the Army awaiting a demobilisation date. Yorkshire had already got off to a strong start to the new season before Willie was demobbed in the second week of June. The summer was wet and cold and Yorkshire's bowling success came from right- and left-arm spin bowlers, Ellis Robinson and 43-year-old Arthur Booth. That season, the batting was mainly dependent on Hutton, who scored four of the seven centuries accrued by the county.

An England trial match was held at Canterbury on July 12. Willie Watson was chosen to play for the rest, probably with the support of captain Brian Sellers. He played well in the second innings, scoring 61, but he did not progress and, in fact, would wait five years for a Test call.

Yorkshire seemed likely to suffer their first defeat against Worcester at Headingley in mid-July. With both Len Hutton and Sellers missing, the county needed only 89 runs to win in their second innings, but found themselves eight down for 73. Willie Watson, with a top score of 29, provided the backbone of the winning total but needed tailenders Robinson and then Smailes to achieve victory by one wicket. In the following match against the Indian tourists, Willie Watson opened with Hutton but while his captain made 183, Watson's contribution to the innings and 82-run victory was just 7 and the catch that removed the Nawab of Pataudi in the first Indian innings.

In all, Willie Watson played 15 innings for Yorkshire without making a century before returning to football training. Meantime, his county had retained the championship.

When Willie Watson was released by Sunderland the following year and arrived back in Yorkshire, he could not have anticipated that cricket would enjoy such a glorious summer. The South Africans were the tourists and it would be the season of Denis Compton and Bill Edrich. Middlesex were to be unstoppable in the County championship. Yorkshire had lost Leyland, Wilf Barber and Cyril Turner to retirement, while Paul Gibb gave up first-class cricket in 1947 before joining Essex in 1951. This meant unfamiliar problems for captain Brian Sellers particularly, when so many new and inexperienced cricketers had to be absorbed into the team. The largely experimental team was heavily dependent on Len Hutton and Normal Yardley.

Willie Watson's first match was at Oxford University, where he batted at number three. In May, Hutton was in tremendous form and soon had four centuries, including one at Oxford. Later the same month Willie Watson moved into form, scoring 78 against Glamorgan and sharing with Norman Yardley a stand of 163 for the third wicket. Against Lancashire at Old Trafford, Watson opened the innings with Hutton and, together, they put on 110 in the first innings and 117 in the second.

At the end of May, Gloucestershire's Charlie Barnett chose the match with Yorkshire at Ashley Down, Bristol, as his benefit match. Unfortunately for Barnett rain reduced it to two days but Yorkshire lost by nine wickets. Willie Watson scored 52 in the first innings and 26 in the second, sharing stands of 77 and 90 with Norman Yardley (43 and 58), but they were put to the sword by Sam Cook taking nine wickets for 42 in the first innings. Cook didn't take a wicket in 33 overs in the second innings but Tom Goddard weighed in with 6-35.

This, however, proved to be a false indication of Watson's form but an accurate reflection of the way his team were performing. They went two months in the championship without a win, a sequence which included a run of four defeats. Against Middlesex and Kent Watson managed only 0, 1, 0 and 1. He did not play against the touring South Africans, but returned to the team for the match with Surrey at The Oval, where, batting at five, he made 153 not out – his maiden first-class century – in his team's total of 350-8.

In the evening, he rang his wife, Barbara, partly to tell her his news and partly to hear how his son, Howard, was. He knew the boy had been unwell again, but he soon learned that he was seriously ill and his wife wanted him to come home immediately. So Willie Watson was faced with a terrible dilemma. There was his loyalty to Yorkshire and the duty to his wife and family. In recent months Howard had been seriously ill several times with a kidney disease and, deciding there was nothing he could have done about it even had he gone home, Willie Watson stayed in London to continue his innings. He finished not out on the same score as Alec Bedser struck twice and the match was drawn. When he did arrive back home, Watson found that his son had recovered from a serious spell. Unfortunately, despite being transferred from Huddersfield Infirmary to Pendlebury Children's Hospital in Manchester, Howard survived only for a few more months.

Another young batsman making an impact in the second half of the season was Ted Lester, who made 657 runs in seven matches, convincing him he should play full-time in the future. Willie Watson made a second century, 147 at New Road, Worcester in mid August, passing 1,000 runs for the season (1,331) when he reached nine. Yardley also made more than a thousand runs that season (1,906) although no one could match Len Hutton. He amassed 2,585 with a highest score of 270 not out at Hampshire in the last championship match.

Despite his heroics Yorkshire fell to eighth place, their lowest position for 37 years. Willie Watson had been awarded his Yorkshire County cap and had maintained the promise of 1946, although not to the extent expected by his warmest advocates. Back in Sunderland, as early as July, the *Echo* was speculating about Willie Watson being picked for the last two Tests as a batsman of international class although the paper was more anxious about his possible selection for the MCC tour party to India in the autumn and the impact that might have on the town's football club. Argus, in the *Echo*, was sure the Sunderland directors would not be impressed by such a prospect. They did, however, agree to give Watson permission to report late for football training – Yorkshire even wanting him to play in the end-of-season encounter with the MCC at Scarborough in early September. As it happened, he was not chosen for the Indian Tour, so no clash of loyalties arose.

The *Sunderland Echo* sounded sceptical when it noted that Willie Watson, who had not played any football since February 14 1948, was able to play cricket on the last day of the football season. It also pointed out that, since signing for the club, he had played in 54 matches out of a possible 84. Three days later the sports page headline speculated that Willie Watson would leave Sunderland before the start of the next season. The big issue appeared to be the player's permanent move to the area in order to train at Roker Park and to eliminate the travel from Huddersfield.

Brian Sellers had resigned from the Yorkshire captaincy at the end of the 1947 season and, as expected, the amateur all-rounder, Norman Yardley, was appointed in his place. He was a product of the pre-War years but now faced the challenge of an emerging team. His responsibilities were further complicated when he was chosen to lead England against the powerful Australian tourists.

The Yorkshire team was quickly exposed to Bradman's Australians, although they were led this time by Lindsay Hassett, at Park Avenue, Bradford. Willie Watson thought it the most thrilling match of the season, even though it ended in defeat by tea-time on the second day. The Bradford wicket was notorious when it took spin. Yorkshire were shot out for 71 with only Harry Halliday of the recognised batsmen reaching double figures. Fast-bowling all-rounder Keith Miller adapted to off spin and took 6 for 42. The Australian batting was also soon in trouble until Miller came to the rescue with a quick 34. The Australians declared at 101 for 9, Frank Smailes taking 6 for 51. Yorkshire did no better in the second innings and were all out for 89, leaving the tourists to make 60 to win. That target became more demanding when half the Australians were out for 20, but Neil Harvey came to their rescue to ensure a four-wicket win. This defeat highlighted many frailties in the Yorkshire staff.

On the positive side, Vic Wilson, a strong, tall left-hander, established himself at number three. While he lacked the style and class of Willie Watson, he became a very good county batsman. Watson's batting got off to a slow start in May but later in the month he scored 59 not out and 52 against Warwickshire at Edgbaston although he was unable to prevent defeat by 54 runs. Yorkshire's form was inconsistent, especially in the bowling department. Len Hutton was, as usual, the outstanding batsman. His batting average would be almost double that of the next batsman (Watson).

Willie Watson had to wait until near the end of July for his first century of the summer, although he had reached the nineties more than once. There was a 92 not out at Lord's as Yorkshire beat Middlesex by an innings and 80 runs. A footnote to this victory is that Denis Compton took his 200th wicket when Yardley was out hit wicket.

Later in June Watson again scored 92 in a six-wicket victory over Kent at Bradford and there was a 95 not out against Surrey at Bramall Lane as Yorkshire triumphed by an innings and 139 runs. When he reached 63, Watson had scored 2,500 runs in first-class cricket.

He really went to town at Northampton on July 21. Opening with Harry Halliday he helped put on 233, making 108 himself. Less than three weeks later against Derbyshire at Scarborough, Willie Watson made his biggest score to date: 172, putting on 302 in a second wicket stand with Vic Wilson although rain prevented Derbyshire from even going into bat.

The Yorkshire challenge for the championship petered out over the last four fixtures and they had to settle for fourth place. They only lost four games but they drew eleven and won eleven. Some consolation could be derived from the full emergence of Johnny Wardle as a top-class left-arm spin bowler. His 150 wickets at 19.4 were nearly double what he had achieved in his first season in 1947.

Willie Watson had the personal satisfaction of passing a thousand runs again and exceeding his 1947 total of 1,331 by 21. He could also take some pride in coming second in the Yorkshire averages with 37.55, even if it was way behind the great Len Hutton's 64.73.

The summer of 1949 was a frustrating one for Willie Watson, while it was surprisingly fruitful for Yorkshire. In terms of weather it was one of England's better summers and Yorkshire continued to rely heavily on Len Hutton for their batting. Despite being described by Anthony Woodhouse (*History of Yorks CCC*) as 'one of the handsomest left-handers ever to have graced the game', Willie Watson had a disappointing season (average 25.84), especially during the middle section where he missed seven County games. He was not the only one; both Johnny Wardle and Vic Wilson shared the experience of a spell in the second team. It turned out to be a salutary episode because they all returned to make a significant contribution to Yorkshire's exciting challenge for the championship. The county lost only two matches but were pursued to the line by Middlesex. Newcomers Frank Lowson, Brian Close and Fred Trueman demonstrated Test match potential.

While Willie Watson was struggling to keep his Yorkshire place, Sunderland Cricket Club asked the Durham Senior League management committee if the Yorkshireman could play for them in league matches as an amateur. Watson was prepared to supply a certificate to say that he would play without payment. Before the management committee met, the Sunderland club received permission from Yorkshire to play him. So they took the plunge and picked him against Wearmouth Cricket Club on July 2. Wearmouth, in turn, had signed Len Shackleton, then playing for Newcastle United but later to become a Sunderland icon, so that the fixture would be doubly attractive to the public. So, for three weeks, there was a mixture of Yorkshire second team games and Sunderland Durham Senior league matches for the future Test cricketer. Then, on July 21, the management committee decided that Willie Watson could not play for Sunderland cricket club while he was a Yorkshire professional.

Perhaps the experience of playing cricket in Durham helped to restore Willie Watson to form. On August 3 he scored 119 at Leicester, following it with 97 opening against Derbyshire at Bradford ten days later before 115 against Warwickshire at Scarborough, sharing a stand of 178 with Ted Lester. He amassed 853 runs for the season, down some 500 on the two previous seasons. The very exciting championship race went to Yorkshire's final fixture, which had to be won to share the title with Middlesex. Victory was achieved, the championship tied and Yardley's captaincy reached its peak.

CHAPTER 6

END OF THE WAR
AND FOOTBALL

IN SEPTEMBER 1945, the war was over but Willie Watson's next representative match was for the Combined Services in Ireland. He was a reserve in Belfast but chosen on the left wing for the Dublin game, being partnered by 21-year-old Billy Wright, with whom he had played for the Western Command. Despite fielding a strong team, including Stan Matthews, Stan Mortensen, Neil Franklin and Tom Lawton, the Combined Services lost to the Irish League 1-0. The next day in the *Daily Sketch*, the prominent journalist, Lionel Manning, wrote: 'Watson should stick to cricket and Wright will be well advised to go back to school and start soccer from the beginning again.' Wright, of course, went on to win 105 full caps.

The next Victory International was against Wales at West Bromwich Albion on October 25 1945. For Willie Watson, this was a genuine international selection, albeit still without a full cap. There were 56,000 spectators packed into The Hawthorns, and Willie was picked ahead of Leslie Smith, Jimmy Mullen and Denis Compton, all talented and experienced left wingers. Once again, despite fielding a strong side, including Joe Mercer, Neil Franklin, Stan Matthews and Albert Stubbins, England disappointed and lost 1-0. In particular, Willie Watson and his partner, Malcolm Barrass of Bolton Wanderers, failed to live up to expectations. Many people at the time were ready to write them both off as internationals but both came back to win full caps. However, to do so, both players changed positions; Willie Watson returned as a wing half while Barrass converted to centre half.

In fact, Watson was seriously considering what his best position was. He was increasingly dissatisfied with his role as a left winger. His experience in a variety of forward positions with Huddersfield Town and in Army teams had convinced him that he was much happier at inside forward where there was more chance of getting the ball and working with it. On the wing, he found there were long periods when he was out of the game because he was dependent on colleagues to bring him into it. This ambition to play as an inside forward had a major impact on his football because Huddersfield were unimpressed with his request. The Town seemed to be stuck in a late 1930s view that Willie Watson was principally a winger. This impasse led to a transfer request, clearly a great wrench for the player. Huddersfield was his home town club, where his father and elder brother had played.

In the meantime, between representative matches, Willie played for Huddersfield Town in the autumn of 1945 while his future was settled. He scored in an impressive 8-2 away win at Middlesbrough, where he played on the wing. He scored again when the double over Middlesbrough was completed by 7-0. However, clubs who may have been interested in the unsettled winger had to reckon with his wish to continue his cricket career. This seems to have ruled out all London and southern clubs.

Once Huddersfield Town had agreed to his transfer, the move was limited to those clubs within easy reach of Yorkshire. Only Leeds United, Middlesbrough and Sheffield United represented Yorkshire in Division One, while seven clubs came from neighbouring Lancashire. In fact, it was the *Sunderland Echo*, on February 13 1946, which speculated about the signing of a Huddersfield forward. The newspaper went on to say that Sunderland manager, Bill Murray, had interviewed Willie Watson. There was no problem about Watson's willingness to move to the north east but there were issues about his wish to continue his cricket career. Yorkshire's desire to control their professionals might have been a stumbling block.

The other outstanding question was Willie Watson's aim to become an inside forward and Sunderland's lack of evidence that the former winger could do the job for them as an inside forward. Sunderland had already acquired Huddersfield's wing half, Ken Willingham, who had a high opinion of Watson's football abilities. The Sunderland press were not impressed with the way the club had cheaply sold off their captain, Raich Carter, to Derby County. Could the Yorkshireman fill that important gap? The *Echo* was convinced that the club needed to spend £20,000 on two inside forwards if it was to survive the re-introduction of relegation in the season 1946–47.

In mid-March, Willie Watson was given a 48-hour pass by the Army and, with Huddersfield's permission, he guested for Sunderland at Gigg Lane, Bury. It was not an auspicious debut because neither the team nor Watson played well. There were doubts about whether the newcomer was worth the £7,500 quoted as his transfer fee. But, eventually, at the end of April, the transfer took place. Willie Watson remained determined to concentrate on the inside forward position, which was why no deal could be done with Middlesbrough, who had enough inside forwards. The deal was done at York, where Watson was playing in a benefit match for Huddersfield Town. The fee was £7,000 and the signature was completed on May 1.

It was hoped that Watson's commanding officer would give him permission to make his debut as a Sunderland player against Middlesbrough on Saturday May 5. In the meantime, the Sunderland cricket club at Ashbrooke made the new recruit a generous offer to become their professional, but they were out of luck because his cricket ambitions remained with Yorkshire. Sunderland lost to Middlesbrough and observers decided it was too early to judge Willie Watson, especially as he had played only 15 games during the season and was short of match fitness. So it was back to Yorkshire to pick up his cricketing career as soon as the Army demobbed him.

As soon as his back was turned, the *Sunderland Echo* raised the issue of how the player would manage to combine playing two sports as a professional. Before the First World War, great amateur sportsmen like Alfred Lyttelton, Leslie Gay, CB Fry and Reginald Foster managed to combine both games to the highest level and became 'double internationals'. Between the World Wars, four professionals, Harry Makepeace, Wally Hardinge, Andy Ducat and John Arnold also reached the top of both games. However, the games did not overlap as much as they would post-1945. In particular, the Football Association had not entered the World Cups of 1930, 1934 and 1938 and the MCC played Test cricket against only Australia, South Africa, the West Indies and New Zealand.

In July, the *Echo* pondered the question of what would happen should Willie Watson establish himself in the Yorkshire side, as seemed likely, since he was selected for a Test Trial. Would he then report to Roker Park in August, when the professionals were required for pre-season training? After all, the newspaper noted, the club was paying him £7.10s per week summer wages. Even more contentious was the outside chance that Watson might be selected for the tour of Australia in 1946–47. If he were selected so soon after Sunderland had invested £7,000 in him, it would certainly be in breach of contract if the club did not grant him permission to tour. The dilemma did not materialise on this occasion because he was not chosen.

Early in August, 13 of Sunderland's 24 professionals returned for training, including three, Johnny Mapson, Len Duns and Eddie Burbanks, who were pre-war Cup and League winners. Willie Watson would report back within a fortnight. While manager Bill Murray and his trainer were supervising the football training, Willie Watson was leading Yorkshire's rearguard action in the Roses match, where his 40 runs ensured a draw.

Watson reported for training at Roker Park on August 19 1946. He was soon involved in a pre-season trial match between the Stripes and the Whites and also in a charity cricket match between Sunderland footballers and Sunderland Cricket Club. He led the victorious soccer players at Ashbrooke, contributing 62 runs. The attendance was the largest since the Australian tourists played there in 1921.

There was an interesting twist to the fixtures for the first match of the post-war Football League season 1946–47. Sunderland's visitors were Derby County. This meant that Raich Carter would return to his native town to play for the first time against the club who made him. Derby marked the occasion by making Carter their captain. At the same time, Willie Watson was playing his first full League match for his new club. Unfortunately, the day before the match, Watson managed to strain a muscle but decided to risk playing with the leg well strapped. The *Sunderland Echo* reported that Willie Watson's first half was impressive, although he faded in the second. The new recruit showed plenty of football craft but needed more menace behind his attacks. Derby County were over elaborate in the build-up of their attacks, thereby contributing to their 3-2 defeat. The gates had to be closed with the official attendance calculated at 48,500.

Four days later, the fixture list was again producing an intriguing match. This time, Willie Watson's home town club was due at Roker Park. Once again, Watson was chosen at inside left, as agreed in his transfer negotiations. He was also developing an understanding with veteran left winger, Eddie Burbanks. The result was a convincing 3-0 victory for the home team. Further good performances saw Sunderland beaten only twice in the opening ten fixtures and Willie Watson missed those defeats because he was injured. During this period, press reports about his performances were generally favourable, especially about his work rate helping in midfield, his stamina and determination. The only question mark was over his lack of menace near goal, because he had not scored in the first 14 games.

In mid-October, Sunderland hit a bad spell that continued into the New Year, and especially affected form at Roker Park. Despite acquiring Jackie Robinson, an inside right from Sheffield United, the club slid steadily down the table. Willie Watson did open his goalscoring account at Sheffield United on November 23, but by mid-December the critics were in full flow. The *Echo* commented that, 'In spite of his cleverness in mid-field, nothing Willie Watson has done yet has convinced me that everyone else was wrong and that he was right – that he was in inside left and not an outside left.' The fact that the team had gained only five points from a possible

18, and that they had all been gained away from home must have worried manager Bill Murray. Nevertheless, until the end of the season, the manager continued to pick Willie Watson at number ten whenever he was fit.

The next line of attack was on Willie Watson's continued residence in Huddersfield. This was seen as a particular disadvantage when the player was injured and needed treatment, which trainer George Grey was able to provide. By early January, Sunderland were getting close to the relegation zone and their confidence was further undermined by an immediate exit from the FA Cup at Chesterfield. Once again, Argus, in the *Echo*, insisted that Watson's goalscoring record was not good enough for an inside forward and that he could make his name by returning to the wing. The general pessimism was to some degree lifted by a 5-0 win against Blackpool on January 18 and a week later Willie Watson scored his second goal in a consecutive away win, versus Blackburn Rovers.

It was not until February 8 that Sunderland's dreadful run of seven home defeats came to an end with a goalless draw against Portsmouth. March 15 brought the first home win for five months against Middlesbrough. Gradually, results were improving and so were the comments about Willie Watson's contribution. 'Some of Willie Watson's footwork was amazingly clever'; 'He gave his wing half a lot of assistance'; were two quotes in the *Echo*. By April 4, in the 4-1 victory over Aston Villa, the acclaim reached unprecedented levels: 'Willie Watson was the game's star player. He crowned a brilliant game with two goals.' The *Echo* went on to rate this game as Watson's best in a Sunderland shirt. His tackling was far better than either wing half; his distribution was accurate and his opening goal after 40 seconds was one of the quickest seen at Roker Park for years. Only the Villa goalkeeper, Joe Rutherford, prevented Watson scoring a hat-trick.

The winter of 1946–47 was particularly severe and there were serious fuel shortages. In mid-March, the Government required the Football Association and Football League to ban all mid-week football. This meant that any backlog of fixtures caused by postponements could not be cleared up within the deadline for the season's conclusion. This in turn meant that the football authorities had to agree to an extension of the season. Consequently, Sunderland's last fixture against Brentford was not played until May 24. By that time, of course, Willie Watson was needed by Yorkshire. In fact, he did not play in any of the last three games because Sunderland's directors, no longer worried by the threat of relegation, had released him to play cricket. But Willie Watson had much more serious worries, for this was when his young son was so seriously ill.

Willie Watson's late arrival on August 25 in 1947 for training meant that he would definitely miss the opening two games of the season against Arsenal and Aston Villa, and was doubtful for the third game versus Grimsby Town. In fact, he did not play until the sixth fixture away at Chelsea. 'That's the handicap of having a pro-cricketer on your books,' lamented Argus in the *Echo*. The first five games had produced only one win for Sunderland, so the club were very anxious for Willie Watson to play at Stamford Bridge even though he was not match fit. But the gamble paid off with the team giving a much improved performance and Watson providing an outstanding performance with no sign of fading, as he ran further than any other Sunderland forward. Also impressed by this return to the game must have been the England selectors, because they named him as travelling reserve for the match against Belgium in Brussels.

Football reunions were the feature of Sunderland's next few matches. First, Willie Watson missed the away game at Blackpool because he was England's reserve in a 5-2 win over Belgium. This experience must have encouraged him to believe that he could win honours in peace time as well as war time. Then, in two successive matches, Willie Watson was in opposition to former colleagues. In the home draw with Derby County, Sunderland supporters had the opportunity to compare their old star and captain, Raich Carter, with their fairly new investment, Willie Watson. The following Saturday he was back in Huddersfield, where he was marked by his elder brother, Albert. The game ended in a draw, but Willie Watson could take some credit from the two goals scored by his left-wing partner, Tommy Reynolds.

Once again, Sunderland's disappointing start to the season (two wins in 12 matches) drew attention to Willie Watson's goalscoring record, which was five goals in 32 games the previous season and no goals in eight games this time. To be fair, the press was equally critical of inside-right, Jackie Robinson, who had only scored twice in ten appearances.

The other cause of dissatisfaction, in Willie Watson's case, was that not only did he continue to live in Huddersfield but he still trained there. This issue was highlighted in the *Echo* in late October and the newspaper believed the club was about to instruct Willie Watson to move to Sunderland. Argus believed such action was overdue and could not understand why the player had been granted this dispensation. There were, however, two very good reasons for the delay in moving to the north east. The first was Howard's chronic illness. The child was treated first in Huddersfield, then moved to specialists in Manchester. Secondly, Willie Watson was committed to Yorkshire Cricket Club in the summer and Huddersfield was convenient for the six-day schedule which the County Championship demanded. By the end of October, the *Echo* reported that the issue of training at Roker Park could lead to a dispute between club and player. On this occasion, the local paper was more sympathetic to Willie Watson, saying, '...there is one thing with him, wherever he trains: you can depend on him taking care of his physical condition.'

In November, the club tried to lure Tommy Lawton to Roker Park from Chelsea in an attempt to solve their goalscoring problem, But the player preferred, of all things, a move from the First Division to the Third and joined Notts County. As a result of a chance meeting between Bill Murray and the Huddersfield manager, Clem Stephenson, the Sunderland manager learned that Willie Watson's best game for Huddersfield during the War was when he played at centre forward against Hartlepool. So, on November 15 for the home match against Liverpool, Bill Murray picked Willie Watson to lead the attack. What a transformation. Sunderland mauled, by 5-1, a Liverpool side containing Billy Liddell, Bob Paisley, Albert Stubbins and Phil Taylor. Willie Watson adapted well to his new role and scored his first goal of the season. But the experiment lasted only two games because Sunderland plunged into the transfer market and signed Ronnie Turnbull, a centre forward from Dundee. So Willie Watson moved back to inside left and Turnbull had a sensational debut against Portsmouth, scoring all four of Sunderland's goals.

The speculation in December was that three or four top division clubs had made offers for Willie Watson. The club rejected them all because of an imminent FA Cup tie and there was no prospect of securing a replacement before it. Just before Christmas, Arsenal were the visitors and Roker Park was packed with its second highest gate for a league game of 58,391. The match was drawn, with Leslie Compton Arsenal's man of the match, completely subduing striker Ronnie Turnbull. Like Willie Watson and like his more famous brother, Denis, Leslie Compton pursued two careers – one at Arsenal and the other at Middlesex County Cricket Club.

At this difficult time in his family life, Willie Watson was reported to have agreed with the club directors that he should no longer insist on playing at inside forward and would play in any position which suited the manager. Argus in the *Echo* welcomed this conciliatory move and predicted that the player could represent England on the left wing. More prophetically, he suggested that Willie Watson could play at right or left half, because '...he has two good feet and can tackle'. Another important change for the Watsons came in January 1948. They sold their house in Huddersfield and moved lock, stock and barrel to Sunderland. But, because the cricket season was only four months away, they did not immediately buy a property; instead, they moved into the Seaburn Hotel. This would allow them to relocate to Yorkshire for the cricket season.

Once again, the FA Cup brought no consolation for Sunderland. In a third-round tie at second division Southampton, the north east club was humiliated 1-0. A fortnight later, at home in late January to Bolton Wanderers, Willie Watson was moved to his third forward position in two months. He replaced Jackie Robinson at inside right. This was a desperate move, since Robinson had scored twice in 12 games, while Watson had managed one goal in 19 games. The experiment was not successful, as Bolton won at Roker Park, and it was immediately abandoned. Willie Watson was dispatched to the left wing for the first time since his Huddersfield Town days.

At the end of January, the shock news in the football world was Len Shackleton's transfer request from Newcastle only 15 months after his arrival from Bradford Park Avenue. The Newcastle board was expecting a record fee for their flamboyant inside forward. 'The Clown Prince of Soccer', as he was later to become called, cost Sunderland £20,050. Willie Watson welcomed the arrival of a fellow Yorkshireman and also admired Sunderland's determination to get their man whatever the cost.

This was particularly applicable in February 1948 as Sunderland struggled to preserve their continued presence in Division One. However, things did not get off to a positive start in Shackleton's debut, with Willie Watson partnering him on the left wing. At Derby County, they faced a team which included Raich Carter, Billy Steel, Jackie Stamps and Leon Leuty, and lost 5-1. Especially galling for Sunderland were Raich Carter's four goals. Argus regretfully wrote that Shackleton may have cost £20,000, but Carter, at 34, was still the greatest inside forward in England. To complete Sunderland's misery, Willie Watson was carried off for the second time in a fortnight.

While Sunderland struggled to avoid relegation, Willie Watson nursed an ankle injury. It was four weeks before he seemed to be recovering sufficiently to return, but this proved to be an over-optimistic prediction. At the end of March, the *Echo* was at a loss to know why he was not fit. Sunderland made seven changes against Stoke in a desperate attempt to halt their poor results, but to no avail. Willie Watson's recovery was further delayed by dermatitis to his toes, but the club's fortunes recovered with a 2-0 home victory over Burnley.

Sunderland's relief was echoed in London where the Government welcomed 'The Marshall Plan', a multi-million-dollar American programme for European Recovery agreed on April 16 1948.

Another league victory over Blackpool meant that in Sunderland's penultimate fixture at home to Middlesbrough, a draw would be sufficient to avoid relegation. They won 3-0. Although fit for the final game at Charlton, Willie Watson was not risked. Instead, he was released to Yorkshire to play cricket against the MCC at Lord's.

At the start of the 1948–49 season, Willie Watson and Sunderland AFC were in dispute. He was so disillusioned that he even considered giving up football to concentrate on cricket. He refused to re-sign for the club and decided to have a two-week break from sport by taking his wife to Ireland. Already, Middlesbrough had made an offer for his transfer but the Sunderland board had turned it down. The speculation in mid-August had moved to Hull City, where Raich Carter was the recently appointed player-manager. Again, a Yorkshire club seemed most likely to accommodate a Yorkshire cricketer. A further issue was the MCC's selection of its tour party to South Africa. If Willie Watson were chosen, where would that leave his football career, wondered the *Sunderland Echo*? As it happened, he was not selected.

For the opening game of the new 1948–49 season on August 21, the Sunderland team, which faced Bolton Wanderers, was very familiar. In fact, ten players were the same as for the final game of the previous season. Willie Watson was still playing cricket with his future at Sunderland unsure. Over the first nine fixtures, Sunderland's well-established team lost only one match, away at Anfield. Len Shackleton and Arthur Wright were so outstanding that they were chosen to play for the Football League. In the background, manager Bill Murray was quietly negotiating Willie Watson's re-signing for the club. Despite further rumours about a move to Aston Villa, Barnsley or even Goole Town, the remaining issue was the choice of a club house, so that Willie Watson could live and train in the town.

Murray's powers of persuasion succeeded on September 22, when Willie Watson re-signed. Meanwhile, Len Shackleton's brilliant display for the Football League gained him a full England cap against Denmark. So, conveniently, the return of Willie Watson could fill the gap at inside left created by the international absence of Shackleton. The match was away to none other than Huddersfield Town. There was no happy return for Willie Watson, because the game was lost 2-0. Nor did everything go Shackleton's way against the Danish amateurs for, despite the presence of Stanley Matthews, Tommy Lawton, Jimmy Hagan and Bobby Langton in the forward line, the game was drawn 0-0.

Much more important to Willie Watson's future as an international were Bill Murray's persuasive powers in another area. The manager wanted Willie Watson to try a positional move to right half. The player had already shown his versatility by playing in all the forward positions but this move to midfield was a more radical change. However, in order to overcome his differences with the club, he was prepared to try anything, even goalkeeper!

The first opportunity to test the experiment was the home match against Manchester United. Since the resumption of peace-time football, United had twice been runners-up in the First Division and were also the Cup holders. What's more, Willie Watson would be directly up against the international inside forward, Stan Pearson. This would be as good a test as any for a novice wing half. To be fair to Argus, in the *Sunderland Echo* he had suggested such a move for Willie Watson many months before.

The match on October 2 was played before 54,400 spectators. The visitors included Jack Rowley, Johnny Carey and Henry Cockburn as well as Stan Pearson. According to the press, Willie Watson made 'a most satisfactory and promising debut'. 'The experiment,' Argus thought, 'was one which had a good chance of putting Watson's unquestionable good ball play into excellent service for the club.' Sunderland took both points and, unsurprisingly, Willie Watson was retained at wing half for the next match. This was no ordinary fixture, but the return of the Tyne–Weir league derby, the first since March 1934.

For this game, both clubs fielded six players born in either Durham or Northumberland. To add to the tension, just one point separated them. The queues started outside Roker Park at 4.00pm on Friday, when three women arrived acting for their husbands. During the evening and night time, the crowds grew. In fact, the long queues probably put some people off coming because the gate was below capacity at 51,400. The match was played like a cup tie, fast and furious. Newcastle were missing Jackie Milburn, their star striker, playing for England, but still took an early lead. The equaliser soon followed, a wonderful strike from Len Shackleton, while Joe Harvey and Frank Brennan were strong in defence for Newcastle, who fully deserved a draw. The *Sunderland Echo* complained that wing halves Arthur Wright and Willie Watson were too attack-minded and so exposed their full backs to the Newcastle attack. Despite this criticism, the newspaper was soon proposing Arthur Wright for a full England cap (to go with his schoolboy cap).

The experiment of playing Willie Watson at wing half lasted initially for three games. Then he was moved to his Huddersfield position of left wing to partner Len Shackleton. The match against Manchester City was won 3-0 and Argus praised the left-wing pairing.

Across the Atlantic, the American press and public were shocked to find on November 2 that they had elected Harry Truman as their President instead of the favourite, Republican Governor Dewey.

For three successive matches in November, Willie Watson played on the left wing before being switched to the right. From these games, Sunderland lost three times, drawing the other. It was time for manager, Bill Murray, to complete the experiment of converting Willie Watson to wing half. For the next 12 games, Willie steadily adapted to his new position but results were discouraging with only three wins. Also, there would be a sensational FA Cup result.

In December 1948, two important announcements were made by the Football Association that would very much affect the career of Willie Watson. The first was the decision that England should take part in the World Cup competition of 1950 in Brazil. The first three World Cups in 1930, 1934 and 1938 had been boycotted by the Football Association because of an unnecessary dispute with FIFA. The second was more immediate: Sunderland were drawn away to Crewe Alexandra on January 8 in the third round of the FA Cup. So far in his Sunderland career, Willie Watson had twice in the Cup been on the losing side. The game at Crewe would be the first ever meeting of the clubs and a chance for Willie Watson to break his cup-tie duck.

For the cup tie, Sunderland made one change from the team that had lost at home to Liverpool, bringing back Arthur Hudgell to left back. This was a full-strength team but Crewe, from the Third Division North, were no respecters of reputations. They were physical opponents and Sunderland players did well not to depart from their football. The *Echo* picked out Willie Watson as one of the most gentlemanly players in the game, who was provoked several times by harsh treatment from one opponent but did not retaliate. Eventually, the First Division visitors prevailed 2-0.

The draw for the fourth round produced non-league opponents, Yeovil, who had beaten Bury of the Second Division 3-1 in the previous round. The *Echo* thought immediately that 'the stage was set for giant killers'. Yeovil were sixth from bottom of the Southern League while Sunderland were eighth from top of the old First Division. Yeovil had a reputation for embarrassing league teams, especially at home, where their pitch had a notorious slope. Furthermore, the *Echo* readers were warned that the return trip to Somerset would be 672 miles. Yeovil's already small chance of success was further reduced by an injury to their regular goalkeeper in the week before the match. His replacement was a 23-year-old solicitor's clerk, Dickie Dyke, with only one previous first-team game.

A great deal of responsibility fell on Yeovil's only full-time employee, player-manager Alec Stock, formerly an Army major. His club had become the centre of national attention and he explained that 'player-managership is violent exercise on top of a pile of worries'. Now aged 30, he had played for Charlton and Queens Park Rangers before the War. His immediate problem was how to accommodate the thousands of potential spectators, once cup fever swept through the West Country. Also, a hundred pressmen had to be located with no facilities except borrowed school desks.

The gate that was crammed in was between 13,500 and 17,000 and they spread up to the touchline. Jack Stelling, Sunderland's right back, later admitted that 'We weren't used to that sort of thing.' Also to the home team's psychological advantage was the pitch's slope, which had been repeatedly exaggerated over the last few days before the game. The *Echo* dismissed the pitch as having nothing but propaganda value. However, one thing was sure: if the match was drawn after 90 minutes, then extra time would be played in order to avoid replays as far as possible. This was still a time of post-war austerity.

In the 26th minute, a cracking shot from Alec Stock opened the scoring. At the other end, reserve keeper, Dickie Dyke, was having a great match defying Shackleton, Robinson and Watson. In fact, the *Echo* described it as Shackleton's worst game ever. But, in the 62nd minute, Dyke was beaten by Robinson, so the game was drawn after 90 minutes. During extra time, fog began to swirl around the Huish ground. Then, in the 104th minute, Shackleton made a mistake, which Eric Bryant intercepted, and beat Johnny Mapson to restore the Yeovil lead. In the second part of extra time, Sunderland threw everything into attack, while Yeovil defenders hacked the ball as far out of the ground as they could. On the day, the *Echo* admitted the better team won, while Willie Watson had a game he tried hard to forget. But, wherever he went in Sunderland for the next six months, the whispered tease would be heard – what about Yeovil? Yeovil's dream did not last. In the fifth round there were 81,000 at Maine Road, no slope and an 8-0 drubbing from Manchester United. However, it was not the end of Major Stock, who left Wessex to make his name in management at Luton Town and Fulham.

Sunderland's reaction to the shock cup defeat was to sign the Carlisle player-manager, Ivor Broadis, despite the competition from ten other clubs. The transfer fee was £18,000 but the *Echo* still reckoned the club had got a good bargain. The response of the team was disappointing. They lost four games in a row, including a 5-0 crushing at Highbury and an unfortunate 2-1 defeat in the derby with Newcastle. 'Geordies' numbering 58,200 saw their team given a lesson by wing halves Willie Watson and Arthur Wright, ably supported in midfield by Len Shackleton and Ivor Broadis. However, in the first minute of the second half, Billy Walsh was injured and had to leave the field of play. So Sunderland's ten men conceded two goals to lose the match. As the club slipped towards the relegation zone, the directors responded with another move into the transfer market with the acquisition of Tommy Wright from Partick Thistle.

Despite Willie Watson's increasingly impressive performances at wing half, manager Bill Murray moved him back to the left wing when Tommy Reynolds was injured. The game was at Preston in mid-March. The *Sunderland Echo* reported that Reynolds sat in the stand and '...got a lesson in left-wing play from Willie Watson. One would have thought that he had never played in any other position this season – but is that not what one would expect from such a football artist?' On the right wing, Tommy Wright also impressed in an important 3-1 win. Sunderland's survival from relegation was based on a record run of six draws followed by an away win over Manchester United on April 21. Willie Watson was back at right half and a win at Charlton meant the directors could release him to play cricket from April 24. Sunderland went on to finish eighth behind champions Portsmouth. Argus noted that while four forwards had been bought in 18 months, Sunderland's goals scored at 49 was their lowest in the 20th century. Nevertheless, a reputation for high spending was being acquired and soon it would make Sunderland known as the 'Bank of England' club.

Once again, Willie Watson's arrival at Roker Park the next season was delayed. However, his position was clarified by Yorkshire and Sunderland because, soon after the football club had held its second trial match, Willie Watson's two employers agreed 'a give and take arrangement' which took into account Sunderland's relegation or championship involvement at the end of the season and Yorkshire's County Championship prospects at the end of August.

Willie Watson missed the opening five games of the 1949–50 season. His understudy at right half was Reg Scotson. After the fourth match on August 31, in which Sunderland beat Burnley 2-1, Argus noted in the *Echo* that, 'while Scotson gives you everything he has in him, that lack of construction in his football makeup is very noticeable. The return of Willie Watson to duty will help there'. His return against Chelsea at Stamford Bridge gave promise of things to come. By October 1, the full-strength Sunderland team were in excellent form against Manchester United, whom they beat 3-1. All the United stars – Carey, Aston, Chilton, Cockburn, Delaney, Pearson and Rowley – were included but it was Sunderland who produced the best football seen in Manchester that season.

The following weekend, Sunderland had two important visitors. First to arrive was the Health & Housing Minister, Aneurin 'Nye' Bevan, a radical and controversial member of Clement Attlee's post-war cabinet. On this occasion he had the pleasant duty of opening the 3,000th post-war house built in Sunderland. The next day, a record of almost 65,000 fans packed Roker Park to welcome Blackpool and the legendary Stanley Matthews. However, the *Echo* reported that it was Willie Watson who was the outstanding man of the match. The newspaper believed that no Sunderland player had produced such a great display of wing half skills before. 'He ran himself almost to a standstill.'

The following week was the local derby against Newcastle at St James' Park, a game seemingly diminished by the absence of Jackie Milburn and Len Shackleton, both representing England against Wales. Before the game, the two clubs had similar League records, with eleven points from eleven games. Newcastle took a two-goal lead but Sunderland, who lost star man Arthur Wright with a pulled muscle and played the second half with ten men, fought back to draw 2-2. The *Sunderland Echo* praised every player in the team for pulling out that extra bit of effort, but 'the man who stood out as the class half-back was Willie Watson, who subdued Houghton, the Newcastle inside left.' Argus believed that in this form Willie Watson was close to an England cap. The Football Association were equally impressed because they selected him and Arthur Wright to play for the FA against the Army on November 2.

The match was played at The Valley and three Sunderland directors and the manager were present to support their two wing halves. Willie Watson was appointed captain of the FA team and had an outstanding game. The England selectors were made aware that he was one of the finest wing halves in the country. Not only the *Sunderland Echo* was convinced that he should be selected for England, especially as he was such a clean player. Charles

Sampson, writing in the *Sporting Chronicle*, stated that Willie Watson's class stood out. 'He continually brought his forwards into play with well controlled passes and repeatedly broke up the opposition's attacks.'

On November 7 1949, the *Sunderland Echo* announced that Willie Watson had been selected to play against Northern Ireland at Maine Road Manchester on November 16. The England team showed five changes from their previous match and included two other new caps: Jack Froggatt (Portsmouth) and Bernard Streten (Luton Town). The home internationals were particularly important in this season because they were being used as qualifiers for the World Cup in Rio. The top two countries would be invited to the finals in Brazil.

Watson's selection gave a great deal of pleasure to Sunderland supporters, for whom he had become one of the most popular players. Since his conversion from a versatile forward to wing half, he had become the complete footballer. What Argus, in the *Echo*, liked about him was that, despite his success at cricket and football, he had not changed and was still the same quiet, thoughtful chap 'who is more seen than heard'.

For the selectors to accommodate Willie Watson at right half, they had to move Billy Wright across to left half. Since the War, Billy Wright had become a fixture in the England team with 19 caps at right half and four at left half. Before Willie Watson's debut, only two other players, Tim Ward and Phil Taylor, had represented England at right half since 1945. Billy Wright of course would go on to be the first player to win 100 caps for England.

The match at Maine Road was watched by a crowd of more than 69,700. It was a one-sided contest from the outset with England four nil up at halftime. The *Echo* thought that Willie Watson had fully justified his cap with a polished performance which was as good as or better than Billy Wright's performance on the left-hand side. But it was not a real test for England and Willie Watson himself believed that it was 'a game where you could not go wrong'. The full-time score was 9-2 with Jack Rowley scoring four, this being an important first step on the road to Rio.

The *Echo* suggested that it would not be a bad idea to pick the same England team against Italy later in November. In the meantime, Wolverhampton Wanderers were the visitors to Roker Park, which meant that Willie Watson would be up against his England colleague, Billy Wright. Together with the other Sunderland defenders, Watson ensured the famous Wolves attack of Hancock, Pye, Smyth and Mullen were outplayed. Sunderland's 3-1 win was their seventh victory of the season and maintained their unbeaten home record.

Willie Watson was chosen for England's match with Italy at White Hart Lane but he became doubtful because of a groin injury. He missed Sunderland's next match at Portsmouth, where he would have opposed Jimmy Dickinson, the man he had replaced in the England team. Eventually it was decided to risk his fitness because the match was a friendly. Bert Mozley was less lucky with his injury and had to be replaced at right back by Alf Ramsey of Tottenham. The crowd of about 70,000 saw the Italians dominate the first half without scoring. Two important innovations were proposed at halftime: a white ball was introduced without dissent but the use of a substitute, other than for a goalkeeper by the Italians, was challenged. The halftime interval had to be extended in order to consult Sir Stanley Rous, the Football Association's secretary. His adjudication resulted in the Italian team resuming the match unchanged. England went on to win 2-0 and Willie Watson was thought to have had another good game until the last 15 minutes, when his groin injury re-occurred and he hobbled on to the wing.

CHAPTER 7

THE ROAD TO RIO

FOLLOWING HIS INJURY against Italy, Willie Watson missed two more matches for Sunderland. Nevertheless, the results continued to be mainly positive, which raised the possibility of the club having its best season since the War. While still recovering from injury, Watson announced the opening of a new sports outfitters shop. This was a joint venture with brother, Albert, whose own playing career with Huddersfield and Oldham Athletic had come to an end because of injury. The business was initially established in Ash Place, opposite Thompson Park on Newcastle Road, not far from the home of Willie and Barbara Watson.

Willie Watson returned to the Sunderland team on December 17 1949 for the home game against Liverpool, the league leaders. The *Sunderland Echo* welcomed his return with admiration and praise. 'His was an exhibition of football which combined skill in defence and attack, plus stamina – the complete half back in every respect, even down to his captaincy of the side.' To complete the satisfaction for Sunderland supporters, the team fought back from 2-0 down to win 3-2. The great Billy Liddell was on the wing for Liverpool but Arthur Hudgell was more than a match for him.

The remaining games of 1949 brought two home wins and two away defeats, including a humiliating 5-0 defeat at Highbury. The New Year brought the third round of the FA Cup and, for Willie Watson, a chance to play against Huddersfield. Sunderland swept into the fourth round, winning 6-1 with inside forwards Ivor

Broadis, Dickie Davis and Len Shackleton each scoring twice. Before the next round, Sunderland won two league matches, which kept them in touch with the leading teams.

The opposition in the next round of the cup were Arthur Rowe's legendary Tottenham, well on their way to promotion back to the top flight. The North Londoners included several of their all-time greats: goalkeeper Ted Ditchburn; full-back Alf Ramsey; wing halves Bill Nicholson and Ronnie Burgess; and forwards Eddie Bailey and Les Medley. The match was all-ticket and was limited to 65,000. Spurs sold their allocation in three hours. The tie reminded Sunderland supporters of the sixth round match at White Hart Lane in 1938, which was won with a single goal by Raich Carter. Unfortunately, that result was not repeated in 1950; instead, Tottenham triumphed 5-1.

Back in the league, Sunderland had three consecutive away wins in February which meant they were only three points behind the leaders, Manchester United and Liverpool. Another close-fought contest was the general election of February 23 1950, in which Labour's huge 1945 majority was cut to just six seats and Winston Churchill narrowly failed to replace Clement Attlee as Prime Minster.

The first game in March was the return Tyne–Wear derby at Roker Park. Supporters of both clubs flocked to the ground in their thousands. The final count was 68,004, a record for a league game at Sunderland. Before the game, Sunderland were third with 37 points, while Newcastle had seven fewer. But the form book is rarely relevant in a local derby and in this case Sunderland dropped a home point in drawing 2-2. For the next match away to Wolves, Billy Walsh was dropped and Fred Hall restored to centre half, but Willie Watson retained the captaincy. The 3-1 victory was a triumph for centre forward Dickie Davis, who scored a hat-trick.

With only ten games left, the competition at the top of the table was intriguing. Sunderland's home match with Portsmouth was their third successive draw at Roker Park. Blackpool had joined Sunderland in challenging Manchester United and Liverpool for top place. April brought three successive wins for Sunderland, which included a derby match with Middlesbrough. In that game, the opposition looked to Wilf Mannion to create something, but Willie Watson saw to it that he did not get the chance. Sunderland now topped the table and Argus wrote, 'Watson carries a discoloured eye from the game but if any pair of wing halves can produce anything better than Watson and Arthur Wright produced in the way of science and graft, I don't know where they are.'

The league position on April 11 1950 had Manchester United with 48 points and three games to play, while Sunderland also had 48 points, but with four games to play. Liverpool and Portsmouth had 47 points with four and three games respectively to play, while Blackpool had 46 points with five games left. Sunderland's next match was at home to Manchester City, who had not won away from home and who were already relegated. Sunderland were unbeaten at home, but captain and midfield driving force Willie Watson would be absent because he was England's reserve at Hampden Park. Also missing was Dickie Davis, top scorer with 23 goals.

Completely against form, Sunderland lost 2-1, their first defeat at home that season. To add to the melodrama, Sunderland were awarded a penalty kick, which Jack Stelling took and which the referee ordered to be re-taken. Stelling took the second kick, which Bert Trautmann saved. Argus wondered what Willie Watson might have done had he been captain, because it was known that Stelling always placed the ball to the same side of the goalkeeper.

Watson resumed his place for the next game away to Huddersfield. Sunderland lost, and so their title hopes were virtually gone. Not even a late flourish of two home wins over Everton and Chelsea, in which eight goals were scored, was enough. The title went to the holders, Portsmouth, on goal average, from Wolverhampton, with Sunderland a point behind in third place. Little consolation could be found in being top scorers in the division with 83 goals, or from Dickie Davis being the top individual marksman on 25.

Against Chelsea, Willie Watson was able to mark Roy Bentley out of the game. He was one of many talented inside forwards to be subdued by the Sunderland captain during the season, including Wilf Mannion (Middlesbrough), Stan Pearson (Manchester United) and Billy Steel (Derby County). It had been Sunderland's best season in the league since they were champions in 1935–36.

Although the league programme was completed, football was moving on to another stage. The first post-war World Cup finals were to be held during the summer of 1950 in Brazil. England had qualified by winning the home championship. The deciding match was against Scotland, the one Willie Watson watched as the England reserve, while Sunderland had been floundering at home to Manchester City. The Scots were also entitled to a place in Rio by being runners-up in the home championship but declined to go. This confirmed what they had already announced: that they would only travel as champions – a decision which today would be regarded as short-sighted and introverted.

This was the first time that cricketer–footballers had faced the choice between a summer with their counties and possibly a Test cap or an international football tournament for the Jules Rimet trophy. On this occasion, the only sportsman facing this dilemma was Willie Watson. Denis Compton, who had not played for England at football since the Victory International against Scotland in 1946, had just announced his retirement after the 1950 FA Cup final. Arthur Milton was only 22 and had not yet established himself in the Arsenal team, although he had had two seasons with Gloucestershire. So, when the FA announced two England squads to tour Europe in May 1950, Willie Watson was selected for the B team. From these two groups the FA would choose the party to travel to Rio.

Willie Watson knew that a reasonable performance with the B team would ensure his place in the World Cup squad, but he was also doing quite well at cricket and had the chance to become a double international. He was also intensely loyal to Yorkshire. After careful thought, he decided that, if he was serious about his double career, then it had to be cricket in the summer and football in the winter.

So he wrote to the FA to say that he would prefer to play cricket in the summer and not to go to Rio, in which case he said that it would not be fair for him to go on the European tour. In reply, the FA sought to persuade him to change his mind and go on the European tour because they were confident he could make the World Cup side. Watson was in a real quandary and so elected to contact the Yorkshire committee and asked them to decide his future in consultation with the Football Association. The response of the committee was positive. They wrote, 'Willie, it's all right by us if you play soccer during the summer. After all, it's England who need you.'

Willie Watson was very impressed with the reaction of the Yorkshire committee. They believed that 'loyalty to one's team was essential but nothing should interfere with one's loyalty to one's country.' So Willie Watson joined the England B party to tour Italy, Holland and Luxembourg. The England first team was due to play in Portugal and Belgium, but they would be deprived of their outstanding defender, Neil Franklin. He had sensationally decided to quit English football and join Bogota in Columbia. Franklin had played in all 27 of England's post-war internationals and was regarded as a very talented centre half.

The two European tours were watched with particular interest around the world because this was England's first experience in the World Cup and they were considered to be one of the favourites. However, Willie Watson noted that several observers believed that England had lagged behind some of the continental teams in the development of football technique. The two tours produced mixed results. The A tour was reasonably successful with two victories: 5-3 over Portugal and 4-1 over Belgium on May 14 and 18. The B team tour was a disaster. The Italians slaughtered them 5-0 while in Holland the defeat was 3-0 against amateurs. The team scraped home against tiny Luxembourg, which provided little consolation. Willie Watson played in all three games at left half, his father's old position.

After the tours, two training sessions were held in London before the departure to Brazil. The FA would compensate players for their travel expenses to London. On the second journey to London, Willie Watson was unable to find a seat, so he upgraded his ticket to first class as he did not think it right to stand all the way south before such an important training session. When his claim was submitted, the FA deducted the 16/3d (81p) upgrading charge from his expenses. Willie Watson was furious because his payment for being in the World Cup squad was £60 whereas he would have received £300 for playing cricket for Yorkshire.

The squad that the FA chose for Rio was 21-strong and Willie Watson was one of the five wing halves included. The *Sunderland Echo* believed that Watson had been one of the few successes on the B team tour. However, the competition for places was very stiff, especially from the experienced Billy Wright and Jimmy Dickinson, plus the future Spurs manager, Bill Nicholson, and Manchester United's Henry Cockburn. Willie Watson recognised that the opposition in Rio would be strong but felt that England's manager, Walter Winterbottom, had been given a talented squad. Nevertheless, the manager had not been given full control over team matters because members of the FA selection committee could interfere.

The main concern of the press and the public was how to fill the large gap left by Neil Franklin's defection. There were doubts about the replacement eventually included. Neither Jim Taylor of Fulham nor Laurie Hughes of Liverpool had played for England yet. Further confusion had been caused by the FA when they selected Stan Matthews and Jim Taylor for a tour of Canada immediately before the start of the World Cup. Eventually, the FA gave way to pressure and arranged to fly them directly from Canada to Rio via New York. The pair arrived three days before England's first match after a flight of 28 hours.

The choice of the Luxor Hotel for the English party was soon found to be inappropriate. It was close to the noisy Copacabana beach and was full of journalists, guests and fans, and so it was very difficult to rest. The food did not suit English stomachs conditioned by years of rationing. Most of the party had a tummy upset at some time while others survived on bananas alone. The soaring temperatures added to the English problems.

Only 13 countries took part in the finals and England were drawn into a group with Chile, Spain and the United States. This meant that they would avoid the most dangerous teams until the later stages. In fact, the first game against Chile was a comfortable but unconvincing 2-0 victory. Willie Watson was not selected as the players who had succeeded on the A tour were preferred. This meant that Stanley Matthews was also overlooked but a forward line of Tom Finney, Wilf Mannion, Roy Bentley, Stan Mortensen and Jimmy Mullen was expected to excel. In fact, it disappointed and there was a call for changes in the second game against the USA. The *Sunderland Echo* suggested that Jackie Milburn of Newcastle could replace Roy Bentley at centre forward, while Walter Winterbottom favoured the recall of Stanley Matthews. However, Arthur Drewry, a fish merchant from Grimsby and a member of the FA selection committee, believed that a winning team should not be changed and his view prevailed. This also meant no place for Watson. The match against the United States was seen by everyone as a foregone conclusion. The American part-timers were not highly rated even though they had put up a hard fight against Spain in their first match. The game was scheduled to be played at Belo Horizonte, 300 miles inland, and while it was a relief to be leaving the Luxor, because as Jackie Milburn said, 'You can only eat so many bananas', turbulence meant the flight from Rio was unnerving and the 16-mile journey from the airport by road to the training camp was hair-raising.

However, the training camp was owned by a British gold-mining company, Morro Velho, which employed 2,000 Britons, and its facilities were excellent and luxurious. Included in the sporting provision was a cricket ground. Willie Watson and Roy Bentley were room-mates and got on well. Today Roy remembers Willie as a classy and skilful footballer who was never physical. Although he was naturally left-footed, you could not tell because he had trained his right foot so well. When there was a spare moment at the camp, the two made their way to the nets where Roy bowled to Willie, who practised his batting. When Willie Watson had a tremendous second half to the cricket season with Yorkshire, Roy Bentley was able to claim that his bowling at Morro Velho had contributed to the flow of runs.

The road to Rio

Unfortunately, the match against the USA turned from a formality into a fiasco. The newly-constructed Belo Horizonte Stadium was narrow and the pitch was rutted and strewn with stones. It was completely unsuitable for a World Cup match but it was the same for both sides. England took command from the start and created numerous chances but their finishing was dreadful. Admittedly, the gritty Americans were almost comically lucky and their goalkeeper had a fantastic game. In one of their rare attacks, Joe Gaetjens deflected the ball past Bert Williams in the England goal. There were eight minutes left before halftime and England resumed their bombardment. Several times they hit the woodwork but the outclassed Americans hung on. Up in the stand, Willie Watson sat next to Stanley Matthews. He remembered the winger repeatedly saying, 'They must score!' But they didn't! Even a Jimmy Mullen header which seemed to be well over the goal line was disallowed, as was a penalty claim when Stan Mortensen was wrestled to the ground.

Billy Wright summed up the performance, saying, 'It was simply unbelievable that our finishing could be so poor.' Team manager, Walter Winterbottom, could only echo the general view, 'The team played very badly indeed, especially the forwards.' Willie Watson wrote that the defeat by the unassuming Americans 'knocked the heart out of us'.

The 1-0 defeat caused a tremendous sensation, especially back home. In fact, in London, a sub-editor, on receiving the result from Brazil, assumed there had been an error in transmission and corrected the score to read England 10, USA 1. Reaction to the result inevitably meant changes. Unfortunately for Willie Watson, the major restructuring took place in the forward line where Stan Matthews took over on the right wing and Tom Finney switched to outside left. Also, Eddie Bailey and Jackie Milburn were introduced in place of Wilf Mannion and Roy Bentley. At left back, Bill Eckersley was preferred to Johnny Aston, but the half-back line remained unchanged. England's football against Spain was a great improvement but it did not bring success; they again lost 1-0. Consequently, England were eliminated from the World Cup.

Willie Watson believed England could have progressed to the final stages but there was no way that Brazil or Uruguay could have been beaten. After all Brazil beat Spain, the winners of England's group, 6-1.

Controversy continued to follow the party after the Spanish match. The FA decided that the players plus the manager should leave for home immediately. Looking back, many of the party, including Willie Watson, thought it was probably a mistake not to stay on and watch the finals. He wrote, 'There's nothing like learning from others and there was lots to learn in Rio. The tragedy was not to lose, but to come back without learning anything. If we'd stayed and watched, we might have avoided the punishment which was inflicted on us a few years later, especially by Hungary.'

Walter Winterbottom admitted later that 'I'd passed up an opportunity to be better informed about developments in the game.' Had he stayed, he would have seen football the like of which had never been seen in Europe. But the FA, back in London, did not see the need to learn from Brazilians or from South America generally. Unfortunately, this sort of attitude had a detrimental effect on the English game for the next 15 years.

CHAPTER 8

MAKING UP FOR LOST TIME

ON JULY 10 1950, the *Sunderland Echo* announced the return of the World Cup party. They maintained that Willie Watson had nothing to answer for as he had not played a game. He was quickly recruited to umpire in a match between Durham schools and Lancashire schools. His football colleague, Len Shackleton, was his partner in officiating and it was felt that, as they were both Yorkshiremen, they would be suitably neutral. By July 15, Willie Watson was due back at Headingley to see if Yorkshire needed him. In the meantime he revealed that he had secured the use of a building to use as a winter cricket school. This was a facility much needed in County Durham and Willie Watson's next stop would be to test the market for such a venture.

While Willie was away in Brazil, Yorkshire were having a good season, even though Brian Close was also unavailable due to National Service. Frank Lowson established himself as Len Hutton's opening partner and passed 2,000 runs. Johnny Wardle was having his best season so far and eventually took more than 170 wickets. Also making steady progress was 19-year-old Freddie Trueman. Len Hutton was averaging 50 while sterling support in the batting line-up came from Vic Wilson, Harry Halliday and Ted Lester. Consequently, Willie Watson would have to fight to win back his place.

In order to get some match practice, Willie Watson was invited to play in benefit matches during the last two weeks of July. One match was a Footballers' XI against Len Shackleton's XI, in which Willie Watson and five other Sunderland first team members took part. Finally, the call came from Yorkshire to play for their second XI in a Minor Counties match. Either Roy Bentley's bowling or the benefit matches cricket put Willie Watson into immediate top form. He hit the Lincolnshire bowling for 168. His recall to the first team was assured and he was duly picked to play away against Somerset on August 2.

At Taunton, Yorkshire replied to Somerset's 260 with 279, including a second consecutive century (122) for Willie Watson. Yorkshire were set to score 224 in their second innings, which they achieved with the loss of four wickets, thanks to 120 not out from captain Norman Yardley.

The next fixture was the Roses match at Old Trafford. Cyril Washbrook was in fine form for Lancashire, scoring 88 and 74. Watson's main contribution came in the Yorkshire second innings when he batted superbly for 73 not out in an hour and 50 minutes. The match, however, ended in a draw.

The next fixture on August 9 was at Headingley against Northants. Willie Watson's fine form continued with 132 in Yorkshire's first innings. Frank Lowson was also playing very well and scored 91 and 141. Northamptonshire were able to hang on for a draw, thanks to 103 from Dennis Brookes. The following game at Bradford against Warwickshire was drawn due to the weather. This meant three consecutive draws would not help Yorkshire's challenge for the Championship.

Another home fixture followed, this time on the east coast at Scarborough. The opponents were Kent, who were skittled out in their first innings for 100. Johnny Wardle had the very impressive bowling figures of 6-20. In the Yorkshire innings, Willie Watson's magnificent spell continued with a third, first-class century in 17 days – 114. Kent were quickly dismissed for a second time, resulting in a two-day victory for Yorkshire by an innings and 114 runs. There was even speculation that Willie Watson might fill one of the remaining places in the MCC tour of Australia. But what would Sunderland AFC make of that?

Yorkshire switched next to the south coast at Eastbourne to play Sussex. In the fourth innings of the match, Yorkshire were set a target of 258. Willie Watson, who had only made nine in Yorkshire's first innings, was back in fine form for the run chase. The target was reached with the loss of seven wickets and Willie Watson was unfortunate to miss out on another century, being 96 not out. The next day, August 23, the *Sunderland Echo* was lauding Willie Watson's wonderful late-summer form.

'There's no knowing what he might have achieved if he hadn't wasted precious time watching in Rio where, apparently, the reserves were not even allowed to be present at tactical talks. Watson now has 564 runs from ten innings, two of which were not out (average 70.5). As Yorkshire are out of the running for the title, Willie Watson is expected back in Sunderland next week.'

By this time, of course, Sunderland AFC had begun its 1950–51 season. Their fixtures began on August 19 with a home game against Derby. The Sunderland team had a very familiar look with only Tommy Wright and Willie Watson missing. Wright had been in dispute with the club during the summer; nevertheless, he was back for the next match at Villa Park. Willie Watson would be a little longer as he had two more games to play for Yorkshire. At Cardiff's Sofia Gardens, the game was virtually wiped out by rain, thus leaving only the match against Hampshire left before the return to football. The Yorkshire batsmen were in fine form at Portsmouth, scoring 369 for 4 with Willie Watson's 73 outshone by Lowson's 104 and Halliday's 98. Hampshire were bowled out cheaply twice, giving Yorkshire victory by an innings and 68 runs. Watson departed to the north east while Yorkshire finished third in the County Championship behind Lancashire and Surrey. His batting average of 68.40 from 12 innings in nine matches was ahead of Len Hutton, Frank Worrell and Denis Compton – an amazingly prolific August.

Within a week of returning for training at Roker Park, Watson was selected for Sunderland's match at Wolverhampton on September 6. This rapid recall was a testament to his remarkable fitness. This fixture was Sunderland's sixth game of the season and thus far only one victory had been secured. Willie Watson was restored to the captaincy but he could not prevent another defeat. In mid-week, Sunderland had a friendly match against Galatasaray of Istanbul, only the second continental team to play at Roker Park. The *Echo* was amazed that Watson was fit enough to play another game within four days and shocked that the club was prepared to risk him. The newspaper speculated that Willie Watson might put an extra 5,000 on the gate. The result was that Sunderland won 3-1.

Although Sunderland's form in the autumn of 1950 was inconsistent, there was plenty to stimulate Willie Watson. On a personal level, he opened his winter cricket school at New Silksworth in Sunderland. Argus wrote that the school was one of the best things to happen to cricket in County Durham. Watson was sure there was a demand in the district for such a facility. The excitement at the football club level was Sunderland's dramatic entry into the transfer market. Welsh international Trevor Ford was the most feared striker in the top division and Aston Villa were prepared to sell him at a price. There was a competition from Chelsea and Cardiff so, for the third time, Sunderland broke the transfer record by paying £30,000, which overtook the £26,500 paid for Eddie Quigley by Preston North End. His signing thrilled the Sunderland area and hopes for success were high. Trevor Ford went straight into the team for the match at Chelsea. Ironically the man to lose the number nine shirt was Dickie Davis, the league's top goal scorer with 25 the previous season.

Ford soon showed his potential, scoring a hat-trick in the 5-1 defeat of Sheffield Wednesday at Roker Park. He also dislodged one of the uprights at the Fulwell End. Big-spending Sunderland made a second important signing in October when Billy Bingham arrived from Northern Ireland club Glentoran for £9,000. Both Ford and Bingham were put up by the Watsons until their housing was sorted out.

The third cause of excitement for Willie Watson came in November 1950 with his recall to the England team. The match against Wales was due to be played at Roker Park and initially Willie Watson was chosen as the travelling reserve.

The selectors, still trying to find a replacement for Neil Franklin, chose Leslie Compton of Arsenal at centre half for his first cap at 38. Like his more famous younger brother Denis, Leslie was a first-class cricketer with Middlesex as well as an Arsenal defender. The league fixtures for November 11 produced an Arsenal versus Sunderland clash which would preview the forthcoming international because Compton would mark Ford of Wales. The result was a 5-1 thrashing for Sunderland, so the first round was a success for Compton. Two days later it was announced that Billy Wright would not be fit for the match with Wales and, therefore, a run of 33 successive international caps since the war would come to an end. His misfortune was Willie Watson's opportunity, as he was chosen to play at right half. He joined Les Compton and Jimmy Dickinson in England's half-back line. Behind him at right back was future England manager, Alf Ramsey, who was captain. In front of him was the brilliant right-wing partnership of Tom Finney and Wilf Mannion.

This was the first time England had played Wales in Sunderland since 1891, before Roker Park was built. The town came alive around lunchtime on the day of the international. Large crowds headed for the ground; huge traffic tailbacks developed and long queues were formed. The crowd exceeded 60,000 and the gates were closed. The spectators were rewarded with a splendid match. Wales gave a good account of themselves in what was one of their best displays. However, England were two goals up by halftime and eventually ran out comfortable 4-2 winners, with Eddie Bailey of Spurs scoring twice. Willie Watson had a particularly fine second half in which his through passes caught the eye. There was a second success for Compton over Ford.

Seven days later, on November 22, England had a friendly against Yugoslavia at Highbury. Willie Watson retained his place but Finney, Milburn and Smith were absent. A debut at centre forward was given to Nat Lofthouse of Bolton Wanderers. Tom Finney was replaced by Johnny Hancocks of Wolves. While Willie Watson had little to comment about on the match against Wales, he was stung into a strong defence of his role against the Yugoslavs. Some of the sporting press had wondered if his attacking style would be suited against the speed and ball skills of the Yugoslavs. However, nothing of these concerns was mentioned to Willie Watson, so, in the first half, he played his normal game and England led 2-1 at the interval. Leslie Compton's own goal was all the Yugoslavs could manage. Nevertheless, at halftime, Willie Watson was instructed to go on the defensive, which completely disrupted his game. He had the most wretched second half in his career, so he believed. He felt it was impossible to become defensive at such short notice. In fact, it was probably impossible altogether because it felt so unnatural. He felt it was entirely wrong to ask a player to change his style of play for one game. It would have been much better to choose another player whose style suited the particular circumstances. Obviously, he tried to adjust in the second half, but, because it had not worked, he believed he had been written off as a failure. Unfortunately, his fourth soccer cap was his last. The match with Yugoslavia was a 2-2 draw with Lofthouse scoring both England goals. However, the Yugoslavs became the first team from outside the British Isles to play in England and return home undefeated.

Back in the north east, Sunderland's big-spending policy was not working as only three out of nine home games were won. Against Everton on November 25, Sunderland were able to pick Shackleton, Ford and Broadis together for the first time. Unfortunately, it did not work, because in a 3-1 defeat teamwork was lacking. Willie Watson, at this point, had played two internationals and three league games in 15 days. By early December, manager Bill Murray decided to reverse his biggest success story of converting Willie Watson to a wing half by moving him back to the left wing. The hope was that he would add direction and thrust to the attack. However, the game at West Brom was lost 3-0. The switch continued the following week at Derby where Sunderland scored five times but still managed to lose 6-5. The full impact of the new left winger was revealed over the Christmas holiday. Firstly, Willie Watson scored the only goal in a home win over Liverpool. This was followed by 'doing the double' over Manchester United, by 2-1 at home and by 5-3 in Manchester. Surprisingly, the Sunderland attack lacked both Ford and Shackleton, but Broadis, back after five games, scored a hat-trick. The *Echo* thought 'the forward line was delightful to watch.'

January 1951 soon brought the third round of the FA Cup. Willie Watson's record in the competition with Sunderland was undistinguished. Since January 1947, he had played in six cup ties with only one win, 6-0 against his home town team. This time the draw was a home tie against Coventry City. The non-availability of Tommy McLain meant that Watson was moved back to right half after six games on the wing. The change worked because his steadying influence in defence and his unhurried distribution to his forwards contributed to a 2-0 victory.

Three weeks later, the fourth round saw Sunderland again at home, this time against Southampton although Watson was forced to withdraw from this tie through injury. At Blackpool in a league match the previous week, he had formed a left-wing partnership with Len Shackleton supported by left-half Arthur Wright. The trio produced the quality of football Sunderland had been seeking all season. The result was a 2-2 draw. Without Watson, Sunderland moved into the fifth round by 2-0 in front of a crowd of over 61,000. Between the fourhth and fifth rounds, Spurs were the visitors to Roker Park. It was 16 years since their previous visit and they arrived as the new league leaders, but they left Roker Park with only one point.

The cup draw continued to favour Sunderland. Not only did they have a third home tie, they also, for the third time, had opponents from outside the top division. Norwich City were challenging for promotion out of the Third Division South. They were expected to play good football and they were sure to be well supported as special trains were booked to transport 18,000 'Canaries' fans. So Sunderland would need to be at their best and the return of Willie Watson would help that. An early freak goal gave Sunderland the lead but they were not having it all their own way until Willie Watson set off on a great run, which culminated with a fine goal and an eventual 3-1 victory.

This earned them a sixth round tie at home against cup favourites, Wolverhampton Wanderers. This draw recalled the three stirring battles in 1937, also in the sixth round. Then, of course, Sunderland went on to win the cup for the first time. The tie was played at Roker Park on February 24. Willie Watson failed a late fitness test and had to be replaced. Sunderland produced a grand display, compared with their recent league form, but could manage only to draw 1-1 with the formidable Wolves. The replay was arranged for the following Wednesday at Molineux, leaving Willie Watson four days to prove his fitness. He recovered and resumed the captaincy from the right half position. Sunderland were able to accommodate all their star forwards by playing Shackleton on the left wing with Broadis alongside, while on the right wing Tommy Wright combined with Dickie Davis, leaving Trevor Ford to lead the attack. But it was not good enough because Wolves triumphed 3-1 in front of a capacity gate of 55,000.

Willie Watson missed the next three league games and did not return until the Newcastle derby on Good Friday, March 23. The Tynesiders had reached the FA Cup final and were well placed in the league. For this Bank Holiday fixture, St James' Park was packed with more than 62,000 supporters and the gates were closed more than an hour before kick-off. The crowd witnessed a classic, fluctuating match with four exciting goals and the points shared. Most observers believed that they had seen, in Jackie Milburn and Trevor Ford, the best two centre forwards in Britain. Willie Watson, after his month-long absence, was quickly back to his best form.

The next day, Sunderland were trounced 3-0 at Sheffield Wednesday, which did not seem a very good preparation for the return local derby with Newcastle on Easter Monday. In fact, Sunderland deservedly won that match 2-1, their first competitive victory over their neighbours since 1934, and it virtually ended Newcastle's challenge for the league title. However, Newcastle went on to beat Blackpool 2-0 in the FA Cup final while Sunderland had to make do with a modest mid-table position. As soon as Sunderland were safe from relegation, Willie Watson was released back to Yorkshire.

CHAPTER 9

A DOUBLE INTERNATIONAL AT LAST

WHEN WILLIE WATSON returned to Yorkshire in April 1951, he was just 31 years old and he had four full caps at football for England. At cricket he had had an England trial in 1946 at Canterbury, where he had made one half century. Since then there had only been speculation about a possible Test debut.

The England selectors had had five summers in which to assess Willie Watson's batting credentials. There must have been a great deal over which they could have agreed. Cricket writers, journalists, former players and contemporaries were unanimous in their admiration for the left-hander's batting style. They either described it as graceful or elegant. Bob Appleyard and Vic Wilson, Yorkshire team-mates, described it as 'classical left-hand batting'. Fred Trueman believed Watson to be the most elegant left-hander with whom he had ever played. Trueman, like Dickie Bird, later a Test umpire, emphasised Willie Watson's ability to cope on wet or worn wickets in the era before they were covered.

Bird went on to explain why Willie coped so well, which was because he played the ball so late. He let it come on to him rather than go chasing after it as lesser batsmen tended to do. Jack Birkenshaw noted that Willie stood perfectly still until the bowler released the ball, and this allowed him to play the ball late. Fellow professionals also pointed out that he was a great timer of the ball. Tom Graveney said that Willie was a beautiful player who stroked the ball, whereas Doug Insole used the word 'coaxed'. Trevor Bailey, who knew Willie Watson very well, said he was 'A superb natural athlete and ball player.' Raman Subba Row concurred about the natural athlete and added that there was never any slogging. In Sir Alec Bedser's words, 'His batting was not aggressive but everything he did was graceful.'

Nor did he lack courage and application. Eric Hollies, the Warwickshire spinner, recalled a match against Yorkshire in 1948 when Willie Watson made two half-centuries on a difficult wicket. They were worth more than many centuries according to Hollies, who added that Watson 'had been hit black and blue by Tom Pritchard but stood his ground as though encased in armour'. *Playfair* magazine described him as the most graceful mover in the game. Perhaps the greatest compliment came from Bill Bowes of Yorkshire and England, who later became a respected journalist. He wrote, 'Only occasionally did he exhibit the powerful pull or the stroke to cover as smoothly perfect as any by Frank Woolley.' Woolley was acknowledged as England's greatest left-hand batsman by *Wisden*.

Despite all this evidence, the selectors, up to 1951, had not been convinced. Some observers pointed to the adverse impact of the war years on a player who was only 19 in 1939. They argued that players like Watson had their development as batsmen halted for six critical years. The war had a much greater impact on cricket than it did on football, so Willie Watson came to the notice of football selectors before the cricket selectors. Of course, the demands of the military authorities had a detrimental effect on all sportsmen but those who were under 16 when hostilities began and those who were over 26 suffered less.

A further disadvantage for Willie Watson was how Yorkshire chose to deploy him in their batting order. Trevor Bailey insists that had he batted regularly in positions one to four, he would certainly have scored more runs. Instead he had no settled position, and fluctuated between opening and number five. Was this because Yorkshire never fully appreciated his talent or was it because Yorkshire had an abundance of class batsmen? Len Hutton, Ted Lester, Frank Lowson, Vic Wilson, Norman Yardley and Harry Halliday all averaged more than 31 for Yorkshire but only the magnificent Hutton exceeded Willie Watson's 38.2.

Perhaps Willie Watson's reserved character and undemonstrative personality was a disadvantage. As Bill Bowes wrote, 'His batting suffered from a quiet modesty'; or as JM Kilburn, the historian of Yorkshire County Cricket Club, noted, he lacked the ambition 'to be first among the foremost'.

Undoubtedly, the demands of playing top-class professional football put pressure on Willie Watson's cricket career. This was increasingly the case in the 1950s and 1960s. The competing demands of the two games had become irreconcilable for Watson in 1950 when he was chosen for the World Cup squad for Rio. Despite his excellent batting form when he got back to Yorkshire from Brazil, it came too late in the season for the selectors choosing the party that would tour Australia. Nevertheless, Yorkshire Cricket committee and Sunderland AFC directors had tried to cooperate over Willie Watson's dual careers. In 1951, their efforts were about to succeed.

It was 18 years since Johnny Arnold of Hampshire and Southampton had won his only soccer cap for England to become the tenth man ever to be a double international at cricket and football.

The ultimate obstacle to Watson's objective was the incumbents; the batsmen whom England had selected since 1946. These included the tough and experienced players who made their debuts in the late 1930s and survived the War. Len Hutton, Cyril Washbrook and Denis Compton all first played in Test matches in 1937 while Joe Hardstaff played in 1935 and Bill Edrich in 1938. All five figured prominently in the late 1940s. Another fine batsman, Reg Simpson, was first capped in 1948 while the elegant Jack Robertson was able to make 11 Test appearances from 1947. There was a second group of players who, like Watson, were pressing for their first Test cap. They included Doug Insole and David Sheppard, who had made the breakthrough in 1950, and Tom Graveney and Peter May, who had high hopes of 1951. The pre-war group eventually amassed 256 Test appearances between them so they were difficult to replace. The contemporary group of four would eventually acquire 176 Test caps.

This was the competition for batting positions which Willie Watson faced in 1951.

The spring of 1951 saw President Truman assert his authority when he sacked General MacArthur from his post of Commander of United Nation forces in Korea. In London, ministers Aneurin Bevan and Harold Wilson resigned from Attlee's Labour government and King George VI opened the Festival of Britain on the South Bank of the Thames. The tourists for the cricket season were the South Africans, and Newcastle United won the FA Cup final.

The cricket season began for Willie Watson on April 28 at Lord's. The MCC entertained Yorkshire and plundered them for 411 runs for seven declared. In Yorkshire's reply, Watson, batting at five, made a modest start and was out hit wicket for eight. Yorkshire moved on to Oxford, where the weather limited play and Watson failed again, scoring only nine. The first home match was at Bradford against the South African tourists. The weather again intervened to make a draw inevitable. The tourists were skittled out for 86 but, in the Yorkshire innings, Willie Watson was four not out when the innings closed at 214 for 4.

Yorkshire's first championship game was at Hull where Northants were the visitors. Watson's poor form continued with 12 out of a total of 143-7. At this point, from four innings, he was averaging 11, unlikely to have caught the attention of the selectors. But, perhaps conveniently, he was transported back to the north east. Celebrations of the Festival of Britain took place across the country and included large numbers of friendly football matches. On May 9, England entertained Argentina at Wembley and won 2-1. It was the first meeting of the two countries and England's win depended on late goals from Stan Mortensen and Jackie Milburn. Sunderland's involvement was part of a tour by Red Star of Belgrade, Yugoslavia. Founded in 1945, they became the most powerful club in their country, winning 19 league and cup trophies between 1948 and

1970. The Yugoslavs first played against Manchester United, which resulted in a 1-1 draw. The visitors were described as a brilliant combination who at times outclassed United. Next, Red Star came to Roker Park, where Sunderland fielded their strongest team, including Willie Watson on the left wing. The two teams produced a great game to watch and Sunderland earned a 1-0 victory.

It was not until May 30 that Willie Watson was restored to the Yorkshire side. He had missed five fixtures but he was not at all rusty, because at Bradford he hit the Gloucestershire bowling for 95 and Yorkshire won by nine wickets. On the basis of this one innings, Watson was chosen for the first Test at Trent Bridge.

England's winter Ashes tour of 1950–51 had not been a success. The series had been lost 4-1 and only Len Hutton of the batsmen came out of it with any credit. Even Denis Compton had a disappointing tour. So the selectors must have been seeking replacements for Cyril Washbrook, Gilbert Parkhouse, John Dewes and David Sheppard. In the event, Denis Compton was retained, as his class deserved; Jack Ikin was recalled to open with Len Hutton. Reg Simpson was also retained because he had been second to Hutton in the batting averages and because the first Test was at his county ground. Willie Watson was chosen to bat at number five. The *Sunderland Echo* was quick to point out the paradox between Watson's fine form the previous summer, when he returned from Rio, which did not secure him a place on the Ashes tour, and his modest form in 1951, which resulted in his first Test honour at 31. Johnny Arnold had made his only Test appearance for England when he opened the innings against New Zealand at Lord's in 1931. Two years later, he made his only football appearance for England at outside left against Scotland. Willie Watson was able to travel to Nottingham in the knowledge that he already had four soccer caps.

At Trent Bridge, the England captain was Freddie Brown and the wicketkeeper was the legendary Godfrey Evans. Trevor Bailey and Alec Bedser opened the bowling while spin was provided by Johnny Wardle and Roy Tattersall. The wicket was known to be good for the batsmen, so when the tourists batted first, Willie Watson knew he would be in the field for a long time. In fact, the South Africans batted for almost two days before declaring at 483-9. The innings was dominated by a double century of 208 from Dudley Nourse, the captain. It was South Africa's first double century against England. In all, the England bowlers and fielders toiled for 550 minutes while Nourse was at the crease, but he took no further part in the match because of a damaged thumb. England's reply was led by Reg Simpson, who scored 137, and Denis Compton, who hit 123. Simpson's Test century remains the only one made at Trent Bridge by a Nottinghamshire player. By the time Watson went in, the plumb batsman's wicket had been washed away by the rain. It was about 6pm and the wicket was not helping the bowlers. In the pavilion Willie Watson had been watching the quick bowler Cuan McCarthy and had not been too impressed, so was feeling quite confident. However, as he made his way out of the dressing room door, he heard Alec Bedser call out, 'Watch this fellow McCarthy, Willie!'

With this advice coming from such a great judge of the game, Watson decided to proceed with caution. McCarthy turned out to be much quicker than he looked, certainly faster than any of the England attack. Nevertheless, Willie Watson was able to weather the storm, and, batting with Denis Compton, helped to carry England out of the danger of the follow-on. There was some grand batting on a rain-damaged wicket and Willie Watson could look back on his Test debut with satisfaction. His 57 runs included some fine shots, especially a hook for six off Geoff Chubb, which brought the crowd to its feet. Acting South African captain Eric Rowan crowded eight men round the bat, but neither Compton nor Watson was perturbed. Together they put on 141 for the fourth wicket. Eventually, England declared at 419-9, 64 runs behind.

The game then swung back in England's favour as Alec Bedser demolished the South African second innings, taking 6-27 out of a total of 121. England needed only 186 runs for victory. However, the wicket had continued to deteriorate and England never looked like reaching the target. They were bowled out for 114 and Willie Watson was for the second time out lbw, but this time for only five. Thus ended South Africa's run of 28 Tests without victory since 1935.

Between the first and second Tests, Willie Watson played in two matches for Yorkshire and scored 84 not out, 24, 67 and 28 not out. So he was in good form for Lord's. Again, he batted well with Denis Compton and the pair put on 122 for the third wicket, joint-top scoring with 79 each. The England total reached 311, which proved more than enough because on a slow, wet wicket South Africa were bowled out twice by off-spinner Reg Tattersall, who had match figures of 12-101. England's win by ten wickets meant that the series was now level.

The series continued at Old Trafford on July 5. Willie Watson retained his place but injury prevented Denis Compton from playing. In his place, a debut was given to Tom Graveney of Gloucestershire, a very promising batsman. South Africa won the toss and decided to bat first despite heavy rain before the match. Alec Bedser took full advantage of a lively wicket and took 7-58. The South Africans were dismissed for 158 but England fared little better on a wicket that turned and lifted alarmingly from the start. Chubb did the damage by taking 6-51 to reduce England to 211. Willie Watson was one of Chubb's victims, bowled for 21.

The South African second innings only produced a modest improvement so that England needed only 139 to win. Len Hutton's innings of 98 not out ensured that England had a comfortable nine-wicket victory. However, he narrowly missed the distinction of becoming the first batsman to score his hundredth first-class century in a Test.

Between the third and fourth Tests, Yorkshire played four times, the highlight of which was the match at The Oval against Surrey, where Len Hutton scored his hundredth century, only the 13th batsman to do so. Willie Watson played in three of the games but he was frustrated to be left not out in three of his six innings.

The next Test was at Headingley on July 26. It was an excellent batting wicket and South Africa, having won the toss, took full advantage, amassing 538. Eric Rowan scored a record-breaking 238. In reply, England batted for an equally long time to reach 505 and both Len Hutton and debutant Peter May made centuries. Willie Watson described Peter May's batting as 'majestic, a great young batsman for the future'. Batting on his home wicket, Willie Watson made 32 but rain prevented Rowan from adding a century to his double century in the match. He was on 60 not out when play was abandoned and the match drawn. Watson would have known that, on the day before the fourth Test started, Sunderland AFC players were due back at Roker Park for pre-season training.

Again, between Tests, Yorkshire had four county fixtures. Willie Watson made one century (108) against Derbyshire at Harrogate but otherwise did not distinguish himself. The fifth and final Test was at The Oval and England led in the series 2-1. It was a low-scoring, tightly contested game. The pitch took spin from the outset and off-spinner Jim Laker, playing on his home wicket, took full advantage. South Africa were bowled out for 202 and England replied with 194, with Willie Watson scoring 31 before being run out. When South Africa batted for a second time, they were soon dismissed for 154, leaving England to get 163 for victory. This target seemed straightforward, as Yorkshire's Len Hutton and Frank Lowson moved to 53 without loss. Then everything changed with Hutton's extraordinary dismissal followed by Peter May's duck, caught off bat and pad. The ball that Athol Rowan bowled to Hutton ballooned off the bat's top edge and Hutton, in trying to stop it hitting his stumps, prevented the South African wicketkeeper Russell Endean from making a catch. The umpires adjudged that Hutton was out for obstructing the field, the only time this has happened in Test cricket.

So Lowson was joined by Compton and for 50 exciting minutes they moved the score towards the target. However, they were out soon after each other and the score was only 94-4 at tea. This brought captain Freddie Brown together with Willie Watson. EW Swanton wrote in the *Daily Telegraph* that 'Watson was batting like a rock, imperturbable and admirably efficient.' After tea, Brown sensed that what was needed to take control of the match was a really forceful knock. In 20 minutes, Brown and Watson put on 33 runs but at 132 Watson was caught at the wicket off Chubb. Swanton wrote that his inning had 'a value the figures scarcely hint at'. Brown was out with 12 still needed but Jim Laker and Derek

Shackleton saw England safely pass the target with four wickets to spare. It had been a tense battle, with fortunes swaying from side to side, but the result meant England had won the series 3-1. It seemed that Willie Watson had looked good enough, technically and temperamentally, to establish himself in Test cricket.

As soon as the final Test was over, Willie Watson's attention turned back to Yorkshire, where the county team were still in the running for the championship. This meant, of course, that his return to Sunderland would have to be delayed. In the event Yorkshire were beaten to the title by Warwickshire. However, they could point to the fact that Len Hutton and Willie Watson had been absent for five Tests while Frank Lowson, Johnny Wardle and Don Brennan had been away for two each. At the same time, Norman Yardley's duties as chairman of the Test selectors kept him away from some county fixtures. The season was also memorable for the remarkable first summer of Bob Appleyard, who took more than 200 wickets. To celebrate reaching 200 – in the last county match, Gloucestershire at Bristol – Appleyard took 8-76 in the first innings of the MCC match at Scarborough.

CHAPTER 10

SUNDERLAND STRUGGLE, YORKS THRIVE

THE MCC PARTY to tour India and Pakistan, leaving in the autumn of 1951, was described as 'hardly representing England's second team, let alone the first' (Peter Wynne Thomas, *Englander Tour*). Willie Watson had a better reason than most for his absence: he was needed at Sunderland. But football had to wait because from September 5 to 7 he was in Scarborough playing cricket for the Players against the Gentlemen. Indeed, his innings of 80 was the Players' top score in their first innings. Amazingly, the day after the cricket concluded, Willie Watson was in the Sunderland line-up at Roker Park to face Blackpool in the sixth game of the season. Results so far for Sunderland had been mixed: two wins and three defeats. Watson was given a great reception as he led out the team. The Sunderland side would have been very familiar to the new double international as there had been no activity in the transfer market during the summer. A serious injury to Tommy Wright allowed Billy Bingham to establish himself on the right wing, otherwise it was as the previous season.

Despite the return of their captain, Sunderland's form continued to be mixed. By the end of the year, 24 matches had been played with only seven victories but 11 defeats. This meant that 20 points had been gained out of a possible 48 and that they were in the lower half of the table. Willie Watson played in 18 of the games up to December 29, predominantly at right half but twice at outside left, where the *Echo* admired his combination with Len Shackleton and Arthur Wright. The club were not inactive in the face of the team's mediocre form. In October, they sold Ivor Broadis, who seemed to have lost confidence in the company of Ford and Shackleton, to Manchester City for about £20,000. The move soon led to a fine run of form by Broadis, which resulted in the first of 14 caps, against Austria at Wembley on November 28.

The Sunderland board's response was to acquire John McSeveney from Hamilton Academical in mid-October. He immediately took over the left-wing position so that Willie Watson could concentrate on his wing-half duties. McSeveney's debut was away to Manchester United at Old Trafford, where Sunderland again prevailed against their illustrious hosts. A month later, Sunderland were back in Scotland to acquire the services of George Aitken from Third Lanark for £20,000. The Scottish international made an immediate debut in an important home game against Fulham. The *Echo* noted that there was 'a flow of really good football shaped by the genius of Len Shackleton and prompted by the quiet, unspectacular service of Willie Watson. His service was a model of accuracy.' The match was drawn 2-2 with Bobby Robson opening the scoring for Fulham and Shackleton replying twice for Sunderland.

The press also noticed that for the England game against Austria, ex-Sunderland star Ivor Broadis was making his debut at inside right without being sure who his right-wing partner would be. Injury had deprived the England selectors of Tom Finney, while Stan Matthews was out of favour, so a suitable alternative had to be found at short notice. The match was at Wembley so the selectors turned to Arsenal's young Bristolian winger, Arthur Milton. His rise to international football had been astonishing. Only in the current season had he established himself in the Arsenal team. Although it proved to be Milton's only soccer cap, it was significant because he was a first-class cricketer with Gloucester and would later attract the attention of England cricket selectors. Nevertheless, some observers were unimpressed with his football cap, which was gained only 'because he had his boots with him' (Ken Taylor).

Despite Sunderland's mediocre form in the first half of the season, there were signs of improvement in December 1951. At the start of the month there was a convincing victory at Middlesbrough where Willie Watson opened the scoring. At home to Derby County, the team put on an inspiring exhibition in which Willie Watson's tackles were more vigorous than usual and his linking between defence and attack was admirable. At the end of the year, there was another fine 4-1 win at home to Arsenal. Trevor Ford scored for the sixth consecutive game while Watson worked tirelessly both in defence and attack. However, in between these victories, Sunderland supporters had to suffer two local derbies with Newcastle over the Christmas holiday. Willie Watson was the only Sunderland player to have played in all these derbies since Newcastle's return to the top flight in 1948.

This was to prove a disappointing holiday for Sunderland. On Christmas Day at Roker Park, Newcastle were a very respectable sixth while Sunderland languished in 18th. Even so, a 4-1 home defeat came as a considerable shock to Rokerites, especially as there was little positive to take from the game, apart from the captain Willie Watson's hard work and aggression. The next day, Boxing Day, more than 63,500 spectators squeezed into St James' Park, easily the biggest crowd of the day. Understandably Newcastle were unchanged and included their stars, Jackie Milburn, Joe Harvey, Frank Brennan and Bobby Mitchell. Sunderland made two changes: Jack Hedley and Arthur Wright for Jack Stelling and Harry Kirtley, but the performance was transformed. Sunderland forced a 2-2 draw, thanks in particular to the pace and tenacity of Trevor Ford. Newcastle's challenge for the league title petered out in the New Year as they embarked on another successful cup run.

Sunderland's league form improved in the New Year and they won eight of their 18 games so that they were able to reach 12th, the same position as the previous season. However, there was no progress in the Cup, where the third round draw brought Stoke

City to Roker Park on January 3. The tie was goalless and the replay was played 11 days later. Although the match was lost 3-1, the *Sunderland Echo* paid generous tribute to Willie Watson's contribution: 'The attack was at fault despite the magnificent constructive work by Watson and Aitken…while Shackleton was at his most ineffective, Sunderland's giants were Aitken and Watson. Willie Watson gave the complete answer to any suggestion that a tough 90 minutes would find a weakness in his stamina. He not only stayed the trip, he stayed every inch of it with greater fight and challenge than he commanded when called on by England… Late in the game, when others might have thought the match lost, he switched Shackleton to the left wing and moved himself into the forwards. He was joined by Aitken on every favourable opportunity and if this pair had managed an equalizer it would have been richly deserved – the proverbial Sunderland presentation should have been provided for them – the Town Hall and a medal as big as Mackie's Clock.' (Mackie's was a local jeweller's corner shop.)

Despite this whole-hearted support for Willie Watson's midfield performance, he was immediately shifted back to the left wing for seven games. Home wins over Liverpool and Chelsea and away wins at Portsmouth, the league leaders, and Wolverhampton seemed to justify the move. Nevertheless, on March 15, Willie Watson returned to right half, where he remained for the last nine games. It was not a happy move because the first opponents were the powerful Spurs, playing at White Hart Lane. Alf Ramsey, Bill Nicholson, Ronnie Burgess, Len Duquemin and Eddie Bailey helped Tottenham to a 2-0 victory before more than 60,000 supporters.

In contrast, Good Friday brought a visit from Huddersfield Town, who were mercilessly trounced 7-1. It was one of the very few occasions when spectators witnessed the apparent demoralisation of a side – it seemed they would gladly have thrown in the towel and left the field if that were possible in football. The Yorkshiremen had neither the spirit nor the ability to fight back. The last time Sunderland scored seven had been away to Birmingham City in April 1936 to ensure the league title. Four days later, the return match was played at Leeds Road, Huddersfield, where Sunderland could only manage a 2-2 draw, despite Willie Watson excelling himself against his old club. The point was not enough to save Huddersfield from relegation.

With their league programme completed, Sunderland were invited by Hull City to play for the East Riding Challenge Cup. This was an appropriate invitation because it would be Raich Carter's final game for Hull City. The former England and Sunderland star was retiring from playing at the age of 38. The occasion was marked by a civic tribute to one of the greatest footballers Sunderland had ever produced. The match ended 2-2 and the trophy was shared. The crowd at Boothferry Park was almost 30,000 and they enjoyed a banquet of bright and skilful football. Among the stars of the match were Len Shackleton and Willie Watson for Sunderland and Bill Harris and Viggo Jensen for Hull.

The change-over from football to cricket was complicated in 1952 by Sunderland's seven-day tour of Holland at the start of May. The club were due to play the Holland B team first, followed in 48 hours by a match against the full national side. Willie Watson was already back at cricket against the MCC from April 30 and then at Taunton from Saturday May 3. His best score in these two early games was 79 in the second innings against Somerset. The Sunderland party of 13 left for Holland ahead of Watson, who was due to catch up with them as soon as matters were completed at Taunton. He was permitted to miss the Yorkshire game against Oxford University so long as he was back to play at Fenners against Cambridge University. Remarkably, to the modern student of the game, Sunderland not only took on Holland's second and first XIs within 48 hours, they beat them both. The B team were overrun 7-3 with Trevor Ford scoring four times while the first team were beaten at Rotterdam by the only goal, scored by Dickie Davis.

Only from May 10 was Willie Watson able to focus on his cricket against a very strong Cambridge University side which included the future England captain, Peter May, and the future Bishop of Liverpool, David Sheppard. Watson adjusted to the summer game very quickly, making 50 against the students, but was out scored by May's 171, and Sheppard's 68 and 103 not out. The next three County

Championship games were played in Yorkshire and were all won by an innings. During the third match, the England Test selectors chose Len Hutton to captain his country, the first professional to do so. Yorkshire were still reluctant to make such an appointment and Norman Yardley remained in charge. The tourists were India and on the basis of his batting in the 1951 series against South Africa, Willie Watson was expected to be in the team against them.

However, in the three successive emphatic Yorkshire wins, Willie Watson's best score was 38 so the selectors picked him to be 12th man. Instead, they preferred Peter May and Tom Graveney, two very talented younger batsmen. As soon as Watson was back in the Yorkshire team on June 7 against Derbyshire, his form improved. He held the first innings together, making 50 out of a total of 138, while in the second innings he was promoted from number five to four where his 91 was not enough to prevent the first County Championship defeat of the season.

The next fixture was at Lord's against Middlesex. During this match, it was announced that Billy Wright had been voted 'Footballer of the Year' and had earlier won his 43rd cap, a record. Willie Watson's many admirers may have wondered how many extra caps he might have won had it not been for the competition of Billy Wright. At Lord's, Watson made 79 not out in the Yorkshire second innings but Middlesex held out for a draw. Worcestershire and Leicestershire were comfortably overcome in mid-June but Scotland were able to secure a draw. Against Nottinghamshire, Willie Watson scored his first century of the season, 103 not out, and Yorkshire won comfortably by ten wickets. However, early in July, Yorkshire were beaten by Surrey at The Oval, a result which would prove crucial in the County Championship race.

In mid-July, the tourists, India, came to Bramall Lane to play Yorkshire, but Willie Watson, with innings of 28 and 12, did not impress the selectors. He did make amends in the next two games, against Warwickshire and Nottinghamshire, by scoring 68 and 97, both games won decisively. Towards the end of the month, Middlesex were crushed at Sheffield by ten wickets, while in a closer game against Gloucestershire at Bristol, Yorkshire prevailed, helped by

Willie Watson's 114. The Roses match at Old Trafford was a low-scoring, even draw, in which Watson's 49 was very valuable. At Bradford, he again showed his ability to bat in difficult conditions by making 59 not out against Sussex in a match curtailed by the weather.

The headline in the *Sunderland Echo* on August 11 read, 'Watson for Last Test at Oval'. England were already leading the series by 3-0 and Willie Watson replaced Alan Watkins, the Glamorgan all-rounder, whom Watson considered to be unlucky to be dropped. This was seen as an opportunity for the Yorkshireman to re-establish himself as a Test batsman, but batting at number six restricted his chances. England reached 264-2 on the first day and went on to 326-6 the following day when they declared, leaving Willie Watson on 18 not out. India were bowled out for 98, Freddie Trueman taking 5-48, but only ten hours of play were possible because of rain and consequently the match was drawn. It was a disappointing tour for the Indians, who were unlucky to face England's new fast bowler, Trueman, who took 29 wickets in the four-match series.

Following his Test recall, Willie Watson played in four more fixtures for Yorkshire. The highlight for him was another century, 107 not out at Clacton against Essex. The match was won, as was the final championship match against Kent, at Canterbury, but it was all to no avail as Surrey won the title with 256 points to Yorkshire's 224. This was the first of Surrey's seven-year reign as county champions, much to Yorkshire's frustration, as they were four times runners-up and once third. Yorkshire's Wardle was the leading bowler and his 158 wickets were at cost of only 14 runs each.

However, there was one more first-class fixture for Willie Watson, at the Scarborough Cricket festival for Yorkshire against the MCC. The late Trevor Bailey recalls that players like he and Willie Watson, who were preparing for the new football season, packed their boots with them and trained after breakfast at the Scarborough FC ground. He admitted that the festival spirit and fitness did not fit together comfortably but they certainly worked for Willie Watson, as he was able to play in the top flight for Sunderland within a few days of his return.

CHAPTER 11

WONDERFUL
WILLIE WATSON

WHEN WILLIE WATSON arrived back at Roker Park on September 6 1952, he was just in time to join the Sunderland team for lunch prior to the home match with Derby County. He watched the game from the stand to see Sunderland win for the third time in four games. The only unfamiliar face would have been the new goalkeeper from Chester, Harry Threadgold. For the first time in 16 years, Johnny Mapson was no longer the number one choice. Against Derby County, Sunderland had a big advantage at wing half, where George Aitken and Arthur Wright were in top form. The next fixture was a mid-week derby at Newcastle. Sunderland delayed their team selection to the last minute because Len Shackleton was recovering from injury and Willie Watson was now available. There was a feeling that Willie should not be rushed back into the team for such a vital match without a warm-up game in the reserves. Ultimately both players were accommodated in a re-arranged forward line with Watson at inside left and Shackleton at inside right.

Before 60,000 fans at St James' Park, Willie Watson was Sunderland's inspiration. According to the *Sunderland Echo*, 'He gave one of the finest displays of inside forward technique seen in the club colours since the war. He was terrific... He put Sunderland ahead from a corner by Len Shackleton – he beat two defenders in two yards and calmly placed the ball past the keeper.'

Sunderland led by this goal at halftime but Newcastle fought back in the second half to take a 2-1 lead. Not until the 81st minute did Sunderland equalise with a goal from the impressive right winger, Tommy Wright. Before the return a week later Sunderland were defeated at Blackpool where Stanley Matthews, Stan Mortensen and Harry Johnson provided strong opposition. Back at Roker Park, 59,600 supporters saw two well-matched teams in an exciting end-to-end contest. Newcastle took a chance in each half, despite Sunderland's greater territorial dominance.

Following this disappointment, Sunderland enjoyed a run of eight games without defeat. They secured home wins over Chelsea and Liverpool and away wins over Manchester United and Middlesbrough. Willie Watson missed the home draw with Portsmouth because he was in Belfast as England's travelling reserve. This gave the club the chance to pick Stan Anderson for his league debut. This would be the first of 447 league and cup games for the future England international from the mining village of Horden.

After the win at Ayresome Park, the *Sunderland Echo* described Willie Watson as 'The man who plays and looks like an international whatever position the manager picks him for.' By the end of October, Sunderland were in second place. During these months, Willie Watson's extra-curricular activities were in the news. His winter cricket coaching school at Silksworth was flourishing with excellent coaching by brother Albert (professional at Seaham Park) and Alec Coxon (professional at Sunderland cricket club and formerly with Yorkshire). Early in November 1952, Willie and Albert Watson moved their sports shop from Newcastle Road to the New Arcade in the town centre.

Sunderland's unbeaten run ended when Preston won at Deepdale but the following week, Willie Watson opened the scoring in a win over Burnley, which returned the club to second. Sunderland remained in close contention with the leaders until the end of 1952. Their closest rivals were West Bromwich Albion and Wolves, thrashed 5-2 over the Christmas holidays. Also in December, floodlit football came to Roker Park when Dundee were the guests and helped to provide 34,300 supporters with a great exhibition of football.

The new year of 1953 brought the third round of the FA Cup. A favourable draw meant a home tie against Scunthorpe from the Third Division North. Before the cup match, on January 3, Sunderland completed the double over Arsenal at Roker Park by 3-1. England's only post-war double internationals were in opposition and Willie Watson was on the winning side against Arthur Milton. This victory also took Sunderland to the top of the First Division and should have been excellent preparation for the cup match. As it happened, Willie Watson was forced to withdraw from the Scunthorpe tie after aggravating a groin injury against Arsenal.

Sunderland struggled to draw the tie, both teams scoring once towards the end of a fog-blighted game. Five days later, and still without their captain, Sunderland travelled to Lincolnshire for the replay, where Scunthorpe put up a strenuous fight and Trevor Ford broke his ankle. Amazingly, he remained on the pitch and scored the winning goal.

Sunderland played two league games before the fourth round at Burnley. They lost at Derby and drew with Blackpool at home. These results were indicative of Sunderland's league form in 1953. The cup run was equally disappointing as Burnley knocked them out 2-0. Trevor Ford, of course, was out of action but Willie Watson was back on the left wing as Stan Anderson was retained at right half.

Immediately following Sunderland's exit from the cup, widespread flooding hit the east coast of England. From Lincolnshire to Kent, sea defences were breached in 1,200 places. Three hundred and seven people were drowned and 40,000 evacuated from their homes. There was widespread damage to property and disruption to communications. It was one of the greatest peace-time disasters in British history.

After Sunderland's second game with Scunthorpe, they did not win a league match for 13 games. Any challenge for the title was effectively destroyed. They did manage six draws in that spell but also conceded five goals twice, at Portsmouth and Bolton.

Consequently, the club slid down the table to ninth. It was an evenly contested season in which seven different clubs topped the table at some stage.

The eventual champions were Arsenal, on goal difference from Preston North End. Willie Watson made 25 league appearances in a season that was affected by injury, illness and cricket. He once again proved his great versatility by playing in four different positions. There was increasing competition from Stan Anderson for the right half place, but Willie Watson was still able to produce impressive displays on the left wing or at inside forward.

The saddest football news, in the second half of the season, was the injury to Sheffield Wednesday's prolific young striker, Derek Dooley, injured at Preston and subsequently losing a leg after gangrene set into the wound.

Willie Watson was soon in action in his most momentous cricket season. He scored 38 for Yorkshire against the MCC at Lord's, soon to be the scene of an epic Test. The Australian tourists, here to retain the Ashes, had already warmed up against Worcestershire.

However, for football fans, the season was not quite finished because Blackpool and Bolton were at Wembley for the FA Cup final. This was Blackpool's third final in six seasons, so far without success. In the Blackpool team was Stanley Matthews, aged 38 and making his third bid for a winner's medal. So Blackpool's 4-3 victory over Bolton became the Matthews final, despite the fact Stan Mortensen scored a hat-trick to win the game.

Willie Watson was soon in action against the Australians as they arrived in Bradford to play Yorkshire on May 6. The home county were crushed by an innings and 94 with only 11 and 15 runs coming from Watson. That was the first round to the tourists, especially Keith Miller, who scored 159, and Richie Benaud, who took 7-46. Willie Watson did not hit form until the middle of May, when he scored 162 not out against Somerset. But the match was drawn so that Yorkshire had to wait until the next match, against Worcestershire at Huddersfield's Fartown, for their first championship win. Willie Watson made 68 in the second innings having been run out for 11 in the first.

Towards the end of the month, the selectors held a Test trial, England v the Rest. There was no room for Willie Watson in the England line-up that included Len Hutton, Reg Simpson, Peter May and Denis Compton, so he batted at number four for the Rest. The match was curtailed by the weather and the only outcome was that Len Hutton was appointed England captain for the first Test.

Yorkshire's gloomy season continued with two more drawn championship games. The second game was overshadowed by the Coronation, which took place on a damp June 2. All cricket followers were delighted to find a knighthood for Jack Hobbs in the Coronation Honours List.

The next fixture was against Middlesex and, once again, Willie Watson enjoyed Lord's where he made 83, having moved up the order from five to four. However, this performance did not convince the Test selectors, whose 12 for the first Test against Australia did not include him. The first Test was at Trent Bridge, while Yorkshire were at home to Nottinghamshire. The batsmen chosen for the Nottingham Test were Len Hutton, Don Kenyon, Peter May, Denis Compton, Reg Simpson and Tom Graveney, which meant they had to rely on only four bowlers, Alec Bedser, Trevor Bailey, Roy Tattersall and Johnny Wardle. It was a low-scoring game dominated by the superb bowling of Bedser (14-99). England were 120-1 in the final innings, needing to make 229 to win when the weather washed out play.

Between the first and second Tests, the Australians went to Sheffield to play Yorkshire again. This was Willie Watson's opportunity to remind the selectors that he was a class, left-handed batsman. He made 61 in Yorkshire's first innings – but would that be enough?

CHAPTER 12

THE SECOND TEST – LORD'S JUNE 1953

COMMENTATORS WERE GENERALLY agreed that the selectors should strengthen the bowling to support Alec Bedser. This would involve replacing a batsman by a quality all-rounder or by a bowler. In their search for a genuine Test all-rounder, the selectors made the controversial choice of Freddie Brown, their own chairman. It was certainly unprecedented for the chairman of selectors to play for England during his term of office and also for a former amateur captain to play for a professional captain. There was the added fact that Brown was 42 and had retired from Test cricket two years before. The popular press were not impressed and one called the selection 'crazy'. However, the decision to include Willie Watson in the 12 for Lord's was generally welcomed, particularly because as a left-hander he could deal with leg-spinners. To make way for Brown and Watson, Peter May and Reg Simpson were unlucky to be dropped. This time Brian Statham's pace was preferred to Roy Tattersall's spin.

One lesson learned in the first Test at Trent Bridge was that the Australians were not invincible and that Lindsay Hassett's side, while talented, did not possess the outstanding quality of Don Bradman's 1948 team. In fact, the Test at Lord's demonstrated a remarkable evenness between the two sides, which produced a match of rapidly changing fortunes. The swinging pendulum was apparent on day one, Thursday June 25. The Australians batted first with Hassett acting as an emergency opener alongside Arthur Morris. The innings seemed very well established when the Australians reached 190-1. Then Neil Harvey was out to Bedser for 59, shortly followed by Hassett's retirement with cramp, having batted beautifully for 104. With these cornerstones removed, Johnny Wardle took three quick wickets and the match fluctuated towards England. But Australia rallied and finished the day on 263-5.

In the morning of day two England took the remaining five wickets for 83, despite dropping six catches. Alan Davidson gave a stinging left-hand catch to Willie Watson at short extra cover and then Len Hutton put down both Davidson and Ray Lindwall. However, Alec Bedser took his 200th Test wicket thanks to a good catch at backward short leg by Watson. The Australians were all out for 346 and England's response was to reach 177-1, thanks to the classic batsmanship of Len Hutton and Tom Graveney. Willie Watson wrote about them, saying, 'They shouldered the responsibility majestically.'

On Saturday June 27, the third day of this absorbing and fluctuating Test, Lindwall bowled the first over and, with his fourth ball, yorked Tom Graveney for 78. This brought together England's two greatest batsmen since the War, Len Hutton and Denis Compton. They were destined to make one of their rare century partnerships. With ten minutes to go before lunch, Hutton was caught for 145 and England were 279-3. The whole ground rose to salute one of Hutton's finest centuries against the Australians. England seemed poised for a very large score but this was the pinnacle of their ascendancy in this game.

Willie Watson made his Test debut against the Australians when thoughts had turned to food. There would be no time to settle, no time to feel your way in, to develop your concentration. He survived until lunch without scoring.

But the decline in England's fortunes began in the first hour after lunch. Bill Johnston, a great Test bowler, opened against Willie Watson, who swept a loose ball for four. A fine way to start an innings, while the crowd cheered encouragement and

Johnston bowled again. This seemed like a similar delivery but it was deceptive. Watson tried to sweep again but missed and overbalanced. The ball struck the wicketkeeper's pads and cruelly rebounded onto the stumps. Watson out stumped for four. The last seven English wickets could only manage 93 and of these 31 came from a last-wicket partnership between Johnny Wardle and Brian Statham.

England's first innings lead was 26 and they would have to bat fourth. The evening of the third day belonged to Australia as Arthur Morris and Keith Miller took the score to 96-1. Miller, one of the world's greatest all-rounders, was the dominating partner and revelled in the tense situation.

Sunday, as always in those days, was a rest day and on Monday morning the overnight batsmen added another 72 precious runs. Len Hutton was forced to introduce occasional bowler, Denis Compton, who broke the partnership by getting Morris brilliantly caught by Statham for 89. Between lunch and tea, the Australians were contained by Bedser, Brown and Wardle, so that their score put them 279 ahead with three wickets standing.

However, after tea, Ray Lindwall launched a savage assault on the English attack to make exactly 50 in 45 minutes. He had lifted England's target from substantial to massive. When Len Hutton and Don Kenyon opened England's second innings, there were 55 minutes left plus the fifth day and the target was 343. The question asked was, could any side make that many runs in the fourth innings against Australia? The answer came swiftly and sickeningly for England as Lindwall dispatched both openers in three overs while Johnston had Graveney caught at the wicket. The scoreboard had a desperate 12-3 and still half-an-hour to play. Willie Watson joined Denis Compton at the wicket. He had not watched the wickets tumble because such misfortunes 'played havoc with his nerves'. He preferred to read a newspaper or a magazine.

Once the batsmen reached the wicket, everything changed because it was the batsmen against bowlers and fielders. Willie Watson felt just as accomplished as the opposition and 'knew as many tricks'. He was not feeling boastful but relieved that he could be involved in saving the day. However, there was still one more awful moment to survive when Doug Ring bowled the final over and Watson gave a half chance to Lindwall, standing at his right shoulder at backward short leg. Ray Lindwall, who had bowled and batted brilliantly that day, dropped the catch.

At close of play, England were 20-3, with Compton on five and Watson on three. EW Swanton, in his *Test Matches of 1953*, summed up the fourth day perceptively, as the game seemed to have been won and lost in the final two hours 'But this has been such a remarkable, and in many ways, magnificent, fight that, against all reason, no doubt, I will not believe that it is over until the scoreboard proclaims the fact.'

The fifth and final day arrived with England needing 323 to win. The morning newspapers were agreed that England's position was hopeless. According to most people, the best that could be hoped for was a draw. This pessimism was reflected in the crowd which was only a fraction of the huge numbers in attendance during the first four days. The odds were more than 50-1 against England getting a draw.

Willie Watson kept his spirits up by wondering if England could stick it out. He reckoned that if he and Compton could get their eye in again there was hope. The start of the great defensive action was mounted by the overnight pair. For Compton it was a role foreign to his nature, nevertheless he carried it out for 95 minutes. He batted beautifully but at 12.40pm he was lbw to Johnston for 33. The crowd cheered him in: the score was 73-4. Now Trevor Bailey made his way to the wicket. He was the third batsman, following Compton and Watson, who was an accomplished footballer. Willie Watson thought that Trevor Bailey was the perfect man for a crisis. He had intense concentration and whatever the bowlers did, they would not be able to tempt him into a rash shot. He was a man who would revel in this sort of situation.

Despite the importance of defence, Willie Watson was prepared to hit the safe ball hard, which ensured the fielders were spread away from the wicket when a ball lifted off the dust. Three times he hit Johnston to the leg-side boundary and twice Ring got the same treatment. Trevor Bailey, at the other end, dealt with Davidson and Benaud without any interest in scoring runs. The two reached lunch safely: the score was 116-4; Watson on 54 and Bailey on 10. While the two partners were at one with their concentrated defence, there were contrasts. At lunch, Willie Watson could not face the food, but Trevor Bailey is said to have managed both plates. Both batsmen batted capless: Watson taller, fair, elegant and with a silent, phlegmatic temperament; Bailey, dark haired, determined but gregarious enough to pass the time of day with close fielders.

The next big milestone would be the arrival of the new ball. It was vital that both these batsmen were still together around three o'clock when Lindsay Hassett could call for it. Not surprisingly in the 50 minutes after lunch only 33 were added to the total. Hassett then called on Lindwall and Miller, who had not bowled since lunch, for a full onslaught. However, by this stage, the batsmen were more confident and, as Willie Watson described, 'The ball seemed as big as a football.' The Lord's crowd was growing by the hour as news of England's resistance filtered through London. It was said that there were no taxis left in the City for the trip to St John's Wood. Lindwall's only successes in this spell of 40 minutes were to inflict two painful blows to Bailey's right hand. This was one of those rare occasions when a cricket crowd revelled in defence for defence's sake. The new ball had been resisted and the partnership patiently reached tea. At this stage, the score stood at 183-4 with Willie Watson on 84 and Trevor Bailey on 39. At no time was a voice raised against the slow scoring rate, even though it was only just over 30 runs per hour.

When play resumed after tea, the prospect of a draw seemed increasingly possible. Certainly Willie Watson felt quietly composed. As the partnership had lasted so long, he could see no reason to fail. The main danger he could identify was tiredness, which could cause a relaxation in concentration. He even raised the possibility of going for victory with Bailey, who simply turned his back and returned to his crease without a word. Eventually, Trevor Bailey reached his half century after three and a half hours. A tremendous piece of concentration that the crowd greeted with terrific cheers.

Lindsay Hassett tried all his bowlers to break the partnership but it was the least-considered, Davidson, who came closest when Willie Watson, on 88, snicked the ball just short of Graeme Hole at slip. The next ball, pitching in the rough just outside Watson's off stump, beat him fair and square. However, such false strokes stood out because they were so rare.

Just before half-past five, Doug Ring pitched a ball outside Watson's legs which he swung hard and high to long leg. Richie Benaud made a tremendous leap to try to make the catch, but the ball pitched well in front of him and sped to the Tavern boundary. This gave Willie Watson a century in his first Test against Australia. All around the ground spectators stood and cheered him; this was an heroic hundred which would remain in the memory of everyone who saw it. The innings had taken five-and-a-quarter hours. The partnership continued for another 20 minutes with Watson, fair haired, cool and upstanding, concentrating on getting the ball plumb in the middle of the bat. But at ten minutes to six, Ring turned a ball which Watson nicked on to his pads and which Hole caught at slip. The stand had lasted for four hours and ten minutes and Watson had made 109. The crowd gave him a standing ovation. There were 40 minutes of play left and England were 236-5.

Freddie Brown, padded up all day, rose to his feet in the pavilion, turned to Barbara Watson and bowed before proceeding to the wicket. But hardly had he arrived in the middle than Bailey was caught off Ring. As so often happens, when one member of a big partnership is out, the other soon follows. In fact, Willie Watson had just stepped into a bath when he heard the great roar which greeted Bailey's dismissal for 71. Watson scrambled out of the bath to watch the last half hour. Godfrey Evans had joined Brown at the wicket; both had lasted for one ball against Ray Lindwall in the first innings. Surely Hassett would turn to the great fast bowler? He had not bowled for two hours, but the captain preferred an all spin attack.

Doug Ring bowled to Brown with three slips. The all-rounder decided that for him the best form of defence was attack. His five hits for four gave the crowd something to cheer about, while his several mis-hits caused them much anguish. Meanwhile, Evans suppressed his natural ebullience and defended. Between each ball all eyes were focused on the clock as the minute hand approached the half hour and close of play. At 27 minutes past six, Brown was caught off Richie Benaud. So, it was still possible for the Australians to win as Benaud had four balls left. However, Johnny Wardle, a more than competent batsman, played the remaining balls safely. England finished on 282-7. The fluctuating battle, which had held the attention of millions for five days, was over.

However, the commotion about the Watson–Bailey stand went on for weeks. People could not stop talking about it. The papers, too, were full of it. Even Sir Don Bradman was heard to say that, 'If we get any more Tests like this, I shan't be able to stand the strain!'

For Willie Watson, there was no time for celebrations. He left Lord's for a train to Taunton where Yorkshire were due to play Somerset.

CHAPTER 13

THE FIGHT FOR
THE ASHES

THERE WAS TIME for only two Yorkshire matches between the second and third Test matches. The series was evenly balanced after two closely fought draws. The England selectors would hope to strengthen their team for the third Test without taking any risks. Willie Watson confirmed his good form by scoring 92 not out at Taunton, although the match with Somerset was drawn. The Yorkshire team moved on to The Oval, where they were bowled out twice for less than 200 by a strong Surrey side who won by ten wickets.

To take advantage of his Test century, an advert appeared in the *Sunderland Echo* for the Willie Watson Sports shop in the New Arcade, which stocked all the summer sports equipment available. The biggest worry for the selectors now was the fitness of captain Len Hutton, who was being treated for fibrositis. Fortunately, he was declared fit to play and joined the 12 selected. There were four changes from the second Test, including a recall for Bill Edrich and Jim Laker.

The match was ruined by the weather. At the close of the second day, Australia's first innings had reached 221 for three, with Neil Harvey unbeaten on 102. On day three, the remaining Australian wickets were taken for 97 runs, making a total of 318. Len Hutton opened for England with Bill Edrich, but two wickets fell cheaply.

This brought together Len Hutton and Denis Compton in 'an almost flawless display of batsmanship on a doubtful wicket' (EW Swanton).

The loss of both their wickets brought together Willie Watson and night watchman, Johnny Wardle. They survived until the close of play with Watson 0 not out. Rain prevented any play on day four and threatened day five. The match did not resume until after lunch on the final day. Willie Watson and Johnny Wardle stayed together for a quiet three-quarters of an hour, adding 23 runs. Then both were yorked, by Alan Davidson and Ray Lindwall respectively. This was followed by a stand between Reg Simpson and Trevor Bailey, which prevented England from being asked to follow on. Eventually England were all out for 276, so a draw was inevitable, or so it seemed. There followed an hour of pure fantasy when Australia went in to bat to play out time. Instead, they were almost bowled out in an hour, reaching just 35 for 8. Johnny Wardle, exploiting the turning wicket, had the remarkable figures of five overs, two maidens, seven runs and four wickets. The crowds had had a lot to put up with from the weather at Old Trafford but the completely unexpected finale must have sent them home in fine spirits.

The day following the third Test, Willie Watson was at Lord's for the Gentlemen v Players fixture. He joined Denis Compton, Cyril Washbrook, Tom Graveney, Godfrey Evans and Alec Bedser in a strong Players team. The Gentlemen were equally well represented with Test cricketers including Bill Edrich, Peter May, David Sheppard, Reg Simpson, Trevor Bailey and Doug Insole. The Gentlemen were bowled out for 129 with Alec Bedser and Roy Tattersall sharing the wickets five each. However, the Players were unable to take advantage and were dismissed for 123; Willie Watson's 29 runs made him second top scorer. In the second innings, the batsmen bounced back and the Gentlemen totaled 311, including a century by Reg Simpson. The Players faced a target of 317 but could not cope with the spin of Robin Marlar (7-79), and were finally beaten by 95 runs. Willie Watson managed only nine runs in the second innings.

He left London immediately en route to Chesterfield, where Yorkshire faced Derbyshire on July 18. Yorkshire were completely outplayed and lost by ten wickets. Watson managed 43 in the first innings out of a total of 121.

For the fourth Test, the selectors dropped Fred Trueman and Johnny Wardle from the 12 selected and recalled Brian Statham and Tony Lock. The old problem facing the selectors was whether they should choose an extra bowler, in which case a batsman would have to be left out. Some commentators, like EW Swanton, reluctantly concluded that Willie Watson should be omitted. They believed that he had not been at his best since the Lord's Test. Willie later revealed that he had felt his form slip away after that match; probably because the fourth Test would be at Headingley, his home ground, he survived.

Lindsay Hassett won the toss and put England in to bat. They struggled all morning, having lost Len Hutton, yorked second ball for 0. Willie Watson stemmed the tide, batting resolutely; but almost strokelessly he made 24 in two-and-three-quarter hours. His dismissal was unfortunate because a ball from Lindwall struck him on the ankle and rolled slowly to his stumps. On day two, England's first innings ended on 167, with Tom Graveney top scorer on 55. The Australians replied with 266 with Alec Bedser taking 6-95. Watson was unable to bat after lunch.

The visitors had scored at twice England's rate and, with a first innings lead of 99, were undeniably in a strong position. On the third day, the rain interrupted play, as it had done many times in this series. At the close, England were 62-1, but Len Hutton was out. On day four, Denis Compton and Bill Edrich came together and their batting recalled their halcyon days shortly after the War. Lindwall, with the new ball, dismissed Edrich, caught brilliantly at slip by Jim de Courcy for 64. Willie Watson's arrival at the wicket put England back in their shell in the 25 minutes before tea. The Australians surrounded him with close fielders so that, by tea, he had made only two. John Arlott described him as looking assured and unruffled in the face of Australia's attacking fields. Together with Denis Compton, the score was 170-3 when rain and bad light stopped play at 5.20. When play resumed, the shower had livened up the pitch and Keith Miller was bowling at top speed. He got a good-length ball to lift and Willie Watson was caught magnificently at fourth slip by Alan Davidson for 15.

On the final day, England's second innings closed at 275, of which Compton made 61 and Trevor Bailey 38 in over four hours. The time was 4.13pm and Australia needed 177 to win in just under two hours. The Australian approach was to go for a win, but accurate bowling by Trevor Bailey and Alec Bedser contained them to 147 for four. The drawn match meant the two sides were all square as they approached the final Test.

Between the fourth and fifth Tests, Yorkshire played four matches. Gradually, Willie Watson found his form and confidence returned. At Leicester, he managed 75 and 66, top scoring in both innings. At Bradford, he scored 42 not out and 83, opening the innings against Warwickshire; while finally, at Scarborough, again opening the batting, he made 10 and 47 against Derbyshire. Unfortunately, this revival came too late for the selectors, who had decided to recall Peter May. John Arlott found the dropping of Willie Watson a little surprising. After all, he argued, only Len Hutton and Willie Watson had made centuries for England in this series. Arlott said, 'There is some criticism of Watson on the grounds that he is a slow scorer but he has just played a very fast innings, going in first for Yorkshire and, after all, the positions in which he has come in during this series have not given him much opportunity or justification for taking risks. He has also twice been most unluckily out, stumped off Langley's pads and bowled off his ankle by a ball going wide. Above all, he can play Lindwall and that must be the criterion for selection as an English batsman in this series. Peter May is in magnificent form just now against County attacks which lack the pace of Lindwall... There is no doubt that the instant May comes to the wicket, Hassett will throw Lindwall – and probably Miller – at him.'

Doug Wright, Kent and England spin bowler, quoted in the *Sunderland Echo*, believed the selectors faced a difficult task. He would have brought in an extra bowler and lost a batsman. The bowler would be Fred Trueman, who was returning to form. But it was not easy to decide which batsman should go. He would drop 'the sheet anchor' Willie Watson. Doug Wright knew it was risky but thought the match demanded some risks. The *Echo* thought England might regret the omission of Willie Watson, should things go badly for the early batsmen. 'On the evidence of the last three tests, defence is clearly Watson's forte.'

The Australian Board of Control agreed that the fifth Test at The Oval should be extended to six days. In the event, extra time was not needed. England bowled Australia out on day one for 275, thanks to the extra bowler, Fred Trueman, who took 4-86 and, on day two, England managed 235-7 with a captain's innings of 82 by Len Hutton. The England score reached 306 on day three while Australia were skittled by Laker and Lock for 162. So England needed only 131 for victory and the Ashes but, at 6.10, Len Hutton went for a suicidal second run and was clearly run out. A great silence descended over The Oval as Peter May came in to play out time.

On day four, England batted resolutely to make the final 94 runs. It took them two hours and 40 minutes and the Australians had only one success, when they removed Peter May. That meant that victory was achieved with Bill Edrich and Denis Compton at the wicket, and the Ashes were regained after 19 years.

Over the five-match series, Len Hutton was England's outstanding batsman, averaging 55.37 (442 runs from nine innings), while Alec Bedser's bowling was crucial (39 wickets at 17.48). The contribution of Trevor Bailey (222 runs at 37.71) was essential to victory. But the unluckiest player to miss the final Test at The Oval was Willie Watson. His wife, Barbara, was more upset by his dropping than her husband, 'who never pushed himself forward'. She was also disappointed by Brian Johnston's radio summing up of the Ashes series because he did not mention Willie Watson's contribution until Trevor Bailey reminded him. Fifty years later in 2003, the MCC made a presentation at Lord's to Willie Watson and Trevor Bailey to commemorate their stand against the Australians in 1953.

There was no time for Willie Watson to mope over The Oval Test because he was immediately on the road to Dover to play Kent. This was the first of three drawn matches in what was proving to be one of Yorkshire's worst seasons. The absence for the whole summer of Bob Appleyard, and the injury which restricted Brian Close to just two games, meant Yorkshire's bowling was depleted. Against Kent, Watson made 41; at Edgbaston he made 65; while at Worcester he made 67 in the second innings. The final championship match was at Bournemouth, at the end of August, when Hampshire were beaten by an innings and 45 runs and Watson again contributed 67 runs.

The Yorkshire season finished as usual at the Scarborough festival with a match against the MCC. This brought Trevor Bailey and Willie Watson together again but this time as opponents. Perhaps their early morning football training together at Scarborough FC toned up their batting skills because Bailey made 80 for the MCC while Watson made 64 not out for Yorkshire. In the Yorkshire batting averages, Len Hutton, as usual, led the way (63.02 with 2,458 from 44 innings) with Willie Watson second scoring, 1,126 runs at an average of 46.91.

Before returning to the winter game, Willie Watson had one last fling in the cricket season of 1953. He was chosen again to represent the Players against the Gentlemen, this time at Scarborough. As in the previous Scarborough match against the MCC, Willie Watson and Trevor Bailey were in opposition. A strong Players XI batted first and amassed 532-5 declared. The Yorkshire pair led the way, with Len Hutton scoring 241 and Willie Watson adding 143 not out. The Gentlemen were not deterred and replied with 447-8 declared. Peter May (157) and Colin Cowdrey (100) scored centuries for the Gentlemen while Willie Watson was outstanding in the field, catching both centurions and also Bill Edrich. In the Players' second innings, Willie Watson top scored with 47 not out as a sporting declaration came at 165-6. Immediately, the Gentlemen took up the challenge and made a victorious 252-5 with Edrich scoring 133.

CHAPTER 14

EXIT FROM ROKER PARK

WHILE THE ASHES series took centre stage in the summer of 1953, there was plenty of activity in the football close season, and it centred on Roker Park. Between June 10 and 23, Sunderland plunged dramatically into the transfer market. First they bought the Scottish international goalkeeper, Jimmy Cowan, from Greenock Morton for £9,000, a Sunderland record fee for the position. A few days later, they turned their attention to London and bought from Arsenal their Welsh international centre back, Ray Daniel, for £30,000. Next they moved to Lancashire and paid £27,500 to Burnley for forward Billy Elliott. The board and manager Bill Murray had been shocked by the steep decline during the previous season, and their response was extravagant transfer deals which revived the term 'Bank of England team'.

While batting for England and Yorkshire, Willie Watson was the centre of speculation in the *Sunderland Echo*. If he succeeded at Test level, then the newspaper believed his career at Roker Park hung by a thread, as he would have a strong claim to tour the West Indies with the MCC in December 1953. On July 30, the *Echo*'s headline asked, 'Will Watson Now Leave Soccer Behind?' His name was included on a list of ten players invited by the MCC to tour the West Indies. He had no doubts about the tour and he jumped at the chance to travel and play cricket abroad, but it did mean he had to consider carefully his football career at Sunderland. For three months he would be able to play football but whether he would return for the 1954–55 season seemed doubtful.

Sunderland's season began a couple of days after the Ashes victory at The Oval. The fixture was at The Valley against Charlton Athletic, and Sunderland included all three of their summer signings in a full-strength team (apart from absent cricketer Willie Watson). Ray Daniel led out the Sunderland side before 50,000 fans packing The Valley. The result was an entertaining 5-3 victory for the south Londoners but the press thought the Sunderland defence had never been poorer. Three days later, Sunderland lost the local derby at Newcastle 2-1, the first time Willie Watson had missed this fixture since his move to the north east. It proved to be a disastrous opening to the season for Sunderland. In the first nine fixtures before Willie Watson was restored to the team, they won only two games, one of which was a 7-1 record defeat for Arsenal.

Willie Watson did not complete his cricket season until September 9. Despite the team's disappointing early season form, he had to wait for his first-team recall. Young Stan Anderson was beginning to make the right-half position his own and the new recruit, Billy Elliott, was first choice on the left wing. So it needed an injury to Len Shackleton at Portsmouth, where Sunderland lost 4-1, to create an opening. So it was on September 26 at Roker Park that Watson returned to the Sunderland line-up against Blackpool. The *Sunderland Echo* described the occasion as 'Matthews' Day', the annual chance to watch the maestro play. Almost 61,000 spectators turned up to watch a match involving 13 internationals. Sunderland grabbed a last-minute winner but nothing in the game matched the brilliance of the Stanley Matthews–Ernie Taylor wing. The following week, Sunderland earned a 2-2 draw at Stamford Bridge, when Willie Watson showed his adaptability by starring in two positions. In the first half, he was the cultured inside forward and in the second he took over from the injured Jack Hedley to give a fine exhibition at full-back. Willie Watson's third game at inside left was away to Manchester United and, in the absence of Ray Daniel, he took over as captain. Unfortunately, the match was narrowly lost 1-0. For the home game against Bolton Wanderers, 'utility man' Watson was chosen at centre forward, the first time for six years. His opponent would be Malcolm Barrass, who had been his left-wing partner in the victory international against Wales in 1946! Sunderland's defeat sent them to bottom place in the league for the first time in their 63-year history.

Sunderland reached the depths despite several times fielding an all-international forward line. In the national press, the club was often the target of critical comment, especially with reference to their big spending. Many took pleasure in the failure of the extravagant transfer deals. A distraction from the league position came on October 21 with a floodlit friendly against Racing Club de Paris. For this match, Willie Watson reverted to his midfield role and the visitors were dispatched 5-2. He retained that position against Preston North End but the team were well beaten 6-2. Then on November 7 Willie Watson was chosen to play at right back against West Bromwich Albion in what turned out to be his last game for Sunderland, a 2-0 defeat. This was the seventh position he had played in for the club, a tribute to his versatility.

Eighteen days later, England's proud unbeaten home record against Continental opponents was lost to a great Hungarian team. In fact, the visitors were superior in every aspect of the game and England were thrashed 6-3. The England captain Billy Wright summed it up: 'They were relentless. They were superb.'

In December 1953, Willie Watson was released by Sunderland AFC in order to join the MCC tour party to the West Indies. He had played for the club for seven seasons and two months. He made 211 league appearances and played in 12 FA Cup ties. In total, he scored 16 goals. Cricket commitments to Yorkshire, at the start and end of the football season, meant he missed around 58 Sunderland league fixtures but, to his credit, he was club captain in the latter half of his Roker Park career.

When the *Wisden Cricketers' Almanack* was published for the summer of 1953, it included, as usual, its choice of the Cricketers of the Year. This selection had been made in every year since 1889, except for eight war years, and almost all the great players of the past had been honoured. They included CB Fry, WG Grace, Wilfred Rhodes, Jack Hobbs, Sydney Barnes, Frank Woolley and Donald Bradman. The 1953 Cricketers of the Year were Neil Harvey and Keith Miller, of Australia, and Tony Lock, Johnny Wardle and Willie Watson of England.

CHAPTER 15

CAULDRON IN THE CARIBBEAN

THE MCC TOUR of the West Indies was the first to be captained by a professional cricketer, Len Hutton. It was the first time an England tour party had travelled by air and, for 33-year-old Willie Watson, it was his first MCC tour. On December 14 1953, the party departed for the Caribbean. The 16-strong group included Charles Palmer of Leicestershire as player-manager. The MCC secretary, Ronnie Aird, described it as the strongest party to play overseas since the War, and Len Hutton agreed with him. Only Alec Bedser was omitted so that he could be rested before the Ashes tour the following winter. The selectors had included Ken Suttle of Sussex, who was quite inexperienced, while Hutton would have preferred Bill Edrich.

However, some commentators had their doubts. They pointed out that several players were untried, that there was no accredited opening batsman to partner Len Hutton and that there was no specialist slip fielder or leg spinner. Nevertheless, there was an underlying feeling of optimism based on the recent recovery of the Ashes. Added to this was the desire to get even with the West Indies team, which had won the last series in England in 1950 so comprehensively. Consequently, the series had something of a 'world title' about it, which only added to the tensions that were brewing.

The tour party landed in Bermuda, where three preliminary matches were played. The cricket was of little value, as the wickets were a matting cover on a concrete base but, at least, the players could get accustomed to the heat. Len Hutton struck an early and complete understanding with his new partner, Willie Watson, and their well-judged quick singles were soon to become a feature of their partnership. Unfortunately, Willie Watson tripped over a concrete strip laid for nets and injured his wrist. Initially, he felt little inconvenience but later it caused him pain and soreness. The serious part of the tour began in Jamaica, where the MCC had their first-ever win over the island. The MCC scored a commanding 457-7 declared, which included an innings of 161 by Watson, the maiden century of the tour, plus 82 from Tom Graveney. The match was won by an innings and 21 runs. The bowling of Brian Statham and Fred Trueman was very hostile on the hard wicket.

The first Test was played at Sabina Park, Kingston, Jamaica. England chose four fast bowlers for this game and then found the pitch docile. Len Hutton lost the toss and West Indies batted first and persisted for more than two days for a formidable 417. Willie Watson felt that the tourists were still adjusting to the brightness of the sunlight, as he had missed a chance when he was blinded by the evening sun. He thought this might also have contributed to his dismissal for three when England batted because he was bowled by a perfectly straight ball from Gerry Gomez, which he would never have missed back home in England. The tourists were bowled out for 170; the great spinning pair of Alf Valentine (3-16) and Sonny Ramadhin (4-65) shared seven wickets. England were 247 behind on the first innings but, to everyone's shock and surprise, the West Indies captain, Jeff Stollmeyer, did not enforce the follow-on. Instead, the West Indies declared on 209-6. So England faced a huge task of scoring 457 in nine-and-a-half hours in the fourth innings.

Despite Willie Watson's worries about the conditions, he and Len Hutton put on 130 for the first wicket in confident style. Peter May joined Watson and showed what a fine batsman he was. The pair put on 90 but it was clear the heat was exhausting Watson. He was out caught and bowled by captain Stollmeyer after running three, following a Peter May drive. Willie Watson had made 116 but was disappointed because he felt capable of staying in all day and the next. So England began the last day needing 230 runs to win with eight wickets left. *The Times* saw the match as 'finely balanced' but a mid-order collapse saw England go from 282-4 to 285-9. So England were beaten decisively and shatteringly. To skipper Len Hutton this was both a surprise and a bitter blow. Jeff Stollmeyer's decision not to enforce the follow-on was vindicated. Another unfortunate incident in the Test was the no-balling of Tony Lock, England's left-arm spinner, for throwing.

A two-day match was played against the Leewards before the team moved on to Barbados where, in Bridgetown, the MCC beat Barbados by one wicket off the last ball. The second Test followed on the same ground on February 6 1954. The island was politically less volatile than Jamaica and provided a less tense atmosphere. Nevertheless, throughout the West Indies, Len Hutton and manager Charles Palmer found that racial sensitivity bubbled just below the surface. Also, home rule movements had grown rapidly in the six years since India has been granted independence.

For the second Test, the policy of selecting four fast bowlers had to be reviewed and Fred Trueman and Alan Moss were dropped. Jim Laker was promoted, leaving a place for an extra batsman. The obvious choice was Ken Suttle, who had just returned to form, but surprisingly Len Hutton preferred Charles Palmer. It was all to no avail, as Clyde Walcott recorded his only Test double century (220) in the West Indian total of 383. England batted poorly, making only 181; Watson was stumped off Ramadhin for six. The West Indies second innings was declared at 292-2 (John Holt 166). England again faced a large total in the fourth innings and again failed to get near it despite substantial scores from Hutton (77), May (62), Compton (93) and Graveney (64).

England were now two down in the series and the English press were questioning Len Hutton's captaincy, and also the contribution of the team as a whole. In contrast, the West Indies were now supremely confident. The tour moved on to what was then called British Guiana. The match was played at the Bourda ground in Georgetown and the tourists batted first. The innings included two free-flowing double centuries by Willie Watson and Tom Graveney. Both players hit the top scores of their careers, Watson 257 and Graveney 231. Together they put on 402 for the fourth wicket, a total which might have been much greater had not captain's orders required them to throw away their wickets after reaching two hundred. England reached 607 to win by an innings and 98 runs. Manager Charles Palmer wrote that 'Willie Watson was lovely to watch; he never moved, he glided. He was never in a hurry. He was a smooth performer in every way.' Willie Watson himself believed that this record-breaking stand was the turning point of the tour.

The third Test began on February 24 1954 at the same ground. Hutton won the toss, which was unusual, chose to bat and scored a masterly century, 169, out of a total of 453. Sonny Ramadhin had the incredible bowling figures of 67 overs, 34 maidens, 113 runs for six wickets, which included that of Willie Watson, bowled for 12. The spinner toiled away as gamely as any bowler in Test cricket, but when the West Indies batted, Brian Statham dispatched Frank Worrell, Jeff Stollmeyer and Clyde Walcott in a fine spell of fast bowling. Despite 94 from Everton Weekes wickets continued to fall until Cliff McWatt and John Holt came together for the eighth wicket. As the partnership grew, excitement in the crowd reached fever pitch and the noise was deafening. However, going for the hundredth run of their partnership, McWatt was clearly run out by Peter May. The fiercely partisan crowd, politically encouraged and involved in gambling on the hundred partnership, took exception to the umpire's decision. Suddenly, to Len Hutton's surprise, he saw umpire Badge Menzies running to the pavilion for safety. Until then, the England captain had not seen the bottles and other missiles landing on the outfield. Hutton's reaction was to yell to Willie Watson, fielding on the boundary nearest to the pavilion, to stop the umpire. Hutton feared a lot of lost time or an abandonment if the umpire disappeared. He was not sure his voice would carry to Watson in all the bedlam but the fielder successfully interpreted the signals and stopped Menzies. Willie Watson said that when the umpire came to a halt he was shaking with fright.

Hutton raced across to reassure Menzies that the England team would look after him. Nevertheless, he seemed singularly unconvinced and responded, 'But I have to live here, Mr Hutton.' The mounted police soon arrived but Hutton bravely refused advice to leave the field and he told the president of the local board that 'These people are not going to get us off. I want another wicket or two before close.'

Eventually, order was restored and Jim Laker bowled Ramadhin to get Hutton the wicket he wanted. The West Indies' first innings reached only 251 and the follow-on was enforced. They did fractionally better in their second innings and England needed only 13 to win in three-and-a-half hours. England's victory was achieved when Willie Watson hit Everton Weekes for six. The series now stood at 2-1 to the West Indies.

The MCC moved on to the Windward Isles, where a two-day game was drawn. Next, the tourists had a four-day match with Trinidad at Port of Spain.

The feature of the MCC's first innings was another century by Willie Watson, this time 141. The match was won by seven wickets, good preparation for the fourth Test, to be played on the same ground starting on March 17. Len Hutton was planning to change his opening partner, as the second and third Tests were relative failures for Willie Watson, whose best score had been 27 not out. The captain's first thought was that Peter May might do the job but his form was inconsistent. After watching Watson's magnificent century against Trinidad, Hutton decided to promote Trevor Bailey to opener and move his previous opening partner to an attacking number five.

The Test wicket at Port of Spain was jute matting, which suited the West Indies batsmen, especially the 'three Ws'. They made massive contributions – Weekes (206), Worrell (167) and Walcott (124) – as the innings was declared at 681-8. Brian Statham pulled a rib muscle on the first day and could not bowl again on the tour. England replied with two centuries by Peter May (135) and Denis Compton (133) plus 92 from Tom Graveney in a total of 537. The match dwindled into the anticipated draw. Willie Watson made

4 and 32 so the move to number five had not produced the form shown in the previous game.

Between the fourth and fifth Tests, the MCC drew a two-day match with the Jamaican Colts XI. Willie Watson was hit on the head, the wound needing six stitches, just three days before the Test. That was played at the venue for the first Test, Sabina Park, beginning on March 30 1954. A win was essential for England to square the series although it did not look promising when Len Hutton lost the toss for the fourth time in five Tests. The West Indies chose to bat first on what seemed like a perfect wicket. Instead, the day belonged to Trevor Bailey, who opened the bowling and took 7- 34, which went a long way to bowling out the opposition for 139. Bailey then opened the batting with Len Hutton, who made a brilliant 205. England totalled 414, but Willie Watson was dismissed cheaply, again for 4. The West Indies' second innings reached 346 thanks to a fine 116 from Clyde Walcott, with Jeff Stollmeyer chipping in with 64. So England needed only 72 for victory. Hutton sent in Tom Graveney and Willie Watson to open and although the Gloucestershire batsman went for a five-ball duck, bowled by Frank King, Watson, 20 not out, and Peter May, 40 not out, took England to a nine-wicket win. The series ended on level terms, much better than could have been expected when England lost the first two tests. The *Yorkshire Post* declared that Hutton 'had silenced his critics'.

Willie Watson enjoyed the tour of the West Indies. He had always believed in taking people as you found them and in trying to understand their different temperaments and cultures. With that approach, he thought that you would get along with other people pretty well. With the bat it was a tour of mixed fortunes. For the tour as a whole he scored 892 runs, more than a hundred ahead of the second man, Len Hutton. But his batting average of 68.6 put him well behind Hutton, who averaged 78.0. When it came to Test averages, there was no one within 40 of Len Hutton's magnificent average of 96.71. Willie Watson's Test batting average was a modest 28.00. The MCC party set sail for home on April 4 1954.

CHAPTER 16

RETURN TO YORKSHIRE

IN APRIL 1954, Sunderland were battling against relegation. After their poor start to the season they had won six league fixtures out of 24 by Christmas. Their 63-year membership of the top division seemed likely to end. The desperate situation convinced the club's directors to splash out again in the transfer market. They had sold Trevor Ford to Cardiff in November for £30,000, so funds were available. At the New Year 1953–54, Sunderland bought Ken Chisholm from Cardiff and, a week later, Ted Purdon from Birmingham. This brought two forwards to the club for the revenue raised by Ford. The transfers certainly contributed to 'improved results' in the second half of the season. On April 7 1954, Sunderland were fourth from bottom, equal on points with Sheffield United and Middlesbrough, but seven points clear of Liverpool.

Willie Watson was able to follow Sunderland's fortunes (and misfortunes) through the newspapers in the West Indies. When the MCC party docked back in England, the relegation battle reached its climax over the Easter weekend with two fixtures against Sheffield United. The first at Roker Park was drawn 2-2; the second at Bramall Lane was a 3-1 victory, which meant Sunderland were safe with only one match remaining.

On his arrival back in England on April 22, the *Sunderland Echo* published a photograph of Willie Watson with his three-year-old son, Graham. The newspaper headline was 'Cricket or Football?' 'It depends', was the player's elusive reply. 'I'm not definitely finished with football but if the opportunity is there for a settled cricketing future, then it is an obvious choice. After all, I'm 34.' Much would depend on whether he was selected for the Australian tour of 1954–55. But cricket, he felt, was so unstable. One minute you were in, the next minute you were out! From the tour, Willie Watson said he remembered breaking three bats on the cement-hard wickets, the tension among the MCC players after their poor start, and the amazing enthusiasm of the West Indies spectators for cricket.

Once settled back into his Viewforth Terrace home, Willie Watson was the guest of Sunderland AFC to watch their final game of the season against Burnley at Roker Park. Eight of the team would have been very familiar to him, especially Fred Hall, Arthur Wright, Jack Stelling and Len Shackleton. The three newcomers were goalkeeper Willie Fraser, centre forward Ted Purdon and inside left Ken Chisholm, scorer of both Sunderland goals in a 2-1 victory. So Sunderland finished 18th, while Middlesbrough and Liverpool were relegated.

On April 26, Willie Watson was included in the Yorkshire squad for the games against the MCC and Oxford University. Two days later, together with manager Bill Murray, Willie Watson announced the parting of the ways between club and player. The *Sunderland Echo* had believed the decision had been inevitable for some nine months. However, they emphasised that he left with the club's best wishes. His plan was to use a full cricket season to fulfill his burning ambition: to win a place on the tour to Australia in 1954–55. Bill Murray said he was sad about Willie Watson's decision because he felt that Watson had two good seasons left in him. At the same time, Barbara Watson told the *Yorkshire Evening Post* that she thought they would be moving down to Yorkshire in about a month.

After a touch of flu, the Willie Watson cricket season began on May 5 1954 at The Parks, Oxford. The month produced modest results for Watson. There were no centuries and only three 50s in 13 innings. For the month, he scored 414 runs at an average of 37.6, but, in fairness, the May weather was uncooperative and all the other Yorkshire batsmen struggled to make runs. However, the Yorkshire team were unbeaten during the month and their bowlers, particularly Bob Appleyard, Fred Trueman and Johnny Wardle, were producing outstanding bowling figures.

June did not prove to be any more fruitful for Willie Watson, as there was still no century and only two fifties. He had only ten innings, in which he scored 345 runs at an average of 38.3. His best innings was 80 not out in the exciting tied match against Leicestershire. In the Yorkshire second innings, the Leicester pace bowler, Terry Spencer, had the remarkable figures of 9-63. Yorkshire remained unbeaten, although there were four drawn matches as well as the tie. By July 3, Yorkshire had taken the lead in the County Championship.

The summer of 1954 saw a visit from cricket's newest Test-playing nation – Pakistan. Unfortunately, the tourists did not get a warm welcome from the English weather. Despite his modest form in the early part of the season, Willie Watson was chosen as 12th man for the First Test at Lord's on June 10. The selectors preferred to recall Bill Edrich to bat at number five behind Peter May and Denis Compton. Tom Graveney was overlooked completely. Three days of the Test were lost to the rain and, when Hutton opened the England innings, he was bowled by Khan Mohammed for nought. This was the Pakistanis' first Test wicket in England. However, only eight hours of play were possible so the match finished as a draw.

At the end of June, two substitute captains had to be appointed. Len Hutton's health meant that he had to withdraw from the second Test starting on July 1. The selectors chose David Sheppard, the highly successful Cambridge University batsman and 1953 captain of Sussex, whom he took from 13th to second place in the championship. During 1954, he was reading theology at Cambridge with a view to ordination. However, he was able to find a reasonable amount of time to play cricket. Meanwhile, in Yorkshire, captain Norman Yardley was busy with his duties as a selector and therefore could not play against Northants at Bradford starting on June 30. The Yorkshire committee appointed Willie Watson to captain the county. Although he had led them before, this was the first time in a Championship match. This was a special achievement for Willie Watson, because it meant he had led both Sunderland and Yorkshire in their respective championship competitions. Further satisfaction was gained from beating Northants by 162 runs, thanks mainly to the bowling of Fred Trueman, who took 5-63 in the first innings, and Brian Close, 6-38 in the second innings, although neither came close to Australian left-arm spinner George Tribe's match figures of 12-180 (8-88 in the first innings). David Sheppard was also tasting success as England won the second Test at Trent Bridge by 129 runs. Bob Appleyard took five for 51, so both England and Yorkshire were benefiting from his return to health and fitness.

July saw no improvement in Willie Watson's batting scores; in fact, things got worse. There was still no century and only one half-century, 73, against Derbyshire when he opened. By the middle of the month, his batting average for the season was 32, only fifth in the Yorkshire averages. It was therefore no great surprise when he did not receive an invitation from the MCC to tour Australia. There was surprise, however, over two of the batting selections. Colin Cowdrey was 21 and the Oxford University captain, but he had not scored a championship century and was quite untried at Test level. The news of his selection reached him from the car radio of a stranger and hit him like 'a bolt from the blue'. Also, the decision to select Yorkshireman Vic Wilson ahead of team-mate Willie Watson raised some eyebrows. Trevor Bailey was shocked by the choice, maintaining that Wilson was 'never more than a good county player with a marvellous pair of hands'. He was surprised that neither Len Hutton, the England captain, nor Norman Yardley, the selector, was able to reverse this curious selection. In fact, Vic Wilson played in no Tests in Australia and averaged only 17.7 in the other tour games, just behind fast bowler Frank Tyson. On the other hand, Colin Cowdrey had a successful tour, playing in all five Tests and contributing 319 runs at 35.44. It was to be the first of a record six series in Australia for Cowdrey.

Meantime, the Test series, against Pakistan, had moved to Old Trafford with Sheppard again the skipper in Hutton's absence. Once again, in the summer of 1954, the weather intervened in a match

England dominated but which ended in a draw. Early in August, Len Hutton proved his fitness at Bradford with a century against Nottingham. He was, therefore, recalled for the fourth and final Test against Pakistan at The Oval. In a low-scoring game, England needed to score 168 runs in the fourth innings. They managed only 143 and went down to a shock defeat.

Although there was still no century, August and September proved more productive for Willie Watson than previous months. He scored four half-centuries, including 80 against Essex, who were thrashed by an innings. The regular absence of Hutton, either through illness or Test match duty, meant that Watson was called on to open the innings for Yorkshire. His partner was Frank Lowson, whose perfect batting technique reminded everyone of Len Hutton. In his first six seasons for Yorkshire, he averaged over 40. In August 1954 he hit three big centuries, 165 against Sussex at Hove, 164 against Essex at Scarborough and 150 not out against Kent at Dover, a match in which Fred Trueman took 8-28 before lunch.

Although Willie Watson did not hit a century he accumulated 1,470 first-class runs in 1954, helping Yorkshire bounce back in the County Championship. They moved from 12th the previous summer to second, still behind the title holders, Surrey. The first-class averages for 1954 revealed the county's strengths and weaknesses. No Yorkshire batsman appeared in the top ten places of the batting averages, led by Denis Compton on 58.6. However, there were three Yorkshire men, Bob Appleyard, Fred Trueman and Johnny Wardle, in the top ten places in the bowling averages. Remarkably, these three took 443 wickets between them. However, Surrey had four bowlers of Test class in Alec Bedser, Peter Loader, Jim Laker and Tony Lock, so Yorkshire were stretched to match them. Who knows if they would have made it had Brian Close not been called up for National Service halfway through the season.

Willie Watson completed his 1954 cricket season at Scarborough in early September. He scored 77 in the Players' 50-run victory over the Gentlemen. Now, there was no longer the need to rush up to the north east to catch up with Sunderland's football season. The travel of a professional sportsman could be quite exhausting and the Watsons had wisely reduced that burden by moving back to Yorkshire. They were not sure where to settle but eventually chose to rent accommodation in Bradford. The property was a mansion owned by Sir Anthony Grady, former Lord Mayor, that was divided into three homes. One third was occupied by Sir Anthony's son and another third was the home of the Bradford town clerk – quite unusual neighbours!

CHAPTER 17

WELCOME TO THE SHAY

ONCE IN BRADFORD, Willie Watson found the football season in full swing but, for the first time in 17 years, he had no involvement. It was not long before he became restless, especially on Saturdays. It seemed he could not live without football. His first move was to turn up at Valley Parade, Bradford City's ground, to do some light training. This was followed by contacting Sunderland to inform them that he was willing to make a comeback. Soon, the word was out among the football clubs, with the keenest interest coming from West Ham United and Charlton. However, they were too far south; Willie Watson wished to remain in Yorkshire while he was still playing cricket there. The West Ham manager, Ted Fenton, confirmed that they had made an offer to Sunderland but nothing came from it.

On October 16 1954, Gerald Henry, the manager of Halifax Town, offered his resignation to the directors, who accepted it with regret. Henry, a former player at the club, had become manager in the 1951–52 season. The following season, Halifax had a spectacular success in the FA Cup, beating Cardiff City and Stoke City to reach the fifth round. There they met Tottenham Hotspur at The Shay before a record crowd of almost 37,000 but, unfortunately, went down 3-0. By October 1954, Halifax Town were struggling near the bottom of Division Three North.

Later in October, the Halifax directors decided to advertise the vacant position. At this stage, it was not their intention to seek a player-manager but, at the start of November, they got in touch with Willie Watson and negotiations began quickly. Agreement was reached that Watson should become a player-manager in the tradition of Raich Carter at Hull or Peter Doherty at Doncaster. This meant that a deal also had to be done with Sunderland and a fee of £3,000, a large sum for a Third Division club, was paid. The *Yorkshire Evening Post* believed that the new manager would inherit the inside left position. It also thought that he would take over a useful side that belied its present position at the bottom of the table. On November 8, Willie Watson was in the stand at Crewe to see his new team secure a draw and move off the bottom of the table. A week later, Watson made his debut as a player for Halifax at inside right against Carlisle.

The match turned out to be a thrilling tussle, which Halifax won 5-3. The *Halifax Courier* stated that 'Willie Watson infused his team with a spirit of purpose that brought its own reward. As the game ebbed and flowed, Watson was forward and backward, introducing touches of real soccer class that marks the maestro, although it must have been an ordeal after a fairly long absence from match play.' He also managed to score one goal in front of 6,700 spectators at The Shay.

For Willie Watson, the move to Halifax was a strange transformation. He had been involved in football at the top level since 1938 and at Sunderland he had been with a rich club used to getting plenty of publicity. The financial comparisons with Halifax could not have been more stark, but more immediately apparent was the change in facilities. Roker Park had been a well-equipped stadium capable of hosting vast crowds, including international games. In comparison, The Shay was small and has been described unkindly as 'One of the slums of the Football League'. Matters were made worse by a disastrous fire at the ground soon after Willie Watson arrived. Nevertheless, the new manager could see that there was room for development but, unfortunately, the club lacked the resources for improvement.

Up to Christmas 1954, the Halifax Town season went well, apart from a first round defeat in the FA Cup at Grimsby Town. In the New Year, the weather caused a three-week break in the Halifax fixtures. The first game back was against Bill Shankly's Workington, who secured a point at The Shay. In February, Willie Watson was injured in a 3-3 draw against York City, although he was soon back in action. But results slumped and the club conceded four goals three times in less than a month. Not until Easter did form return to Halifax with their best haul of points over the holiday since the War. At the end of the season, the club had gained 43 points, which earned 14th place in the league, equalling their best position since the War. Willie Watson was not available for the final fixtures because he was back at Headingley for another cricket season. However, he had enjoyed his first season in management and he had built a good relationship with the club chairman, Harry Taylor, and with another director, Cyril Thornber. Thornber was an important chicken breeder and he persuaded the Watsons to take up the business. So they took over a stock of 4,000 to rear chicks. This involved them moving back close to Huddersfield where their house at Lindley Moor came with two acres of land.

The 1955 cricket season benefited from a fine summer and in May Yorkshire got off to a flying start. Under Norman Yardley's experienced leadership, they were confident that Surrey's monopoly could be challenged. Six consecutive championship victories in May seemed to suggest a title year. It was an especially prolific month for Bob Appleyard, who took 49 wickets at eight runs each. Surrey, however, were in no mood to give up the fight and stayed level with their north-country rivals.

Willie Watson's start to the season was disappointing, as in the Yorkshire batting averages, published on May 21, he lay seventh on 23.5. In his first nine innings, he had made only one 50, against Cambridge University, at Fenners, where he had opened with Frank Lowson, and their driving was often 'handsome in its assurance' [Yorkshire Post]. Perhaps he needed the challenge of a Roses match because, at the end of May, Willie Watson scored 94 and 46 at Old Trafford, where Lancashire were beaten by five wickets.

The tourists in the summer of 1955 were from South Africa. Len Hutton had returned from a successful tour of Australia and New Zealand weary and worn. He was also appointed England captain for the whole of the series against South Africa, the first time such a vote of confidence had been given by the selectors since CB Fry in 1912. However, as soon as Hutton returned to county cricket in English spring weather, his lumbago returned more persistently than ever. He was forced to write to the selectors to tell them that he was resigning from international cricket and that he doubted he had a future in the first-class game. The selectors were disappointed but not surprised, and they appointed Peter May to replace him.

By the time of the first Test at Trent Bridge on June 9, Willie Watson had not shown any form which might have attracted the selectors. In fact, the middle-order batting positions were dominated by Peter May, Denis Compton and Tom Graveney, a formidable combination which played in all five Tests. However, the problem for the selectors was to replace Len Hutton and find a second opener. They experimented with Graveney and Bailey as openers and then turned to Don Kenyon, Frank Lowson and Brian Close.

June did not see a revival in Willie Watson's form and, meanwhile, Yorkshire's challenge faltered when, early in the month, they met arch rivals, Surrey, at The Oval. The pitch was treacherous and Appleyard (7 for 29) bowled the home side out for 85. In reply, Willie Watson and Billy Sutcliffe '...followed the classic principles of bad wicket batsmanship in either defending with a dead bat or hitting hard when hitting was possible' [*Yorkshire Post*]. Nevertheless, Yorkshire were twice bowled out for less than 175 and lost by 41 runs.

Willie Watson's best score so far came at the end of the month when he made 68 against Hampshire at Bournemouth. Top score in an innings of 165, it helped Yorkshire win by 96 runs in two days. The most exciting game of the month was the return match against Surrey at Headingley. Surrey had a first innings lead of 102 but were bowled out in their second innings for 75 (Mike Cowan 5-15). Such was the interest in this contest that 17,500 spectators turned up on the third day, and in the fourth innings Yorkshire needed to make 178 in 195 minutes but fell behind the clock so that, after lunch, 150 were needed in 140 minutes. Vic Wilson and Frank Lowson forced the pace to keep victory in sight and next Watson and Billy Sutcliffe came together when 30 runs were needed in the last half hour. The target was finally reached with ten minutes to spare with Watson, unbeaten on 51, scoring the winning run. This was Surrey's first defeat since the summer of 1954 and meant there were just 12 points between the counties.

Batting in July was a revelation for Willie Watson. It began with the match between Yorkshire and the tourists. The South Africans proved too strong and won by 193 runs but Willie made 51 opening for Yorkshire. A week later at Sheffield, his best form was revealed against Sussex with an innings of 163. Watson batted at number four, which is probably where he ought to have batted more regularly. His first century for Yorkshire since May 1953 was, according to the *Yorkshire Post*, a fine innings in which, 'He scarcely made a false shot.' He hit two sixes and 15 fours, batting for five-and-three-quarter hours. The newspaper speculated that this innings had put Willie Watson back into consideration for a place in the Test team.

His next match was at Lord's, for the Players against the Gentlemen. On this occasion, Watson was chosen to open the batting with Don Kenyon of Worcestershire. The combination failed in the first innings but built a partnership of 70 in the second, which contributed to a 20-run victory with five minutes to spare by the Players. The outstanding batting in the match came from two Leicestershire cricketers. For the Players, Maurice Tompkin made 115 in the first innings, while Charles Palmer responded with 154 for the Gentlemen.

There was no travelling for Willie Watson after this win because Yorkshire were due at Lord's to play Middlesex. Unfortunately, in the Yorkshire first innings, he was forced to retire hurt on 16 following a blow to his right arm. Frank Lowson filled the breach with an innings of 116 and Yorkshire went on to win by eight wickets, thanks to the bowling of Fred Trueman and Bob Appleyard. This result moved Yorkshire to within four points of Surrey in the County Championship.

On July 21, the *Yorkshire Post* wondered if England would choose a new opening partnership for the fourth Test at Headingley. The newspaper thought either Frank Lowson or Willie Watson would be brought into the team to join Trevor Bailey to open the innings. In the end, the selectors opted for Lowson as Watson's arm was still recovering. Watson returned to Yorkshire, where he was soon to make his second century of the season (105) at Bradford against Essex, putting on 192 with Vic Wilson (132) for the fourth wicket. The match was won by ten wickets, with Brian Close bowling magnificently to take 7-62 in the Essex second innings. The month ended with a Roses match at Sheffield, where Brian Statham soon had Yorkshire in trouble. At 60-5, Willie Watson came to the rescue with 174 out of a total of 312. The *Yorkshire Post* described the innings: 'There was scarcely a flaw to be discovered in the whole of Watson's stay. He will never do himself more justice and never serve the needs of his side more faithfully.' Lancashire made only 139 and were forced to follow on and, at 203 for seven, they just escaped defeat thanks to the weather.

Early in August 1955, Yorkshire and Surrey were racing neck-and-neck for the County title on 208 points each. On August 9, both Willie Watson and Brian Close were chosen for the final Test against South Africa at The Oval. They were the fifth and sixth Yorkshire players to take part in the Test series. These absentees did not give Surrey any advantage in the Championship because they also made a similar contribution to the England team that summer. The final Test would decide the series because England had won the first two matches while South Africa had won the next two.

Only on the day before The Oval Test was Willie Watson's fitness to play confirmed. The England first innings was an uphill struggle after new openers Brian Close and Jack Ikin were parted at 51. Watson, batting at number five, joined Denis Compton at 69-3. They batted for an hour and a half until Watson was out for 25. Eventually England were dismissed for 151 with Trevor Goddard taking 5-31. South Africa also found the conditions difficult and were bowled out for 112 with Tony Lock taking 4-39. England's second innings reached 204 with Peter May making 89 while Willie

Watson, moved down to number six, scored three. The South Africans were again soon in trouble with the English spinners Jim Laker (5-56) and Lock (4-62) exploiting their home wicket. England won by 92 runs and the series by three games to two.

While the Test progressed, the contest at the top of the county table remained level, with Yorkshire and Surrey on 232 points. Willie Watson returned to the Yorkshire team on August 20 at New Road, Worcester. He came to the wicket in the first innings with Yorkshire at 16-4. He first rescued the team with Ray Illingworth and took the score to 147-5, and then with his next partner, skipper Norman Yardley, put on 214. Eventually Yorkshire declared at 378-7 with Watson not out on 214. This was his only double century for Yorkshire and would be the third highest innings of his career. Johnny Wardle took 11 Worcestershire wickets in the game, ensuring a Yorkshire victory by nine wickets.

Willie Watson played in only one more game for Yorkshire that summer at Southend, where Essex were also beaten by nine wickets. At the end of the season, Yorkshire had won an impressive 21 games; unfortunately, Surrey won 23. In many previous seasons, as few as 15 victories were enough to take the championship. Surrey had the astonishing record of not drawing a single game. This was remarkable in an English summer but also an indication of their positive attitude to the game. Willie Watson had the consolation of heading the Yorkshire averages on 47.73, which also placed him fourth in the national batting averages.

In several ways, the close of the 1955 season ended an era in Yorkshire cricket, as both Len Hutton and Norman Yardley announced their retirement. Hutton's batting achievements had been legendary: 85 centuries for his county and 24,807 runs, despite the years lost to World War II. In all first-class cricket he scored 40,140 runs at an average of 55.51 with 129 hundreds. In 79 Tests he accumulated 6,971 runs at an average of 56.67. Yardley's contribution was more controversial. He was an accomplished all-rounder who captained England in 14 matches. He took over the Yorkshire captaincy in 1948 from Brian Sellers and led the county for eight seasons. In that time, Yorkshire were once joint champions and four times runners-up. In retrospect, this can be regarded as a period of successful captaincy but, at the time, it was viewed as under-achievement. It was particularly unpalatable to find Surrey winning the title repeatedly. The criticism of the Yorkshire performance under Yardley was based on the view that the team, man for man, were as good as if not slightly better than Surrey but, as a team, they were inferior to Stuart Surridge's side. This might have been the result of Yardley's tolerant and lenient approach to the forceful and aggressive attitudes in the Yorkshire dressing room. This contained strong personalities like Bob Appleyard and Johnny Wardle, and one of the team members said of Yardley that 'He was too nice a chap to be the captain we needed.'

With the loss of Hutton and Yardley, Yorkshire had to appoint a new captain. Derek Hodgson, writing later in the *Independent*, noted that, 'a perceptive Yorkshire Committee might have offered Willie Watson the captaincy... but they were still wedded to an amateur appointment'. Brian Close said that his choice would have been Johnny Wardle, a very knowledgeable cricketer, while Ted Lester took the view that Wardle had made too many enemies to do the job properly. Bob Appleyard agreed with Close that Wardle would have made a good captain, but his own choice would have been Willie Watson, who was a very astute cricketer and who was also well respected as a real professional. Ted Lester was doubtful because, 'Willie would have been much too quiet.' Appleyard accepted that Willie Watson did not say a lot but he had shown his character against the Australians. He was a determined fighter. In fact, neither Watson nor Wardle was seriously considered by the Yorkshire Committee. They wanted an amateur and the only one left in the team was Billy Sutcliffe, son of the great Herbert.

CHAPTER 18

IN TIME FOR A BENEFIT

INEVITABLY, THE FOOTBALL season was under way before Willie Watson was released by Yorkshire. During his absence from Halifax, centre half Les Horsman, now player-coach, deputised. The club's final trial match produced some good performances. The opening fixture of the season, August 21 1955, was an away match at Workington and Willie Watson's guiding hand was missed in a 2-0 defeat. The first home match resulted in a 2-2 draw against Carlisle, including a goal for the visitors from England international Ivor Broadis. Willie Watson was released by Yorkshire in time for the home match against York City, who had reached the FA Cup semi-final the previous season. It required a replay before Newcastle could overcome the challenge from the Third Division North club. Halifax expected York to field their full cup 'giant killing' team. Watson's team went down 4-2.

Halifax did not register their first win until their sixth match of the season against Crewe Alexandra, where Willie Watson's contribution was outstanding. The *Halifax Courier* compared his style to that of the great Irish international, Peter Doherty, as he 'exhibited craft and industry both in attack and defence'. The paper hoped he would continue to play at inside forward. But results into the autumn were very mixed, ranging from a heavy defeat, 4-0, at Grimsby Town to a convincing 3-0 victory over Darlington. The FA Cup first round in November produced a tricky away match against non-league club, Goole Town. The Halifax win came after they had fallen a goal behind and included a rare Willie Watson goal. In December, the Cup draw brought a second round tie at home against Burton Albion of the Birmingham and District League. The prospects seemed favourable for Halifax when, a week before the Cup tie, they overcame Bradford Park Avenue by 6-0. This victory was not only a record for this 'derby match' but was also a league record for Halifax. The unchanged Halifax team were held to a goalless draw by Burton and lost the replay 1-0.

At Christmas Halifax's inconsistency was evident. They did the double over Oldham Athletic but lost heavily to York City. Into the New Year, they moved up to 13th place in the league, even though Willie Watson had missed two consecutive games due to injury. Early in March, Halifax Town completed the double over Darlington, their third double of the season, which placed them halfway. At the end of the month it was reported that Willie Watson, who had missed a lot of games through injury, would retire from playing at the end of the season. The club were not considering the appointment of a new player-manager at this stage, the chairman insisted.

However, the issue came to a head a week later on April 7 1956, when Willie Watson resigned. In accepting the decision with regret, the chairman explained that the issue was not to do with injuries or ability to keep playing but the overlapping demands of cricket and football. This long-standing complication for Watson had been intensified by the Yorkshire Committee's decision to award him a benefit in the summer of 1956. In an era in which county cricketers were not very well paid, the organisation of a benefit season, with a variety of functions and fund-raising events, was crucial to the players' financial security. Willie Watson felt unable to devote himself to a benefit season while remaining the manager of Halifax Town. It did soon become apparent that Willie Watson would be retiring from the playing side of the game at the age of 36, but he did not want to think that he had completely finished with the game in some capacity or other. He had made 17 first-team appearances for Halifax Town that season, sometimes when not completely fit. The *Halifax Courier* said that Watson was very popular with the players, and one of them described him as 'The best man in the business as a manager.'

For the Watsons, the saddest part of leaving The Shay was the break with the director Cyril Thornber and his wife Dorothy. There were, however, business links and other sporting connections which allowed the friendship to continue and strengthen. When the Watsons' daughter, Val, was born in Huddersfield in 1957, Cyril and Dorothy Thornber became her godparents. Thornber was from Mytholmroyd, near Hebden Bridge, and in chick-hatching and poultry breeding his firm was the biggest in Europe.

The new cricket season started on April 28 1956. Yorkshire played at Lord's against the MCC with Billy Sutcliffe in charge of the team. He was 29 years old and had made his debut for Yorkshire in 1948. He was a competent batsman but he lived in the shadow of his famous father. He gained the captaincy because he was an amateur, and he knew he faced a dressing room in which, 'there were elements of disharmony' [JM Kilburn, *History of Yorkshire Cricket*]. It seemed doubtful that he was the man to restore discipline and the determination needed to win the championship. In fact Yorkshire fell away significantly in the title race and finished seventh. They did have one good excuse because in a wet summer they did seem to get the worst of the weather.

However, for Willie Watson, his benefit season got off to a perfect start. Against the MCC at Lord's he made 117 out of a Yorkshire total of 186. In the second innings he added another 27 not out. He did not play against Cambridge University and he did not bat against Oxford in an innings victory over the University, while the match on May 9 against the Australian tourists was ruined by the weather. Ten days later at Headingley, the Roses match was a triumph for the Lancashire spinner, Roy Tattersall, who took 14 wickets in the match and helped his team win by 153 runs. In the next game against Warwickshire in Birmingham, Willie Watson scored his second century of the month (103) as Yorkshire won by an innings and 41 runs. When he reached 35 Watson had scored 13,500 runs in first-class cricket. In the final game of the month, he again reached a century, going on to make

149 against Middlesex at Bramall Lane after Yorkshire had been bowled out for 99 in their first innings, John Warr 6-25.

The innings gave Yorkshire new hope and his partnership of 98 in 75 minutes with Bob Appleyard transformed the match. The *Yorkshire Post* reported that Watson's 'first 60 runs were forgettable, but with Appleyard he was magnificent. He drove, pulled and hooked Hurst for four consecutive boundaries.' The match, though, was drawn.

During May, Willie Watson had regularly batted at number four, which may have contributed to his fine form or it may have been the pressure of the benefit season. Already a benefit match at Halifax had had to be postponed and rearranged. At the start of July, Willie Watson stood tenth in the national batting averages on 58.7. Further good news came in the Queen's Birthday Honours list, which awarded a knighthood to Len Hutton. Willie Watson was a great admirer of his Yorkshire team-mate. He believed Hutton to be among the all-time great batsmen and he particularly praised his determination, his concentration and his sense of responsibility. Willie Watson saved his biggest compliment for Len Hutton's batting on 'a sticky wicket' against class spin bowlers. In those conditions, he was the best ever.

Willie Watson's fine batting in May ensured that he kept his England place, won back in the final Test of the previous summer. The MCC's winter tour to Pakistan had been by an A team and did not play any Tests. The first Test, against Australia at Trent Bridge, began on June 7 1956 but more than 12 hours of play were lost to rain and even two declarations by England could not force a result. In the *Yorkshire Post* Len Hutton wrote that, in his first innings, 'Watson received a beautiful, swinging yorker which hit him low on his right pad and had him lbw second ball.'

Hutton added that 'The swinging ball had always been Willie Watson's worst enemy, especially at the start of his innings.' In his second innings, Watson was out for eight to a magnificent diving catch by wicketkeeper Gil Langley, off the bowling of Keith Miller. Peter Richardson, who opened for England with Colin Cowdrey in his debut against Australia, was the first batsman in that position to score a 50 in each innings without going on to make a century.

On his return to county cricket in Sheffield, Willie Watson, standing in as captain, scored 50 and 51 against Gloucestershire at Bramall Lane. Yorkshire's victory, by 143 runs, was their first for three weeks and was secured with only ten minutes left of the extra half hour. Appleyard with 5-78 and 4-24 helped matters with a late hat-trick. The next fixture was at The Oval, for the clash with Surrey, which had developed into a rivalry comparable to the battle of the Roses. Surrey's Jim Laker, a Yorkshireman, had chosen this game as his benefit match and Alex Bedser described the contest between the two counties as 'World class teams, separated by the narrowest threads'. In the previous summer, the two clubs had between them provided England with 13 players. For the 1956 game, Willie Watson continued as captain and put Surrey in to bat. They were bowled out for 99 with Johnny Wardle taking 4-22. In reply, Yorkshire fared little better, making 111, of which Watson made 11 while Tony Lock took 4-29. In Surrey's second innings, the low scoring continued with a total of 135, with Bob Appleyard leading the Yorkshire attack and taking 6-31. The target for Yorkshire was a modest 124, especially when they reached 60 for two. However, Tony Lock with 5-42 and Laker with 4-36 skittled the Yorkshire batting for a total of 100.

From Jim Laker's benefit match, Willie Watson returned to Yorkshire for a match for his benefit fund between the Leeds League XI and a Willie Watson XI, which included West Indies Test stars Frank Worrell and Sonny Ramadhin. The next commitment, in a heavy schedule, was at Lord's for the second Test against Australia. Only Peter May of the English batsmen succeeded against the fine bowling of Keith Miller (10-152) and the record-breaking wicketkeeping of Gil Langley (nine dismissals). In the England first innings, Watson was unlucky to be out when he nicked a ball from Miller on to his pads and then on to Richie Benaud in the gully. Len Hutton wrote that he had lost his wicket once or twice that way and always considered himself very unlucky. Willie had made only six and, in the second innings, he again fell to Miller, this time for 18.

This meant that in two Tests he had scored just 32. The Australians won the match by 185 runs.

Willie Watson returned to Yorkshire to captain his county against his recent adversaries, the Australian tourists. The match at Sheffield was badly hit by the weather after the Australians declared at 306-7 while Yorkshire had made 96-4, Watson six, when the match was abandoned. For the last game in June, against Warwickshire at Bradford, Willie Watson again led his county. Yorkshire were in desperate need of a win, having fallen to 12th in the championship. Fortunately, with the help of fine bowling by Bob Appleyard (7-48) in the first innings, Yorkshire were easy winners by ten wickets. Although Willie Watson's batting in June could not maintain the high standard of May, he remained top of the Yorkshire averages on 42.

Yorkshire's second match in July against Nottingham was memorable firstly for the young Yorkshire opener, Ken Taylor, who was batting with Willie Watson when he reached 99 and faced the Australian leg spinner Bruce Dooland. Taylor survived a teasing over with the 'imperturbable Watson' at the other end. He then hit a fierce cover drive for four and was congratulated by Watson, his fellow Huddersfielder. Taylor went on to make 168 while Watson reached 37 and Nottingham were beaten comfortably by nine wickets.

Yorkshire moved next to Kidderminster for a remarkable match against Worcestershire. At that time in county cricket, there was an unwritten law in three-day matches, that you declared at the end of the first day (or earlier) unless there was rain. Roly Jenkins was the Worcester stand-in captain who won the toss and decided to bat. His opener, Don Kenyon, was a prolific county batsman who had reached 200 at the close of play when Worcestershire had reached 369-4. After worrying all night, Jenkins reached his controversial decision to bat on. It was the only occasion in the 1956 season when a county failed to declare after a full first day. The Yorkshire team were not impressed and could not hide their contempt for the decision. Johnny Wardle was particularly outspoken in his criticism of the home team's tactic. Yorkshire's stand-in captain,

Willie Watson, gave the ball to Wardle for the first over. The left-arm spinner marked out a longer run and bowled six bouncers over the batsman's head. His plan was to prevent Worcester from scoring any additional runs. At the end of the over, Willie Watson came across and said, 'Thanks very much, Johnny' [Stephen Chalke, *Runs in the Memory*]. That was his only over. Don Kenyon went on to make 259, the 20th-century record for an individual score against Yorkshire. The determination of the Yorkshire batsmen to teach Roly Jenkins a lesson backfired badly as they were bowled out twice for less than 200 and lost the match by an innings and 94 runs. Willie Watson's only consolation was to top score with 45 in the Yorkshire first innings.

In their determination to pull back Australia's one-nil lead the England selectors jettisoned Tom Graveney and Willie Watson, who had not scored well in the first two Tests. The surprise replacement was Cyril Washbrook, who had recently been appointed a selector. His co-selectors' confidence in him, after five years' absence, was justified when he scored 98 to go alongside captain Peter May's 101 and England won by an innings and 42 runs. Also in good form were Surrey spinners Jim Laker (11-113) and Tony Lock (7-81). It was England's first Test victory over Australia at Headingley.

The return match between Yorkshire and Surrey was played at Sheffield on July 21 1956, and Willie Watson chose it for his benefit game. It was again a low-scoring match and again Yorkshire squandered the chance of a rare victory over their big rivals. After Surrey were bowled out for 128 – Ray Illingworth 4-38 – Yorkshire went on to establish a first innings lead of 61. On the final day, Yorkshire's position seemed unassailable as they needed only 67 runs with eight wickets standing. Peter Loader and Alec Bedser bowled in tandem for over an hour to Ken Taylor and Willie Watson. Tony Lock was held in reserve until Yorkshire reached 50-4. Lock bowled Brian Close and swept aside the tail, taking 5-11; so Surrey won by 14 against all expectations. Again, Willie Watson had the dubious consolation of top scoring in the Yorkshire debacle. The *Yorkshire Post* reminded its readers that Willie Watson was the last link with the pre-war Yorkshire team.

It also noted that in the absence of Sutcliffe, Watson had captained Yorkshire eight times, more than any Yorkshire professional in a season. Fortunately, the grey skies had not put off the spectators for the testimonial match and more than ten thousand turned up. This resulted in nearly £2,000 being added to the Watson benefit fund. Also, during the match, he passed 1,000 runs for the season.

The fourth Test took place at Old Trafford, becoming a match which has gone down in history as the one in which Jim Laker took 19 wickets for 90 runs and the Australians were destroyed by an innings and 170 runs. Meanwhile, Yorkshire moved to Harrogate to play Somerset and Willie Watson was able to remind the selectors of his form by scoring 139 not out. The match was won by Yorkshire by seven wickets. However, the county's challenge fell away over the next nine games, only one of which was won.

During August, Willie Watson scored 89 in a drawn game at Leicester and 83 not out in the defeat by Essex at Southend. At the end of August and early in September, he was invited to play in three matches at the Scarborough Festival. He represented three teams: Yorkshire, the Players and JN Pearce's XI, their opponents being MCC, the Gentlemen and the Australians. His best innings at Scarborough was 72 for the Players against the Gentlemen, a match which ended in a seven-wicket victory. The innings included a stand of 150 in 100 minutes with Tom Graveney. As Trevor Bailey was playing for the Gentlemen, it is possible that some light soccer training was attempted before cricket commenced.

Generally, professional cricketers of this period did not become wealthy through their cricket. As a capped Yorkshire player, Watson earned about £650 in a domestic season, while out of season Yorkshire paid him about £3 per week. Therefore, a tax-free benefit was a very important source of income. The total raised for Willie Watson was £5,356, not in the same league as Len Hutton's £9,712 in 1950, but comparable with Frank Smailes in 1948 and Vic Wilson ten years later. In fact, Len Hutton's total remained unequalled until Tony Nicholson in 1973.

In the 1956 season, Yorkshire dropped to seventh place in the Championship, while the number of matches won fell from 21 to eight. In his benefit season, with 38.50 Willie Watson topped the Yorkshire batting averages and was 14th in the national batting averages.

CHAPTER 19

WINTER IN THE SUN

NO LONGER COMMITTED to Sunderland or Halifax, Willie Watson was able to enjoy fully the Scarborough Festival. Nor was he selected for the 16-man England party to tour South Africa in October. Peter May captained a strong squad which included Denis Compton, Trevor Bailey, Colin Cowdrey, Johnny Wardle, Brian Statham and Jim Laker. Apart from Watson, the two notable omissions were Tom Graveney and Fred Trueman. Although England won the first two Tests, they shared the series 2-2.

However, the close season was not confined to tours of South Africa because the Bengal Cricket Association was celebrating its silver jubilee and a two-match visit to India was arranged. The party was captained by Bill Edrich and included Willie Watson, Alec Bedser, Tom Graveney and Fred Trueman from England plus Australians Bruce Dooland and George Tribe. The party flew from London on Boxing Day 1956 and returned by air on January 11 1957.

The first match was against the Chief Minister's XI at Kolkata (then Calcutta), starting on December 30. The game was lost by 142 runs and only Bill Edrich with 58 made any runs in either of the tourists' innings. The party then moved on to Bombay to play the President's XI. This match was won by the tourists, thanks to a century in both innings by Tom Graveney. The most effective bowler for the visitors was George Tribe, and the centurions for the home team were Nari Contractor and Polly Umrigar.

Within five weeks of the return home, Willie Watson, Tom Graveney, Alan Moss and George Tribe were ready to depart for another cricket tour. This time the invitation had come from the Jamaican Cricket Association and the tour was organised by the Duke of Norfolk. The captaincy went to Hampshire's Desmond Eagar and other members of the party included Roy Marshall, Doug Wright and Colin Ingleby-Mackenzie. The Duke took with him Lord Cobham of Worcestershire, soon to become Governor General of New Zealand. These two flew to Jamaica while the rest of the party set sail from Liverpool in the banana boat, *Metina*. On arrival at Kingston, the tourists were split into three groups to stay as guests in various private houses before the first match. Willie Watson, Tom Graveney, Alan Moss, Desmond Barrick and Colin Ingleby-Mackenzie were allocated to Brimmer Hall, the home of Major Douglas Vaughan, where they stayed for five days. The host organised a cocktail party for his visitors and one of the guests was near neighbour, Noel Coward, who proved to be as witty as his reputation promised.

The first match against St Mary was won thanks to Willie Watson's 77 in the first innings and Roy Marshall's 106 in the second, while Doug Wright of Kent took the bowling honours with 7-31.

The second game against the Country Districts was also a two-day match, but this time it finished as a draw and, once again, Roy Marshall (87) and Willie Watson (76) dominated the batting. The third match was against Jamaica's 'next eleven' over three days at Sabina Park, where the Jamaicans fielded a very strong side made up of several Test players including Allan Rae, Collie Smith, Roy Gilchrist, Gerry Alexander and Alf Valentine. A draw was not an unsatisfactory result in the circumstances and Willie Watson and Roy Marshall continued their fine form and were joined by Tom Graveney, who made 90.

Still at Sabina Park, the Duke of Norfolk's XI faced All Jamaica. The match was drawn but there were two Jamaican centurions, Neville Bonitto and Easton McMorris. After a trip up-country to Monymusk, the tourists reached Montego Bay to face Cornwall

XVI. Unfortunately, the wicket was too wet for play but local officials decided to mop it up by setting it alight with petrol. This most original, if unorthodox, method worked. Both Lord Cobham and the Duke of Norfolk played in this fixture, which was drawn despite Cornwall's advantage in numbers.

The next opponents were the Combined Estates, who played at Frome, where the match was won by an innings thanks to superb bowling by George Tribe, whose match analysis was 11 for 89. This was excellent preparation for the second match against Jamaica, this time at Melbourne Park. Once again, the Duke of Norfolk's XI relied on the batting of Willie Watson, 71 not out, and Tom Graveney, 51, in the first innings and Roy Marshall, 97, in the second. The tourists were extremely pleased to win by three wickets. The final match of the tour, the third against Jamaica, was again at Sabina Park.

The enthusiasm of the visitors was intensified by the generosity of Stanhope Joel, a very wealthy race-horse owner, who offered cash prizes of £25 (worth more than £120 today) for each 25 runs scored by an individual batsman and the same for each wicket taken and for each catch. The team quickly agreed that all prize money would be pooled. The tourists' second innings proved particularly expensive for Mr Joel because of the five who batted: the lowest score was 46 by Desmond Barrick of Northants. Willie Watson was particularly popular as he completed his half-century just in time. The tourists won by seven wickets and, on April 7, they returned home.

The tour ended as a great success from every point of view. Friendly relations were re-established with the Jamaican cricket community after the strains of the MCC Tour of 1953–54. All the tour party enjoyed themselves enormously and the Duke of Norfolk was very popular as he managed the players with tact and humour. His sense of fun was illustrated on one occasion when one of the locals mistook him for Willie Watson. The well-wishers said, 'My word, you batted well today, Willie!' 'Not at all,' said the Duke, taking it in his stride. 'Being a left-hander, I find helps me out here.' For the return journey, the *Metina* was fully loaded, so the voyage was much smoother. Each player was given a fine stem of bananas so that, when they returned to Liverpool, they looked like soldiers returning from duty in the tropics. A week later, on April 12 1957, the West Indies tourists, led by John Goddard, arrived in England.

CHAPTER 20

GOODBYE TO YORKSHIRE

THE *YORKSHIRE POST* published the view that the 1957 season was a critical one for Yorkshire Cricket Club because it was eight summers since the county had won the championship. The newspaper wrote that it was 'Yorkshire's urgent business to establish a co-operation of talents in a common cause. It's idle to pretend that Yorkshire are not faced by serious problems.' It was the task of Billy Sutcliffe, in his second season as captain, to bring about these changes, which many believed were well overdue. Brian Close, a growing influence at the club, was certain that Sutcliffe was not the man 'to crack the whip'.

Yorkshire made a modest start. They beat Derbyshire and Somerset comfortably but lost the return match with Derbyshire at Chesterfield. Two games were drawn, as was the match with the West Indian tourists. Although Willie Watson scored 73 against the Cambridge students at the start of the month, he did not hit top form until the end of the month when he scored 134 against Scotland. On this occasion, he was promoted to open. However, for the first match in June against Glamorgan, Willie Watson was inexplicably rested despite his return to form. Glamorgan took their chance and won the game by seven wickets. The next fixture was the Roses match at Old Trafford but Willie Watson remained out of favour and, together with four others, Doug Padgett, Bob

Appleyard, Mike Cowan and Bob Platt, all with recent first-team experience, was selected for minor county duties. At this stage of the season, Watson was third in the Yorkshire batting averages. His response to this treatment was to score a century for Yorkshire seconds against Staffordshire.

Willie Watson was restored to the Yorkshire team for the match with Middlesex at Lord's on June 15 when he scored 53 in a ten-wicket Yorkshire victory. However, it was in the next game against Northants that Willie Watson showed his true class, batting at number one. The *Yorkshire Post* reported that 'Watson had a leading part in Yorkshire's big score of 361 for seven declared. His 162 surely must have put him back into permanent favour with the Yorkshire selectors, after being left out earlier in the month. He batted beautifully for five-and-a-half hours, never giving a semblance of a chance or being hurried into a stroke. There was scarcely a shot in the book which was not played. When he was fifth out, the score was 286, which indicates how he dominated proceedings.'

This exhibition was followed by a very different batting context. In the return with Middlesex, at Headingley, Yorkshire experienced their worst day of the summer as they were bowled out for 98. Willie Watson top scored with 41, in which he gave a practical demonstration of how to play good seam bowling by Alan Moss and John Warr. Then, after Middlesex had totalled 381, Watson top scored with 50 in the second innings when Yorkshire finished on 163-3 to save the game. The last game in June was against arch-rivals Surrey, at The Oval. The first day was dispiriting for Yorkshire as Surrey accumulated 365 runs. In reply, Yorkshire could only manage 172, of which Willie Watson made 53. He had batted at number one and he was top scorer but Yorkshire were forced to follow on and, in their second innings, Watson again top scored with 72 but could not prevent a defeat by an innings and 19 runs. Peter May's 125 played a large part in Surrey's success.

July 1957 was a very significant month in the career of Willie Watson, not for events on the pitch but for the discussions in the pavilion. Leicestershire were the visitors to The Circle in Hull and were led by Charles Palmer. Now 38, he had decided to retire at the end of the 1957 season. A new captain was needed to carry the team forward and, with the preoccupation with having an amateur in the post receding, Palmer had spent the first two months of the season on the lookout for a quality player. At the close of play at Hull, Charles Palmer and Willie Watson met for a drink and Palmer asked Watson if he knew anyone on the circuit who might be interested in a five-year contract. Willie Watson knew that Yorkshire could sack him at any time so he answered that, 'Yes, I might be!'

While Willie Watson considered the implications of this possibility, Yorkshire swept aside Leicester by an innings and 12 runs. Watson's contribution was 49 and this confirmed him in 15th place in the national batting averages (41.2). On July 25, the *Yorkshire Post* broke the story that 'Willie Watson may become a county captain', revealing that he had asked Yorkshire to release him to take an appointment with Leicestershire. It also reported that it was with the greatest regret that Willie Watson was leaving Yorkshire but he felt it was only fair to make way for a younger man and that it was also time to consider his future. In Leicester, the club was waiting for Watson to apply formally for the post of assistant secretary and player when his release from Yorkshire was confirmed. The chairman could not disguise his interest in the possibility of a player of Watson's ability and personality applying for the post. At the end of July, the Yorkshire committee announced that 'Permission had been granted for Leicester to engage Willie Watson if they wish.'

While Leicestershire awaited Watson's application, he was on the road, scoring 80 at Worcester and 68 at Hove in matches Yorkshire won comfortably. However, this major career change was not something Willie Watson wished to be rushed into. Back in Yorkshire, he top scored against Worcestershire at Scarborough with 102, batting at number one. On August 11, the situation was further complicated by the announcement that Billy Sutcliffe was resigning from the Yorkshire captaincy after two seasons. Might Yorkshire abandon their policy of appointing amateurs as their captain? Watson was senior professional and had already captained Yorkshire several times when Yardley or Sutcliffe were unavailable.

On the other hand, Billy Sutcliffe had failed to make a cohesive team out of a group of outsized personalities. There were so-called hard men at the club whose rivalry and arguments did not improve the dressing-room atmosphere. Johnny Wardle could be a particularly disruptive influence, as was revealed in his abrupt departure from Yorkshire a year later. Would Willie Watson have welcomed the prospect of taking over such a divided team? Furthermore, there did not seem to be any well-qualified amateur players from whom the Yorkshire Committee might choose a captain.

In the event, Willie Watson agreed the terms of a five-year contract with Leicestershire on August 21 1957. He was quoted as telling the *Leicester Mercury*, 'I am very pleased to be coming to Leicester and I am confident things will go well.' When asked about the Leicester captaincy, he replied, 'If I am invited to captain the side, I would aim to establish the happiest relations through all ranks. From my experience in football and cricket, I realised all too well that no team can be successful unless they get on well together.' This could be interpreted as a veiled comment on the Wardles and Appleyards back in Yorkshire or the Len Shackletons and Trevor Fords at Sunderland AFC.

Willie Watson still had to complete his commitments to Yorkshire and, on August 21, he scored his last century (his 26th) for Yorkshire, 116, against Warwickshire at Edgbaston. Then he travelled to Taunton to make 48 in the second innings, helping Yorkshire to a seven-wicket victory. The final game of the summer was an anti-climax for Willie Watson, as the Cardiff wicket was taking spin and it was Glamorgan's Don Shepherd who took full advantage, taking 12 wickets for 76.

Illingworth and Appleyard could manage only nine each as Yorkshire won by four runs in two days. Yorkshire had to settle for a respectable third place in the County Championship behind Surrey and Northants. Willie Watson scored 1,462 runs in his final season at Yorkshire; he was second in the county batting averages and ninth in the national averages on 36.88. JM Kilburn wrote that 'Watson was the most reliable bat because he was technically the soundest.'

The next hurdle to be cleared was the application for special registration with his new county to be determined by an MCC sub-committee in mid-October. Leicester had offered terms to the Derbyshire stalwart, Alan Revill, who had not been retained. Both were approved. Willie Watson's next engagement in Leicestershire was at the De Montfort Hall, where he made the cricket league presentation before an audience of 600. A week later, on October 18 1957, there was a presentation to Charles Palmer, who had enjoyed eight years with the county. He said that if the captaincy were offered to Willie Watson he would prove to be a tremendous influence at the club and was also an extremely nice chap. He described the Watson batting as being 'In the classic mould and perhaps the best judge of a single in the world.' The Leicestershire Committee did not seem to be in any hurry to make a decision, as their November 1957 meeting did not consider the question of the captaincy at all.

CHAPTER 21

A GLORIOUS FINALE

THE LEICESTERSHIRE COMMITTEE eventually appointed Willie Watson as captain for 1958. In the previous four seasons the county had twice come bottom and once second from bottom, while in 1955 they had been sixth. Back in 1953, they had been third. But clearly, this move from title-chasing Yorkshire to lower-regions Leicester was not encouraging. Furthermore, Leicester's Grace Road cricket ground was not an attractive one in the 1950s. Jim Laker said, 'It looked its usual broken-down shambles; it's incredible that those rickety, worn-out steps that lead into darkness and into the leaky, spasmodic cold shower had not yet completely disintegrated.'

Willie Watson, who continued to live in Yorkshire with his wife and family, paid his first visit to Leicester since being appointed captain on February 28 1958. He said it was to 'pick up the threads, before getting down to the new job'. He attended the Loughborough Town Cricket Club annual dinner and visited the county's indoor cricket school. He said he looked forward to the new season 'with interest and not a little confidence'. The fact that Leicester had a mainly young team made the new captain even keener. In his view, the real enjoyment came from playing the game, whereas at the higher levels it sometimes seemed that the result was all that mattered and, so, when that happened, something was going out of the game.

At the end of March, Watson was back for the Leicestershire AGM. The Lord Mayor of the city attended and said he was hopeful that the club would own its own ground within a year. Willie Watson asked for patience in what he called a 'transitional period'. He was convinced that the policy of selecting a young side would pay dividends in the future and he insisted there would be no lack of endeavour and that everyone in the side must give only his best to the team. For the new championship season, Willie Watson was one of five new county captains. Ronnie Burnet, an amateur and 39 years old, was given the job of ending factionalism at Yorkshire; John Warr took over at Middlesex; Ramon Subba Row, a Cambridge blue, was to lead Northants; and the dashing Colin Ingleby-Mackenzie took charge at Hampshire. Peter May, on the other hand, had the challenge of leading Surrey to their seventh County Championship.

On April 16, Leicestershire made what was probably the quickest award of a county cap to Willie Watson, before he had played a single innings for them. The chairman told the players that his committee believed the team were very lucky to have such a distinguished captain and the response was a reassuring 'Hear hear!' The new captain was to get an early chance to test his batting in the match against the tourists, New Zealand. Unfortunately for Leicester, the New Zealand leg spinner, John Alabaster, was able to exploit the conditions and take 11-80. Although the tourists won by an innings and 64, the *Leicester Mercury* believed the first impressions of the new captain were heartening. They could point to Willie Watson's top score in the second innings of 45.

However, the first month under the new leader did not reverse the mould of the two previous seasons. There were seven first-class games in May and only one produced a victory, at Chesterfield against Derbyshire. The consolation for the new skipper was his own splendid batting form, as he scored 131 not out against Sussex at Hove and 119 and 88 not out against Northants at Grace Road. The contest against Subba Row's team was an exciting one for two new captains. Watson declared the Leicester first innings at 253-6 and Northants declined to pursue their innings to gain first innings points and declared 66 runs behind. Willie Watson and Jack van Geloven put on 100 in 75 minutes, allowing a declaration at 158-1. So Watson set Northants a target of 225 runs in 167 minutes, which they achieved with two balls to spare and three wickets standing. Almost 50 years later, Raman Subba Row recalled that Willie Watson was fair with his declarations. To compensate for this very narrow defeat, Watson could look back on a match in which he had scored 207 runs for once out. The month of May concluded dramatically with Leicestershire needing 144 in the fourth innings to beat Hampshire after they had bowled out the southern county for just 71 in their second innings. It turned into a contest between Derek Shackleton's medium-paced bowling and Willie Watson's batting. The bowler took all the six Leicester wickets to fall for 29 runs while Willie Watson batted for two-and-a-quarter hours for 62 and never made a false stroke, one of the finest innings on a bad wicket that Hants captain, Ingleby-Mackenzie, had seen. The match was drawn and the Leicester captain stood second in the national batting averages. Two factors may have contributed to this batting resurgence: liberation from the Yorkshire dressing room or batting regularly at number three in the order, or a combination of both.

At the beginning of June, the Test selectors did not recall the in-form Watson for the first match against New Zealand, preferring Warwickshire's Mike Smith. This meant that Smith joined Willie Watson as a double international, except that, in Smith's case, it was rugby and cricket.

The month of June was an improvement for Leicester's fortunes as they won two matches and only lost two. These results took the county up into the middle of the table. The summer was cool and wet and many fixtures were drawn. For Willie Watson, the month was not as prolific as May had been but he still contributed regularly, including a 77 not out against Essex at Colchester. He was the third batsman in the country to reach 1,000 runs – only Peter May and Ramon Subba Row were ahead of him.

Certainly, the *Leicester Mercury* was impressed with the fine job the new captain was doing. 'This season, in one great innings after another, he has for the first time realized his great potential. I believe the answer lies simply in the change of clubs. For some years, the Yorkshire atmosphere has been far from what it should be and away from it Watson has become a far different player.

Also, responsibility and leadership are something he thrives on.' The newspaper went on to say of Willie Watson that 'This serious student of the game does not suffer fools gladly and obviously revels in a sticky situation.'

July was a sharp contrast to the month that preceded it. Leicestershire lost three successive matches. At Gillingham, Kent's Dave Halfyard did most of the damage, including a hat-trick, while at Old Trafford Brian Statham also took a hat-trick while adding another 13 wickets. A first-innings 50 from Willie Watson could not save Leicestershire from defeat by an innings and 132 runs and they failed to reach three figures in either innings (99 and 87). The batting was even worse against Derbyshire, at Ashby de la Zouch, with Les Jackson almost unplayable. Leicestershire's totals were 70 and 77 and Jackson bagged 7-30 in the first innings and 5-47 in the second. Derbyshire won by an innings and 42 runs despite scoring only 189!

The captain was spared further pain by an invitation to play for the Players against the Gentlemen at Lord's. The star batsman for the Players was Arthur Milton, who scored 101. He had recently become a double international and will almost certainly be the last player to achieve that distinction. The best form for the Gentlemen came from Raman Subba Row, who made 102 not out, while in the Players' second innings Willie Watson made 31 not out, opening with Roy Marshall. The match was drawn.

The *Leicester Mercury* speculated that the match had been an unofficial trial for the tour of Australia and that Willie Watson was in competition with Mike Smith, Ted Dexter and Raman Subba Row for a batting place 'down under'. On July 10 the MCC asked Watson if he was available. He was very keen but could not give a definite answer until he had sorted out one or two things. The newspaper thought that he thoroughly deserved an invitation for his batting and bold captaincy, which had increased interest in cricket in the county. At 38 years old, he would have to face the physical strain of an Australian tour, but 'He was much fitter than most players of his age and was still a beautiful mover in the field' [*Leicester Mercury*].

His form earned him a recall to the England team for the fourth Test against New Zealand at Old Trafford starting on July 24. At that time, he also informed the MCC that he was available for the Australian tour. His return to the Test team created a record: he became the first ex-Yorkshire cricketer to play for England. At Old Trafford, New Zealand were dismissed for 267 and England's reply was led by two left-handers, Peter Richardson, with 74, and Willie Watson, with 66. Captain Peter May added a century and England totalled 365. In their second innings, New Zealand were bowled out for 85 by Tony Lock, who took 7-35. At the end of July, the MCC Test selectors announced the inclusion of Willie Watson for the tour of Australia. He would be only the fourth Leicestershire player to undertake this tough assignment.

While Willie Watson's career was experiencing a resurgence, Leicestershire's July went from bad to worse, if that were possible. They won one game only, losing five, but it was the scale of the defeats which was depressing. Ironically, Leicester's sole victory came at Snibston Colliery, Coalville, against Essex, when skipper Watson was away on Test duty. This success was largely due to Maurice Hallam's fine 134.

To quote the song, 'Things can only get better' and, in August, they duly did. Northants were beaten by 20 runs in a low-scoring match at Northampton. Surrey's varied and top-class attack was frustrated by Leicester's second innings opening partnership between Hallam, with 60, and Watson, 63 not out, ensuring the match was drawn. Against Nottingham, Willie Watson scored a dominating 141 out of a total of 267-7 declared. Nottingham were then dismissed for 166, which meant a well-timed declaration was needed when Leicester batted again. Watson judged the decision perfectly because Nottinghamshire were bowled out for 166 with five minutes to spare and the match was won by 61 runs. In the next game at Scarborough, Willie Watson met up with his former Yorkshire team-mates for the first time since leaving for Leicester. He would have noted that Ken Taylor was not playing because he had returned to Huddersfield for football training before the new season. Taylor was among a small and declining number of players able, in the post-war period, to earn a living at both games. The weather curtailed play and the match was drawn.

In the match against Glamorgan at Loughborough, the Watson timing of declarations was again close to perfection. Glamorgan were out for 197 in their first innings. Leicester replied with their first opening stand of 176, as both the captain and Maurice Hallam scored 95. Watson declared on 327-8, hoping to have enough time to bowl Glamorgan out and win by an innings. Peter Walker, the Glamorgan all-rounder, remembers the game clearly nearly 50 years later. He described the climax: 'Glamorgan had two wickets standing, with the last over to be bowled. With the first ball another wicket fell, so the last man, Don Shepherd, came in. He blocked the next four balls and then he couldn't resist having a go at the last ball and was caught on the boundary. Our captain, Wilf Wooller, was furious and he turned on Haydn Davies, who had batted sensibly, and sent him home for some dispute which had happened earlier in the day. Haydn's reply was, "You're sending the wrong man home!"'

Willie Watson missed the next fixture at Grace Road in order to play in the fifth Test at The Oval. The match was curtailed by the weather and finished as a draw – Watson's contribution was catching Bert Sutcliffe off Fred Trueman as New Zealand managed 161, and then ten runs in England's reply of 219. The tourists were 91-3 when the match was halted.

Leicestershire topped 100 points in the championship for the first time in three years and climbed to 13th. That put them immediately behind Yorkshire, whose season had ended in turmoil. The temperamental Johnny Wardle had not taken to the appointment of Ronnie Burnet as captain and, as a result of this clash of personalities, the Yorkshire Committee decided to dispense with the bowler's services. Wardle, also chosen to tour Australia, responded in a series of bitter articles in the *Daily Mail*. As a consequence of his public clash with his county committee, the MCC withdrew his invitation.

Willie Watson was top of the Leicester averages and second nationally with 46.62. At the top with 63.74 was Peter May, who led Surrey to their seventh consecutive championship. EE Snow, the Leicestershire historian, wrote, 'The modern generation will not have seen a more graceful batsman than Willie Watson, one of the greatest left-hand bats of all time. He made batting supremely easy and seemed to have all the time in the world to play his shots. He was also a fine runner between the wickets; he moved in the field like the superb athlete he was.'

During Watson's first season at Leicester the ground at Grace Road remained in the ownership of the Local Education Authority. Therefore, the home games played there were concentrated into the school summer holidays in July and August. So, during that period, Barbara Watson and children Graham and Val took a break from Yorkshire and were accommodated in the Grand Hotel in Leicester.

CHAPTER 22

AUSTRALIA AT LAST

IT HAD BEEN a long-held ambition of Willie Watson to tour Australia with the MCC. For the first tour after the War (1946–47) he had been relatively inexperienced, beginning to establish himself in the Yorkshire side. In the event the selectors gave captain Wally Hammond a seasoned and mature party, which the Australians defeated 3-0. For the next tour in 1950–51, the selectors were criticised for choosing too many inexperienced players for captain Freddie Brown, and Watson's chances were frustrated by his selection for the 1950 World Cup and his fine batting form when he returned came too late to impress the MCC selectors. The third post-war tour to Australia in 1954–55 was a serious disappointment for Willie Watson. He had scored a Test century against the Australians and he was no longer contracted to play for Sunderland. However, his form in the summer of 1954 was disappointing and the last two batting places in Len Hutton's party went to Colin Cowdrey and Vic Wilson. Nevertheless, Jim Laker thought him 'downright unlucky not to go.' At 34 years old, it seemed his chance had gone. Instead, it was the resurgence at Leicester that propelled Willie Watson into Peter May's party.

Unfortunately, the story does not have a happy ending for Watson or England – this despite the fact that the tour party was believed to be one of the strongest to represent the MCC abroad. It was seven years since a major series had been lost and Australia had been beaten in three successive Ashes series. Unfortunately, the sacking of Johnny Wardle from the party was a huge distraction before the party started its voyage. The journalist EW Swanton believed that Peter May had been deprived of his most valuable bowler on overseas pitches, but the former Australian Test cricketer and journalist, Jack Fingleton, regarded Wardle as, at best, a moderately useful Test cricketer. The MCC Test selectors decided not to replace him, so the party became 16.

Unbeknown to the selectors (or journalists) the 16 was to be temporarily reduced to 15 before the journey out was completed. The unlikely incident has been described by the man himself, Willie Watson: 'On the ship going over, I sat talking to the physio in the lounge. When I got up from the settee to get dressed for dinner, I turned round and my knee felt funny, but not painful. I found I couldn't bend my knee...The physio tried to put it back but couldn't.' Watson remembered that, back in 1942 when he was in the Army, he had a cartilage operation but he had played football and cricket for 16 years since then without any trouble.

When the tour party reached Aden, Willie Watson saw an RAF doctor, who frightened him by saying he had osteoarthritis. This Watson could not believe. When the ship reached Colombo, in Sri Lanka (then Ceylon), it was decided to fly him to Perth to see a specialist at the city's hospital. After a couple of weeks, the knee was manipulated under anaesthetic but Watson still could not bend it. On the day before the team arrived he was getting out of a taxi when his knee felt different; he could bend it right back but not straighten it. When the specialist was informed, he identified the problem and an operation was deemed necessary. Floating gristle, resulting from the original surgery on the cartilage, had to be removed. As a result of the hospital treatment, Willie Watson could not play cricket until the start of December 1958. By that time, about ten games had been played while the first Test at Brisbane was almost due.

Jack Fingleton wrote that the selection of 38-year-old Watson had always been a gamble and was 'perhaps two tours too late'. For a batsman on his first tour of Australia, 'The eyes have to become accustomed to a much harsher sunlight, the pace from the faster wickets is harder to pick up and the muscles, with a long sporting career behind them, do not respond too well in the morning after a long day in the field.'

The early tour had gone quite well prior to the first Test at Brisbane. The state games against Western Australia, New South Wales and Queensland were drawn while South Australia and Victoria were beaten. During this period, Peter May had batted brilliantly and Jim Laker had bowled very well, taking 10-101 in the victory over South Australia at Adelaide. Meanwhile, the 'new' Don Bradman, Norman O'Neill, looked a powerful and attractive batsman. However, the issue which came to dominate the tour was the alleged throwing by a number of Australian bowlers. The first example came at Melbourne against Victoria early in November. The suspect, Ian Meckiff, whose action had been picked out in advance for special scrutiny, was thought by the MCC batsmen to throw. However, because he did not throw especially well, no complaint was made but, with the benefit of hindsight, this was probably a misguided decision. Five years later, Meckiff was no balled four times in an over for an unfair action and never played first-class cricket again. But, in 1958, Tom Graveney insisted, 'The throwers were kings.'

The Australian selectors made a crucial decision before the Test to select Richie Benaud as captain in preference to the outstanding left-handed batsman, Neil Harvey. Despite his inexperience of captaincy in first-class cricket, he quickly brought a keen mind to the job and developed a superb fielding side that made England look lethargic and tardy. Furthermore, Benaud's own leg-spin bowling had improved out of all recognition.

Willie Watson's long-awaited debut on tour came in the final game before the first Test. The MCC faced Queensland at Brisbane – a match in which Subba Row broke his wrist when fielding, which led to Ted Dexter and John Mortimore being added to the party – and, understandably, Watson's form was undistinguished. He opened with Arthur Milton, making seven in each innings, each time being caught by Wally Grout off Ray Lindwall. Consequently, he was not included in the England line-up for the first Test at the same ground. Peter May won the toss and decided to bat on a quick pitch, and England were soon 79-5. Jim Laker discussed May's decision with Willie Watson, whose cricket judgement and knowledge he greatly respected. Watson's view was, 'In England you put a side in if you have a fair expectation of getting them out for 100. In Australia, it's different. It's worth putting them in if you think you can shoot them out for 200.'

England struggled to reach 134, suggesting they might have benefited from inserting the Australians. However, Australia struggled to pass this total and were out for 186. What followed caused EW Swanton to describe the cricket as the dullest and most depressing he had ever watched. It featured Trevor Bailey scoring 68 in seven hours, 38 minutes, which reinforced his nickname of 'Barnacle Bailey'. En route he established the record for the slowest Test half century (just under six hours). But it was all to no avail, as O'Neill led Australia to victory with a brilliant 71 not out.

Between the first and second Tests, Willie Watson was given a full-scale trial. The tour reached Tasmania for a match against the island at Hobart. Willie Watson opened with Peter Richardson, a batsman who remains a great admirer of his partner to this day. Together they put on 72, Watson making 30. The weather was wet and the match was drawn. Next, the tour moved on to Launceston to play a Tasmanian Combined XI. This time Willie Watson was paired with fellow double international, Arthur Milton. In the first innings, they opened with a stand of 99, of which Watson made 43, and he followed that with 42 in the second innings.

In Adelaide, against South Australia, Willie Watson was moved down to number three and scored only two, but in the second innings he was promoted to open with Peter Richardson and reached 40 before being bowled by John Martin. Meantime, Ted Dexter made nine and seven.

In his preview of the second Test at Melbourne, EW Swanton named three Australian bowlers whom he suspected of throwing: Meckiff, Keith Slater and Jim Burke. This assessment was quickly at the centre of this controversial match. The England selectors made one change, Watson replacing Milton, but they also decided that Trevor Bailey should open with Richardson, while Watson would bat at number three. This move meant Peter May and Colin Cowdrey batting at five and six.

Peter May won the toss and decided to bat on a greenish wicket with plenty of life. The game's sensational start came in a magnificent opening spell of swing bowling by Alan Davidson who, in his second over, had Richardson caught at the wicket. Watson was bowled by a yorker for a duck, and Graveney was out first ball lbw. England were 7-3 but May survived the hat-trick and went on to score 113 out of 259. Australia's reply of 308 was largely thanks to a brilliant 167 by Neil Harvey although England were particularly well served by Brian Statham with 7- 57. However, these excellent achievements were completely overwhelmed by England's second innings of 87, lasting just three hours. Watson was again yorked by Davidson, this time for seven, but it was not Davidson's bowling which caught the attention: it was that of Ian Meckiff. He took the wickets of five of England's top batsmen in his figures of 6-38. EW Swanton wrote that he had never seen anything so blatant as Meckiff's action and he believed the English batsmen were undone as much by feelings of indignation and resentment as by the inherent difficulties of fast left-arm bowling. According to Tom Graveney, batting at number four, throwing had a corrosive effect on the morale of the whole side: 'When you are struggling, it comes as a big extra load.' Jack Fingleton was less sympathetic, describing the English batting as the most pitiable display he had ever seen on a good wicket. The Australians scored the 42 they needed to win, with the loss of two wickets.

England made four changes for the third Test at Sydney, which started four days later. Godfrey Evans had broken a middle finger in Melbourne and was replaced by Roy Swetman as wicketkeeper; Fred Trueman came in for Peter Loader; Arthur Milton was recalled for Peter Richardson; and Ted Dexter came in for Willie Watson. Only a second innings 182-run partnership between May (92) and Cowdrey (100) and the weather prevented another England defeat.

Watson was recalled for the game with Victoria back in Melbourne and he returned to his best form in scoring 141. He used his feet, drove well and also pulled with distinction. Unfortunately, Milton suffered a second finger break and his tour was over.

It seemed Willie Watson was now sure to win back his Test place. Victoria were beaten by nine wickets and the tour moved back to Sydney to play against New South Wales – whoever planned the itinerary did not have travel fatigue in mind. There the MCC batsmen came up against another controversial Australian bowler, Gordon Rorke, a 6ft 5ins right-arm fast bowler who dragged his rear foot several feet over the bowling crease. In fact, his exceptional drag provoked moves in official circles to modify the laws. Not only that but the England players reckoned he was another chucker. At Sydney, his pace proved a handful to Willie Watson, Tom Graveney and others, but fortunately Peter May gave another glorious exhibition of batting, scoring 136. However, the weather had the final say in the outcome and the game was drawn.

The fourth Test in Adelaide was crucial to England. Fail to win, and the Ashes were Australia's. Again the selectors chopped and changed. Peter Richardson replaced the unfortunate Arthur Milton; Willie Watson came in for Ted Dexter; Godfrey Evans took over from Roy Swetman, and Frank Tyson was in for the injured Jim Laker.

Peter May made the surprising decision to put the Australians in to bat and they stayed there until lunch on the third day. They reached 476 – Colin McDonald topping the scoring with 170 – and England's chance was gone. The English batting again proved inadequate. In the first innings, Watson, at number six, soon found himself defending tailenders, as the score moved from 170-4 to 188-9. He batted for two hours 25 minutes, mainly with the help of Brian Statham, to help England reach 240. When England were asked to follow on, May told Watson to keep his pads on and open the second innings with Richardson. The pair put on 89, with Richardson particularly impressive. Watson was out for 40 to Les Favell's brilliant catch deep on the offside off Richie Benaud and, despite fifties from May and Graveney, England slumped to 270, just avoiding an innings defeat. Benaud was the most successful Australian wicket taker, nine wickets in the match, and there could be no English complaints about his action. Jack Fingleton was critical of the English fielding, singling out Peter Richardson as cumbersome and Willie Watson's throwing as weak. He wrote, 'The ball had to be relayed from the deep by a half-way assistant.' So Australia's ten-wicket victory meant they regained the Ashes after five years and 170 days.

Between the fourth and fifth Tests, the MCC comfortably won three matches against weaker opponents. Willie Watson's best contribution in this period was 63 against Southern New South Wales at Wagga Wagga on February 9. However, he was declared unfit on the morning of the first day of the fifth Test in Melbourne and the Australians, impressively led by Benaud, never looked remotely like losing their grip on the match and won the Test by nine wickets.

Tom Graveney described the 1958–59 tour as the saddest mission he had ever been on. He concluded that the party had been cursed. There had been an exceptional number of injuries and a depressing lack of purpose. The major doubt about the party, the opening batting, proved to be well founded. England tried four opening batsmen and only once was more than 30 reached. There were complaints about umpiring, about throwing and about dragging, but they could not explain the size of the Australian victory. Over the whole series, the England team were beaten by 35 wickets. Astonishingly, the fact is that, at the end of not a single day in any of the five Tests, could anyone say that England enjoyed an advantage.

The problems were not confined to the field. May was criticised for taking his fiancée Victoria Gilligan, niece of Arthur Gilligan, who had captained England on nine occasions, and it was felt that manager Freddie Brown drank too much.

The tour moved on to New Zealand where, on February 23, Otago were the opposition at Dunedin. The visitors were successful by an innings and 94 runs, thanks to match figures of 13-79 for Fred Trueman. This was followed by the first Test at Christchurch. Willie Watson opened with his friend, Peter Richardson, but all the batting honours went to Ted Dexter, who made 141. New Zealand were dismissed twice in quick succession, the outstanding bowler in the match being Tony Lock, with 11-84, and England won by an innings and 99 runs. Next, the MCC moved on to Wellington, where the visitors batted first and amassed 511-9 declared. Colin Cowdrey, Peter Richardson and Willie Watson each scored centuries while Tom Graveney was only nine runs short and Wellington were beaten by an innings and 211 runs.

The second Test and final match of the tour was curtailed by the weather, including warnings of cyclones, a depressing way for Willie Watson's Test career to end. It was not a distinguished 23rd and final Test for the Yorkshireman, bowled for 11 by Ken Hough. Peter May scored an unfinished 124 so some crumbs of comfort could be derived from the unbeaten New Zealand section of the tour.

CHAPTER 23

A VINTAGE SUMMER

WILLIE WATSON WAS back in England by March 23 1959. He arrived in a group which included Peter May, who announced that he hoped to continue playing cricket for Surrey and England. He paid tribute to all his players for their excellent team spirit throughout what he termed 'a difficult tour'. The players were instructed not to discuss their feelings about the legality of the actions of some of the Australian fast bowlers and as captain May was not about to break the omerta, just saying, 'We were beaten by a much better team.'

Leicestershire County Cricket Club held their AGM on April 3 and Tony Diment, the secretary, reported that problems over the acquisition of Grace Road were beginning to sort themselves out. He said the club was sometimes criticised for not getting new players but he insisted this was not due to lack of effort. Skipper Willie Watson was given a great reception on his return from Australia and New Zealand. The secretary said that Willie's selection had brought honour and prestige to Leicestershire cricket. Furthermore, he was pleased to report that the 'Watson Knee' had fully recovered and should not cause any problems in the coming season. Willie Watson replied that he was hopeful for the new season and was looking forward to further improvements by the team. In mid-April the *Playfair Cricket Annual* placed Willie Watson in its ten cricketers of the year.

The opening fixture for the 1959 season was against the Indian tourists at Grace Road. It was clear from the Leicestershire selections that there were no significant changes from the previous season, except for the promotion of Ray Julian to wicketkeeper in place of Jack Firth. May proved to be a good month for Willie Watson. He scored 518 runs but it was an exceptional month for Maurice Hallam, the experienced Leicester opener. In the opening month, including the fixture against Glamorgan, which began in May but concluded in June, he scored two double centuries and two centuries. The first century (158) was the draw with the Indians which Leicestershire dominated. Two County Championship matches were won, two were drawn and two were lost: a modestly successful start to Leicestershire's season.

Hallam's first double century – the first of a long career – was exactly 200 in a draw with Derbyshire at Grace Road. He and Willie Watson (101 not out) put on 207 for the fourth wicket. After a home draw with Kent, Watson took his team to Old Trafford and while they won by three wickets, the captain grabbed a 'pair', his first for 21 years, also at Manchester but in a second XI game.

After a nine-wicket defeat at Northampton in which Hallam's form continued with 59 and 48 came the eight-wicket win over Glamorgan at Grace Road. After Glamorgan had won the toss and decided to bat they accumulated 322-9 declared, thanks mainly to 132 from Allan Watkins. Leicestershire replied with 325-5 declared after Hallam bettered his previous highest score by ten. The Welshmen then declared on 271-7, setting the home team a stiff target of 269 in three hours. Leicestershire rattled off 271 for the loss of only two wickets in 49.3 overs with half an hour to spare. Maurice Hallam became only the fifth batsman to score both a double century and a century in a match. He dashed to 157 in the second innings, reaching his century in the fastest time so far that season (71 minutes). Willie Watson weighed in with 59 not out which included two sixes.

Hallam must have been close to a call from the England selectors but, ultimately, Ken Taylor of Yorkshire was preferred.

Leicestershire struggled in the championship in June, losing to Middlesex, Gloucestershire and Somerset by an innings and to Northants by nine wickets. They also lost, by eight wickets, at

Oxford after the students had declared their first innings at 325-8 and Leicestershire suffered the indignity of following on.

The batting was very fragile and, on six occasions, they failed to reach 160. At the start of the month there was a respectable draw with Nottinghamshire in which Willie Watson was left, not out, on 98. At the end there were two commendable victories: the first was at Colchester, where Essex were completely dominated by Terry Spencer, who took 14 wickets. His second innings figures of 8-41 are a Leicester record against Essex. He also scored 51 not out, batting at number eight. Trevor Bailey's splendid bowling for Essex, match figures of 9-108, was largely overlooked.

Jim Laker wrote that in cricket parlance Leicestershire were becoming known as 'Watsonshire'. Hampshire, Leicester's final opponent of the month, would have understood this description because at Grace Road Willie Watson scored 97 and 68 not out to help his team to a five-wicket victory. Overall in June, Watson made 491 runs at an average of more than 44.

Unlike its predecessors, the summer weather in 1959 was glorious. While Maurice Hallam and Willie Watson continued to take advantage of the good batting conditions, the county was unfortunate enough to lose the services of its major strike bowler, Brian Boshier, halfway through July. His damaged Achilles tendon meant the Leicester bowling lost penetration and it resulted in Spencer being over bowled. Twelve championship games followed Boshier's injury and Leicestershire did not gain a single point. Consequently, the county fell steadily down the table. Despite his team's troubles, Willie Watson continued to score heavily during July and managed to hit centuries as an opener in an eight-wicket win over Middlesex at Ashby de la Zouch (109 plus 74 not out), in a draw at The Oval (a rearguard 155 when opening) and in a six-wicket defeat by Essex at Grace Road (110). He added more than 500 runs to his season's aggregate.

While Willie Watson's batting could not be faulted, some 'deckchair critics' had begun to question his decisions to put his opponents into bat. On three occasions, in the first half of July, at Worcester, Edgbaston and The Oval, Watson asked the rival captain to bat first. The *Leicester Mercury's* Bryon Butler gave his full support to Watson who, he pointed out, had 20 years' experience on which to call. Although the three games did not go well, could the captain's decisions be justified? The facts were that Leicester's playing resources were depleted, their opponents were stronger and the wickets were green or wet. As Watson explained to Butler, the captain's decision 'on winning the toss depends on three factors: an assessment of the opponent's strength and of his own team's strength and an examination of the wicket in case it offered some help to the bowlers'. Bryon Butler turned to the relevant match statistics, which showed that Worcester were 162 all out, Warwick were 37-2 and Surrey were 123-4. These facts, he maintained, justified Watson's decisions. Subsequent scoring in the matches was irrelevant to the argument.

As July moved close to August, Willie Watson faced his native county at Grace Road. Yorkshire batted first and made 218 while Charles Palmer, making one of his occasional appearances for Leicester, had the remarkable bowling figures of 11 overs, seven maidens, five runs and one wicket. In reply, the Leicestershire batsmen struggled except for their captain, who scored 79 out of a total of 132. However, it was to no avail as Yorkshire won by 78 runs with 13 minutes to spare.

Although in August injury restricted Willie Watson to only eight innings, he still managed another two championship centuries. At Derby he hit 150 in a draw; against Surrey at Grace Road, another draw, it was 173. He also scored 106 in an eight-wicket victory over Ireland. Over the season, he made seven centuries, which equalled the Leicestershire record set by Les Berry in 1937. He was also only the second batsman to reach 2,000 runs in a season for the county. The first was again Les Berry, in 1937. Leicester's results in August were dismal: five defeats and two draws, which meant they finished 16th. This was a disappointment after the previous season's improvement. Watson was second behind Mike Smith in the first-class averages with 53.50 to 57.94 but Smith had scored 3,245 runs that summer, compared with Willie Watson's 2,212. Although this was the first time, indeed the only time, Watson topped 2,000 runs in a summer, there were 11 more batsmen who scored more runs than him in 1959.

Willie Watson's fine season can be summed up in the words of Bryon Butler, who watched him bat against Surrey, the county champions, on August 19. 'Willie Watson confirmed, if it were needed, what a great player he is. This was an innings in the grand manner, top heavy with responsibility, yet so generously endowed with all the good things of cricket that, even though he was at the wicket for nearly six hours, time never hung heavily... He was always in majestic command, driving and cutting with all the elegant and precise authority that is his real strength.'

(Incidentally, Butler, who died in 2001, later made his name on the *Daily Telegraph* and in 1968 became football correspondent for the BBC.)

Clearly, Leicestershire faced deep-seated, dispiriting problems. The key issue was to recruit new players, but the only immediate source was rejects from other counties. Not many of these were of the necessary quality to strengthen the squad. One clear exception was Test opener, Peter Richardson, who had played for Worcestershire for ten years as an amateur and who wished to pursue his career as a professional. He told the author that Willie Watson was frequently on the phone urging him to join Leicestershire. Eventually Richardson chose Kent, despite Watson's desperate calls. At that time, if counties wished to recruit overseas players there was a three-year qualification period – unfortunately not a solution to Leicestershire's short-term problems. Another possible source was for the county to find and groom their own players. In this area, Leicester were in the vanguard and only time would tell if this route would succeed. Certainly, the county could not expect to progress on the basis of being 'Watsonshire'. It would be unreasonable to expect him to keep repeating the vintage summer of 1959: innings 50, not out 10, highest score 173, total runs 2,212, av 55.30.

If Leicester were not contenders for the County Championship, Willie Watson would have been quietly satisfied with Yorkshire's first outright title since 1946.

CHAPTER 24

RESISTANCE AT SNIBSTON COLLIERY

THE *LEICESTER MERCURY* heralded the new 1960 cricket season with an attack on the MCC, published on March 24. It claimed that the MCC's rules 'make weak counties weaker'. The rules on registering new players were 'hidebound' and resulted in a prominent Test cricketer like Peter Richardson losing a season while he waited to qualify for Kent. As it happened, Leicestershire had given trials to more than 40 players from outside the county over the past year without uncovering any potential recruits.

The newspaper went on to report that club secretary Tony Diment had resigned and would be taking up a post in industry, as his predecessor, Charles Palmer, had done. The post was offered to Mike Turner who, for the next 33 years, became one of the game's most influential administrators. Two days after the paper aired its views Willie Watson visited Leicester from his home and poultry farm near Huddersfield. He told the Mercury that the previous season had been 'very disappointing indeed, not only for the spectators but also to me and the players. .He said that bowlers win matches and the loss of Brian Boshier had seriously weakened the bowling.

By April 8, the players were back for pre-season preparations. The skipper was optimistic but was cautious in his assessment of the county's chances, saying that with luck they could finish five or six places above the bottom. A fortnight later, there was good news about Brian Boshier, who was fully fit again. Furthermore, Yorkshire fast bowler Peter Broughton accepted an invitation to join Leicestershire. He had made six appearances for Yorkshire, all in 1956, where he was competing against nine other fast bowlers for a place. He had trials with Sussex and Nottinghamshire but chose Leicester because they were welcoming, down-to-earth and not dominated by rather snooty amateurs. He also joined because he was a great admirer of Willie Watson, who was liked by everyone in the cricket world.

Before the end of April, another Yorkshire cricketer was heading south to Leicester. He was Harold Bird, an opening batsman who had made 181 not out against Gloucester the previous summer. Today, of course, he is much better known as the very experienced former Test umpire, Dickie Bird. Bird had been upset by the treatment he received from the Yorkshire Committee. He had resigned two or three times from the club but the resignations had not been accepted. Eventually, his request for release was agreed and he was approached by several counties. He chose Leicester because Willie Watson came in first and was very persuasive, even persistent. Years later, with the benefit of hindsight, Dickie Bird thought that joining Leicester was the worst decision he had made in his cricket career. The move from the top county to one near the bottom, he felt, put a lot of pressure on him to succeed.

He was drafted into the Leicester team for the first county game of the season on May 7 1960 against Glamorgan. The match was a baptism of fire for Dickie Bird, as Leicester collapsed to 88 all out: Willie Watson 2, Dickie Bird 4. Glamorgan's reply was 384-7, with centuries by Gilbert Parkhouse (121) and Allan Watkins (107). The Leicester second innings showed only a modest improvement, 152, so Glamorgan were easy winners by an innings and 144 runs. Watson top scored with 37, but Bird managed only six. Outstanding for Glamorgan was Peter Walker, who took 5-25 in the first innings and five catches in the second.

The next two games against Worcestershire and Gloucestershire were drawn, and Dickie Bird (53) made his first 50 for his new county at Stroud. The next game, a low-scoring defeat by Lancashire, was notable for injuries to Bird and Watson. Bird was forced to retire in the first innings and was absent from the second, while Watson battled against an extremely hostile Brian Statham, who took 14-58 in the match. In Leicester's first innings, which reached just 37, wicketkeeper Ray Julian was top scorer with seven!

The Leicester captain had been hit four times by Statham but, although he felt sore, he decided to play in the next game against Hampshire at the Snibston Colliery ground in Coalville.

This proved to be the most memorable match of the year. Willie Watson moved himself up the order to open with Maurice Hallam, while Dickie Bird was at number three. The Leicester captain soon passed his previous top score of the season and completed his first century, 110, out of a total of 285 (Bird got a duck). Hants replied with a rapid 367-4 declared, including centuries by Jimmy Gray (150) and Henry Horton (105). In the field, Watson found that he could not bend down to field on his right-hand side. Unfortunately, unbeknown to him, the duel with Brian Statham had resulted in a cracked rib. For the second innings, the Leicester skipper dropped down the order but the batting disintegrated to 52-8 at the close of play. Leicester still needed 30 runs to avoid an innings defeat and Hampshire believed they were virtual winners. So did the ground staff because next morning before play commenced a truck was at the venue collecting up the deckchairs. However, a heavily-strapped Watson decided to bat at number nine and joined number four, Bob Gardner, at the wicket. Watson knew that Gardner did not like facing Hampshire's best bowler, Derek Shackleton, so he decided to take him as much as possible himself. The stand of 125 lasted from 11.30am to just after tea, the match was saved and Gardner did not have to face Shackleton once in the whole of that time. When the innings ended at 191, Hampshire needed to score 110 in 37 minutes, an impossible task. But the Hampshire captain, Colin Ingleby-Mackenzie, was so frustrated by the Leicestershire fight-back that typically he ordered his batsmen to go for the runs. As a consequence, they finished the day playing for time on 31-4. One national paper suggested that Willie Watson had now become a cricket immortal because of his great innings of 76 at Coalville. The *Leicester Mercury* reminded its readers that Watson had already had his glory day in 1953 at Lord's, against the Australians.

Leicestershire did not win a match in May and, apart from his heroics at Coalville, Willie Watson's form was not comparable with the previous season. In the first game in June at Lord's, his team were forced to follow on against Middlesex. In the second innings, Watson opened with Maurice Hallam because Dickie Bird was dropped after a run of poor scores. Together they put on 196 for the first wicket – Hallam 121, Watson 61 – in a valiant attempt to save the match. However, the rest of the team had no answer to Alan Moss (6-23) and nine wickets fell for 18 runs, so that Middlesex won comfortably by ten wickets.

The next game in June was at Coventry, where Warwickshire held a lead of 29 on the first innings. Willie Watson produced a superbly methodical 60 in the second innings, which allowed him to set Mike Smith's team a challenge of scoring 213 in 130 minutes to win. MJK Smith led by example, however, scoring 84, but Warwick still needed 12 off the last over. Eight runs came from the first five balls, so a boundary was needed off the last ball but only a single was scored. The match was drawn and Leicestershire dropped to the bottom of the table.

But Leicestershire's long wait for their first victory came to an end when Somerset were completely outplayed in the next match. Firstly, the Leicester batsmen were in total command back at Grace Road, declaring at 339-2. For once, Willie Watson was not required to bat, mainly because fellow Yorkshireman, Jack van Geloven, was in splendid form in scoring 157 not out. Hallam had chipped in with 71 and although Bird failed again with just three van Geloven was joined by Robin Gardner (100 not out) as they put on 218. Then it was the bowler's turn to complete Somerset's rout. First, Rodney Pratt took 5-44 to help dismiss the visitors for 106, which meant they were required to follow on. In their second innings, Somerset managed 185, leaving Leicester winners by an innings and 48 runs.

Unfortunately for Willie Watson and Leicestershire, this victory proved to be a false dawn. In the remaining five fixtures in June, there were no wins, one defeat and four draws; nevertheless, there was one exciting finish at Loughborough, where Notts were the visitors. Willie Watson hit his second century of the summer (125) and followed it with 68 in the second innings. He then declared at 258-7, setting Notts to make 312 in 250 minutes. It was a well-judged target because as the runs came and the wickets fell, both teams had a chance of winning. Eventually, Nottinghamshire finished 21 runs short with three wickets standing.

July brought no relief from Leicestershire's poor results, with five matches drawn and two lost, both by an innings. The batting was vulnerable once Watson and possibly Hallam were out. The only encouraging performance during July was against the South African tourists at Grace Road, when Maurice Hallam (164) and Dickie Bird (104) put on 277 for the first wicket. The partnership was the highest against the tourists and Leicestershire's best, for any wicket, since the War. Two shrewd declarations by Willie Watson set the South Africans a target of 169. At the close of play, they were 11 runs short of victory with six wickets standing. In Leicestershire's second innings, Trevor Goddard, South Africa's outstanding all-rounder, took six of the eight wickets to fall for 29 runs.

Towards the end of July, Willie Watson reached 1,000 runs for the season, whilst batting against his old county, Yorkshire. He must have sympathised with one of his Yorkshire opponents, Ken Taylor, a key member of the Huddersfield Town team, but who had been contacted by the MCC about his availability for a winter tour to New Zealand. Obviously, his future Test career could depend on him making the trip and, to their credit, Huddersfield said that if he were to be selected, he should go.

There was no respite for Leicestershire in August 1960. On the first of the month, Willie Watson was out for 91, having shared a century opening stand with Dickie Bird against Warwickshire at Grace Road. The match was drawn but Harry Brown of the *Leicester Mercury* was not optimistic about the remainder of the season. He wrote, 'I shudder to think what would happen to Leicester if Watson was unable to play. With a look at the table, you'd scarcely think they could be worse. Don't believe it! This man is the rock on which the shipwreck leans for support.' The paper's pessimism was immediately justified at Grace Road, where Leicestershire were bowled out for 42 by Sussex, Ian Thomson taking 6-23. This was the first of three defeats by an innings, and completed in two days, during August.

For skipper Watson, in this time of adversity, there was one piece of good news. He was chosen to be the senior professional on the young MCC party to tour New Zealand in the winter of 1960–61. The 14-strong party would be captained by Dennis Silk, the Somerset amateur and Marlborough schoolmaster. Willie Watson's comment to the press was that 'It's a lovely country and should be a most enjoyable tour. I'm looking forward to it.' Apart from Silk and Watson, the selectors chose up-and-coming youngsters who were likely to make their mark in Test cricket in the future.

When the Leicestershire team arrived at Dover on August 31 for their final championship fixture, they had still won only one match. They languished at the foot of the table and faced Kent, who had already won seven times. Leicester batted first and made 206, and Kent replied with 166-8 declared. Next, Willie Watson declared the Leicester second innings at 144-8, leaving Kent to make 185 at about 75 runs an hour. Despite collapsing to 88-5, Kent were not prepared to play for a draw and continued to hit out. They were dismissed for 134, so Leicester achieved a second victory by 50 runs. If Leicester had lost to Kent, they would have ended the season with fewer points than any other county in the Championship since the War.

Not surprisingly there were no Leicestershire batsmen in the top 25 of the national batting averages. Willie Watson led the Leicester averages on 34.23 runs, having scored 1,335 runs, while Dickie Bird scored 1,028 and was awarded his county cap. Boshier headed the bowling averages but injury forced him out of over half the matches. In his absences, Yorkshireman Peter Broughton was given the new ball with Terry Spencer.

Several weeks before the end of the disastrous season, the Leicestershire club were on the lookout for experienced players to reinforce the playing staff. In mid-August, it became known that Lancashire would not be retaining Alan Wharton and, within a week, Leicestershire had made an offer for the Lancashire all-rounder and terms were quickly agreed. The 38-year-old would need a special MCC registration to be able to play for Leicester in 1961.

CHAPTER 25

THE NEW ZEALAND TOUR

THE IDEA OF AN MCC tour in 1960–61 had come from the New Zealand Governor General, Lord Cobham. His objective was for the tourists to bring a positive and attacking brand of cricket to New Zealand that would increase interest and involvement in the game. To spread the message, it was decided to visit as many places as possible, making it the most exacting tour.

However, the introduction of three unofficial 'Tests' changed the emphasis significantly. Instead of a goodwill tour alone, it became an opportunity to blood promising younger players on the international stage, especially with an Australian tour of England scheduled for 1961.

At the close of the 1960 season, Willie Watson could return to his Huddersfield chicken farm for three months, as the tour party was not due to leave until a week before Christmas. Along with captain, Dennis Silk and vice-captain Willie Watson, the selectors chose players such as David Allen, Bob Barber, John Murray, Jim Parks, Doug Padgett and David Smith, who already had Test match experience. They were reinforced by players who would become Test cricketers, like Roger Prideaux, Eric Russell, Don Wilson and David Larter. The team travelled from England by air, the first major MCC party to do so on the outward journey, though several had flown home.

The tourists faced a very busy itinerary that included 22 matches in about 12 weeks. In between games, there was a good deal of travelling in an era before motorways or dual carriageways. Often, the distances involved were much greater than was usual in England. And an even more contentious arrangement was that the players were usually billeted with families, rather than in hotels. This decision was made for economic reasons but it had an impact on team morale, especially when players were placed on their own, 15 to 20 miles from the ground, which meant that team meetings were almost impossible to hold. It tended to go against the building up of team spirit.

The party landed at Auckland and, on Christmas Eve, they played at Eden Park. The match against Auckland was drawn but much more significant was the first of many injuries that were to blight the tour. It began with Dennis Silk, who damaged a hand and, consequently, missed a lot of games. The next first-class match was against Wellington at the Basin Reserve ground, when the tourists were captained by Willie Watson. The tourists won by an innings and 91, thanks to a magnificent innings of 160 in 238 minutes by Roger Prideaux and to hostile bowling by 6ft 7ins David Larter.

The tour moved on to the South Island, where an exciting first-class match was played against Canterbury at Lancaster Park, Christchurch. The home team made 287 in their first innings, which the MCC matched for three wickets declared. Canterbury then made 190, which the MCC had to exceed to win. Captain Watson struggled hard to hold the tourists' second innings together. Only with a brilliant innings of 106 were the visitors able to win with one wicket to spare. It was in the next game against New Zealand colts at Ashburton that the injury list became so long that the tourists could not raise a full team. To overcome this emergency, the MCC co-opted Michael Bear, of Essex, who was coaching in New Zealand. This two-day game was drawn but John Murray hit a fine 80 not out. In the following three-day match against Otago at Dunedin, the injury problems came to a head, when the MCC could field only six completely fit players. Nevertheless, they were able to hold out for a draw, thanks to a commendable 92 not out by Jim Parks.

The next important fixture was the 'unofficial first Test' against New Zealand. Unfortunately, Dennis Silk was again injured, so Willie Watson stepped into his place as skipper. His opposite number was John Reid, a talented all-rounder and experienced captain of New Zealand. This was the ninth match of the tour and it was played at Dunedin, on 20 January, over four days. The home team batted first and made 313-7 declared; the MCC followed that with 277-5 declared. The MCC spinners, Bob Barber and David Allen, took nine wickets in the New Zealand second innings of 169, which set the MCC a target of 205 to win but they could only manage 167-7, so the first unofficial Test was drawn.

Between the first and second 'Tests' there was one first-class fixture against Central Districts at Cook's Gardens in Wanganui. This game involved the tourists in a journey back to the North Island of New Zealand. There was an exciting finish, with the Central Districts needing nine to win with two wickets standing when time ran out. The MCC were delighted with the batting form of Doug Padgett (129) and captain Dennis Silk (81).

The second unofficial Test was staged at the Basin Reserve, and again Willie Watson had to stand in as skipper. The first day's play was lost to rain and when Watson won the toss he put New Zealand into bat. The decision seemed inspired when New Zealand slumped to 43-5, but the lower orders staged a recovery which meant they were all out for 148. This was the fast bowlers' day, with David Larter and David Sayer capturing seven wickets between them. It proved the same for New Zealand's pacemen, Dick Motz and Francis Cameron, who swept the visitors aside for 111. Willie Watson 'strove with a sort of forlorn desperation to hold the innings up, seeking the partner to hold fast with him. But the partner never came,' according to John Reid. Watson was top scorer with 31. In their second innings, New Zealand did much better, even though the pitch remained awkward. They made 228 with Reid scoring 83. Willie Watson's decision to put the opposition in to bat meant the MCC would have to bat fourth on a turning wicket. Unfortunately for Watson and the MCC, New Zealand had just the bowler to exploit the condition, leg-break specialist John Alabaster. He gave the MCC batsmen no peace and they were bowled out for 132, giving New Zealand victory by 133 runs.

There followed three two-day matches in North Island that the MCC won comfortably and they also beat North Districts in a three-day first-class match at Seddon Park, Hamilton. Willie Watson took a rest from this fixture, and the MCC batting was dominated by Doug Padgett, with 125, and by Jim Parks, with 85. The next first-class match was played at Eden Park, Auckland, on February 24, against the Governor General's XI. To the New Zealand public, this game towered over the unofficial 'Tests' played on this tour. Lord Cobham was better known to cricket followers as the Hon JC Lyttelton, who had toured New Zealand with Errol Holmes' MCC party in 1935–36. So the Governor General was well able to lead his team against the tourists and, furthermore, he was able to recruit two cricket legends based in Australia: Ray Lindwall and Martin Donnelly. He also invited Collie Smith and Gerry Alexander, both fresh from the West Indies triumphs in Australia. Included among the six New Zealanders were Bert Sutcliffe and John Reid.

The match attracted a large and enthusiastic crowd who appreciated the vintage batting of Sutcliffe (74) and Watson (41), the fine spin bowling of Barber and Alabaster and the speed and agility in the field of Smith and Donnelly. Batting fourth, the Governor General's team were set to make 253 to win. It proved to be just beyond them and the MCC won by 25 runs.

There were no more first-class matches before the third unofficial Test at Christchurch on March 10. Happily, Dennis Silk was able to lead the MCC into this fixture, which involved the tourists in a journey back to the South Island. Willie Watson and Roger Prideaux opened the batting for the MCC against some fiery fast bowling from Gary Bartlett. He had all the batsmen struggling with a mass of rapped pads, thighs and boots. In Watson's case it was an injured hand, but he resumed his innings and made a courageous 61. The MCC were out for 223 and, in reply, New Zealand made 249-8 when Reid declared. In their second innings, the tourists were restricted to 45-1 as the weather wiped out the final day's play.

There was an attempt by a visiting journalist to sour relations between the tourists and New Zealanders by claiming, in an article for the *Daily Mirror*, that the fast bowler Gary Bartlett threw the ball. The writer claimed that this charge came from the MCC players, but this suggestion was quickly and angrily refuted by Dennis Silk. However, the story was out and the label 'Chucker' was attached to Bartlett. This was unfortunate because both teams had agreed that Gary Bartlett did not throw and were convinced that the journalist concerned was not present to report cricket but to find sensation.

In his report back to the MCC, captain Dennis Silk described the unprecedented levels of injuries sustained by the tour party and he referred particularly to the Otago match at Dunedin, the one in which there were only six completely fit players available. He was critical of the fixture list because there were too many second- and third-class matches, especially in the second half of the tour. Silk was particularly scathing about the billeting system that had been devised for the tour. He felt that the whole essence of a tour was lost by being split up into separate accommodation. The team spirit and morale of the side rapidly blossomed on the rare occasions that a hotel booking was provided.

In complete contrast, Dennis Silk could not have been more generous in his report about his vice-captain, Willie Watson. He wrote, 'There are not limits to the debt that the MCC and I personally owe to Willie Watson. The main burden of the tour fell squarely on his shoulders the moment I was injured. The way in which he responded was remarkable. His loyalty, friendliness and cricket knowledge made my task light. His batting, fielding and captaining of the side were superb, and his quiet good sense and wise advice to young players made him the idol of the team. He was the perfect ambassador, a reminder of a golden pre-war age.'

Forty-seven years later, Jim Parks remembers a happy tour of New Zealand, despite all the difficulties pointed out by Dennis Silk at the time. All the tourists agreed that Willie Watson's calm, wise leadership had helped to make it a positive and rewarding experience.

CHAPTER 26

GREAT PROGRESS AT GRACE ROAD

WHEN WILLIE WATSON arrived in Leicester on March 24 1961, he joined two others on the injured list. Maurice Hallam was recovering from injury, as was newcomer John Mitten – son of a famous father, Charlie, the Manchester United and Fulham left winger – who had been hurt playing for Newcastle United. All three were expected to recover before the start of the cricket season. Club secretary Mike Turner was able to announce that the Grace Road ground would become the permanent home of Leicestershire Cricket Club in 1963. He was also able to report that a lot had been going on behind the scenes in the close season, including a bid to bring Gloucestershire's Tom Graveney to the county. Despite his damaged finger, Willie Watson looked bronzed and fit after his recent tour to New Zealand.

He apologised for the disappointing playing results the previous summer and maintained that they were not a true reflection of the team's ability. He put it down to a lack of confidence among the younger players, for which he accepted responsibility.

In the first week of April, the MCC announced that Tom Graveney had been refused a special registration to play for Worcestershire, so he would need a year's residence before he could play in the County Championship again. When the Leicester playing staff reported to the indoor cricket school on April 10, they included Clive Inman, a trialist from Ceylon (now Sri Lanka). He would have to qualify in the second XI but eventually would score more than 12,000 runs for the county.

The Leicester committee were keen to ensure the club offered attractive cricket and Willie Watson supported them, cautioning, 'We have been too timid in the past. This year we must decide to take the bit between the teeth.' However, the opening games in May did not provide much opportunity for the bolder approach, as the first three matches were interrupted by rain, and were all drawn. A further set-back, in the third game at Trent Bridge, was another injury for Willie Watson. As a result of this mishap he missed Leicestershire's remaining six matches in May. The next two matches, against Cambridge University and Ireland, were comfortably won but the four championship matches that followed produced one narrow victory over Glamorgan and three heavy defeats. The bowling, particularly by Terry Spencer, was not at fault but the batting was very fragile, without the steadying influence of the captain. The only good news for the club in May was the successful bid to bring Yorkshireman Jack Birkenshaw to Leicester. When Yorkshire decided to release him, secretary Turner was quick off the mark and travelled to Leeds for talks. The negotiations moved to Huddersfield, where Willie Watson was able to support Mike Turner's proposals. The deal was done, subject to Birkenshaw receiving a special registration from the MCC. This process delayed his debut till the June 3 at The Parks, Oxford.

June turned out to be a memorable month for Willie Watson and Alan Wharton, whose combined age of nearly 80 brought a wealth of experience to the Leicestershire batting. They were both attractive, left-handed batsmen capable of producing an exhibition of stroke making. Watson returned to captain the side against Oxford University. He had been injured for three weeks and his skill and experience had been missed, especially by younger batsmen. However, it was Wharton who used the students' bowling to run into form by making 134 not out. There followed two consecutive County Championship victories, the first over Worcestershire at Coalville and the second over Northants at Kettering. Here, Watson got into form with 64 against Northants, opening the innings with Maurice Hallam, and Leicester moved up into the top half of the table.

Back at Grace Road, the county proved no match for the Australian tourists, who won by ten wickets. Robin Gardner scored 102 not out in the first innings but the home supporters watched Colin McDonald (105) and Peter Burge (137) score centuries for the Australians, who won by ten wickets. Gardner apart the match gave no premonition of Leicestershire's record-breaking batting, which would embellish the second half of June. The county's team left Grace Road for Taunton to play Somerset on June. 17 The home team batted first and were bowled out for 239, while in the Leicester reply, Watson and Wharton came together at 48-2 to remain unbeaten 316 runs later with Watson on 217 not out and Wharton 120 not out.

Leicestershire declared at 364-2, the third wicket stand having beaten a 57-year-old record set by John King and Albert Knight. Willie Watson hit a six and 28 fours and, when he reached a hundred, he completed 23,000 first-class runs. It was his first double century for Leicester and the 47th century of his career. Alan Wharton hit a six and 18 fours to complete his 26th century. Not surprisingly, perhaps, Watson's batting average for the season so far went up from 26.8 to 48.5. However, Leicestershire were unable to overcome Somerset's dogged resistance to the spin attack of Jack Birkenshaw and John Savage, who bowled more than 80 overs between them.

Leicestershire then travelled to Hinckley to face a strong Hampshire side led by the ever extrovert and sociable Colin Ingleby-Mackenzie. While Ingleby-Mackenzie believed that Hampshire would win, he knew his friend and opposition captain, Willie Watson, usually did well against Hants. This proved to be the case, as Watson hit 79 out of a weak Leicester score of 140, while Hampshire replied with 310 despite fine bowling by John Savage, who took 6-66. Hampshire won comfortably by ten wickets after Leicester's second innings produced only 181.

The next fixture was at Grace Road against Lancashire on June 24. Leicestershire batted first and, on this occasion, the 'two Ws' came together for the second wicket. There followed a feast of stroke making which, according to the *Leicester Mercury* 'included every shot in the book'. This time Watson and Wharton put on 287, of which Watson made 158 and Wharton 135. This stand broke the 1935 record for the second wicket set by Les Berry and Norman Armstrong. Alan Wharton took more pleasure in this partnership because it was against his old county. He had departed the north west with a degree of resentment so, as he left the field, he gave a wave to the Lancashire committee men whom he had spotted on the pavilion balcony. Lancashire were then dismissed for 201, which meant that Willie Watson could declare the Leicester second innings at 140 -3 (Watson hitting 47) and set Lancashire a target of 298. They only reached 156-4 by close of play and the match was drawn.

The period between June 17 and 27 was a purple patch in Willie Watson's career. It involved three County Championship matches in which he had five innings, one of which was not out. In total he scored 508 runs at an average of 127. Of course, this is an artificial statistic but it does show what a rich vein of form the 41-year-old veteran was still capable of.

However, Willie Watson's heavy scoring came to an abrupt halt at Derby in July. Against a lively Derbyshire attack he was forced to retire hurt on 15 in the second innings. Derbyshire went on to win with ease by nine wickets and Watson missed the next three Leicester fixtures, but he had the consolation of two successive Leicestershire championship victories. The first, by 41 runs, was over Somerset at Loughborough, where Jack Birkenshaw made 81 not out, his career best score to date, and Maurice Hallam (93) passed 13,000 runs when he reached 54 and 1,000 for the summer when he got to 80. The second was at The Oval over the still mighty Surrey, when Peter Loader faced Terry Spencer, needing one to draw or two to win. The bowler knew Loader backed to leg when the bowling was quick, so he sent down a yorker on the leg stump and the match was won by one run.

Willie Watson's return to fitness came just in time to lead the Players against the Gentleman at Lord's on July 19. This would prove to be the penultimate fixture between these two teams at Lord's before the MCC abolished the distinction between amateur and professional cricketers in 1962. Willie Watson captained a strong Players team that included Ken Barrington, Brian Close, Tony Lock, Fred Trueman and Bill Alley. The Gentlemen were led by Peter May, who had an equally impressive line-up including Mike Smith, Ted Dexter, John Brearley and Trevor Bailey. The Players batted first and were bowled out for 203; Ken Barrington top scored on 53 while Watson hit 30. The Gentlemen replied with 177, Trueman taking 5-47. Willie Watson declared the Players' second innings at 263-6; unfortunately, Brian Close was on 94 when the declaration was made. The Gentlemen could manage only 117, so the Players won by 172. Ted Dexter had the misfortune of making a King pair.

This was Willie Watson's tenth and final appearance in the Gentlemen v Players fixture and captaining the team must be considered one of the high points of his career. His batting average for the Players was 53.4, which placed him seventh in averages for this fixture between 1900 and 1962. Among those above him were several great batsmen, such as Sir Jack Hobbs, Sir Len Hutton, Andy Sandham and Douglas Jardine.

From Lord's, Willie Watson travelled straight back to Grace Road for the Leicestershire fixture against Northants. In this game Watson was described by the Leicester historian EE Snow, as being 'in a class of his own.' This was because he top scored with 64 in the Leicester first innings and made 104 retired hurt, out of a second innings score of 204-3 declared. For Watson, this century must have seemed very much like hard work, as he received a succession of blows to his right knee which swelled up like a balloon. The *Leicester Mercury* took the opportunity of comparing Willie Watson with the opposition's skipper Raman Subba Row, who at that time opened for England. The newspaper maintained that 'for class, command and technique, our Willie Watson had the edge on all counts. Surely he is one of the straightest batted left handers for many a generation?' Despite Watson's heroics, Subba Row's team managed to hang on for a draw.

Once again, injury forced Willie Watson to miss the three games at the end of July and the start of August. He must have been disappointed not to play in the match at Grace Road where Yorkshire were comprehensively outplayed and beaten by 149. This was Leicester's best post-war victory over the 'Tykes'. The captain and the county could take particular pleasure from their bowlers Brian Boshier, John Savage and Terry Spencer taking third, fourth and fifth positions in the national bowling averages.

Despite very fine batting by Alan Wharton, Leicestershire lost their first three games in August. Two of the defeats involved close finishes. Middlesex won at Grace Road by 28 runs despite Wharton making a century in each inning. At Edgbaston, Willie Watson set Warwick a target of 222 in 150 minutes and, despite Jack van Geloven's fine bowling figures of 6-85, the home team won by two wickets with two minutes to spare. The result had hung in the balance all day and, despite the defeat, the *Mercury* admired the 'stirring type of cricket the County are supplying these days'.

Leicestershire faced six more championship fixtures before the end of the season. Against Derbyshire, Willie Watson made a fine 53 in Leicester's first innings of 145 but Derbyshire then declared their second innings, setting the home side 327 to win. Despite Alan Wharton's 62 they never looked like achieving the feat. However, two emphatic wins at Grace Road followed. In their first innings, Kent were skittled out merrily for 67 by Terry Spencer's 5-16 while Leicestershire then took a first-innings lead of 104. Kent recovered in their second innings but were still well beaten by seven wickets. At this point, in mid-August, Maurice Hallam, Alan Wharton and Willie Watson had passed a thousand runs and Watson stood seventh in the natural averages.

The second successive victory at Grace Road was against Nottinghamshire, when Leicestershire were set to make 266 runs in 170 minutes to win the game. Captain Watson promoted himself to open with Hallam and they put on 60 for the first wicket. Hallam went on to make an unbeaten 130 and victory was achieved with seven minutes to spare and five wickets standing. Leicestershire travelled on to Portsmouth to face Hampshire, who led the championship table. As usual, the opposition skipper had only one worry when facing Leicestershire – Willie Watson. Ingleby-Mackenzie admired Watson as a shrewd bridge player and as a fine advert for professional cricket. On this occasion, Watson top scored in both innings (25 and 38), which was not enough to prevent Hampshire from winning by 152 runs.

The season's penultimate game against Gloucestershire at Grace Road was a much closer contest. It also featured another splendid century by Maurice Hallam, 152 not out, out of a total of 231. The visitors declared their second innings at 247-6, setting Leicestershire a target of 306. They fell 17 runs short of victory with Willie Watson top scoring with 69 and David Allen taking seven for 78.

At this point, August 23 1961, Willie Watson announced that he would give up the captaincy at the end of the season. He would, however, continue to play for the county in the final year of his contract. But he did expect to retire from playing cricket at the end of the 1962 season. There was immediate speculation in the *Mercury* about who would be appointed as Watson's successor. The choice seemed to be between Cambridge blue David Kirby and the vastly experienced local lad Maurice Hallam.

Willie Watson did not play in Leicestershire's final match at Worthing against Sussex. In his absence, Hallam took the opportunity to reinforce his qualities with the county committee, while they considered the appointment of a new captain. He overshadowed everyone, first by scoring 203 not out in Leicester's innings of 376-7 declared, then by making 143 not out in the second innings. Consequently, he was on the field of play throughout the match and Sussex were beaten by 62 runs. Leicestershire finished ninth with 146 points in the Championship, which was won by Hampshire.

At the close of the season, Watson was able to report to the committee that, 'For the first time in four years here, I can honestly say we have made progress this season. Though this is a team game, I really must stress the bowling strength which has been so tremendous. Also the fielding has really underlined the big improvement in results.'

Willie Watson again led the Leicester batting averages on 43.64 and he was ninth in the national averages, while Maurice Hallam's 346 runs, without dismissal, at Worthing pushed his average up to 39.60. The bowlers Brian Boshier, Terry Spencer and John Savage all took more than 100 wickets and finished in the top nine places in the national bowling averages.

After the victory over Sussex on September 1, the former England captain Arthur Gilligan said that Leicestershire need look no further than Hallam for a replacement for Watson as captain. However, the Leicestershire committee had other ideas; one week later they announced that 22-year-old amateur David Kirby would captain the county in 1962. Hallam was given the consolation of a benefit in the forthcoming season. Kirby would become Leicester's youngest captain.

An important factor in Willie Watson's decision to resign from the captaincy was his appointment as a Test selector. This meant that, among other requirements, he would have to miss some county games. His chairman of selectors was the former Middlesex and England captain Walter Robbins, a dynamic and influential cricketer and administrator.

CHAPTER 27

TEST SELECTOR

THE 1962 SUMMER was historic in two respects. Firstly, the MCC decided to end the ancient distinction between amateur and professional cricketers. Consequently the fixtures at Lord's in July and at Scarborough in September between the Gentlemen and the Players were the last to be played. Leicestershire's only representative in either match was their new captain David Kirby, who played at Scarborough where the Players won by seven wickets.

Secondly, the first experimental steps were taken to organise limited-overs county matches. These steps were in response to an interim report by an MCC committee enquiring into the financial state of county cricket. Mike Turner, the Leicestershire secretary, was an early supporter of one-day matches and, in order to test the idea, he arranged a competition between four Midland counties in May 1962. The competitors were Derbyshire, Nottinghamshire, Northants and Leicestershire and the first two matches took place on a freezing May 2 at Grace Road and Trent Bridge. Leicestershire and Northants prevailed and met in the final a week later when Northants were victorious by five wickets. The matches were studied with great interest and the rules adjusted for the introduction of the Gillette Cup, involving all counties in 1963. Mike Turner deserves much credit for advocating and promoting the development of one-day cricket at county level.

For Willie Watson, 1962 was also an eventful season. His appointment as a Test selector was a considerable honour, but the financial rewards were restricted to travel expenses. He was freed from the burden of Leicestershire's captaincy but he was now 42 years old. He felt he had, in his own words, 'reached the stage when I would go in and score 20 or 30, whereas before I felt I could bat all day.' He began to feel it was time to pack it in. Yet he would top the county's batting averages once again in 1962.

In mid-April Leicestershire belatedly awarded their new captain his county cap. Some observers felt it had come much more easily to him than to others.

Willie Watson was back in Leicester on April 15 to prepare for the new season. He was also hoping to be appointed coach and this was confirmed at the start of May. Also at this time he was preoccupied with the death of his father, Billy Watson, the great survivor of Huddersfield Town's golden age.

With the qualification of Stanley Jayasinghe of Sri Lanka completed, the Leicester side of 1962 should have improved on the results of the previous summer. However, the results in May, four draws and two defeats, were not auspicious. The highlight of the month for Willie Watson was an opening partnership of 186 with Maurice Hallam, who made 106, but the match at Dean Park, Bournemouth, against Hants was lost by four wickets. Watson missed the last game of the month against Surrey because his selectorial duties took him to Edgbaston, where England played their first Test of the summer against Pakistan. At Birmingham he would be joined by co-selectors Walter Robbins, chairman, Alec Bedser, the legendary opening bowler, and Doug Insole, who had been a double blue at Cambridge and played in the FA Amateur Cup final for Corinthian Casuals. They would all be pleased with England's crushing victory by an innings and 24 runs. The batting of Cowdrey (159), Peter Parfitt (101 not out), Tom Graveney (97) and Ted Dexter (72) was particularly impressive. The team was captained by Dexter.

Back in the County Championship, Leicestershire continued to struggle and June became another month without a win, and several of the defeats were heavy. The new leader David Kirby, who lacked first-class experience, found his batting form was faltering with the strains of captaincy. Also important was another unfortunate injury to the main strike bowler Brian Boshier, who played in only seven games, and the absences of Willie Watson, who played only 16 games. He did, however, score his first century of the season (101) against Essex at the start of June but the match was lost by eight wickets. Three consecutive matches were lost and the club hit the bottom of the table. Against Derbyshire, Leicestershire faced Les Jackson bowling at his best. He took 6-26 in the first innings and 7-47 in the second. Only Willie Watson put up any resistance, scoring 142, supported by Jack Birkenshaw with 54. The losing sequence was broken against Hampshire at Grace Road, where Leicester were set 197 in 120 minutes to win. They finished seven runs short with six wickets in hand and the *Leicester Mercury* reported accusations of gamesmanship because Hampshire's David 'Butch' White bowled four bumpers in an over in the closing minutes.

Willie Watson missed the remaining five games in June. Without him and Brian Boshier the county faced Cambridge University. Such was David Kirby's desperation, in trying to bowl the students out in their first innings, that he used eight bowlers. Included in the University side were future England captain Mike Brearley and the son of an England captain, Richard Hutton. Near the end of June, at Grace Road, Kirby rediscovered his batting form with 118 against Kent and declared at 351 with four wickets gone. Also scoring well, with 77, was Dickie Bird, who had so far had a disappointing time at Leicester. He had the ability, but his nerves let him down and his average at the county was only 19.72. Kent replied with 551-9 declared including 162 from Tony Catt and 112 not out by the Charlton Athletic footballer Stuart Leary. Leicestershire lost the match by an innings and 32 runs and were the only team in the championship without a win.

For the second Test against Pakistan at Lord's, the selectors made two changes. Geoff Pullar, the Lancashire opener, was replaced by Micky Stewart of Surrey, and Len Coldwell made his Test debut in place of Brian Statham who was injured. Walter Robbins proposed that selectors Bedser and Watson should each act as manager of for two of the remaining four tests. The MCC were due to tour Australia in the winter and Robbins was not available to manage the England party. The selectors were rewarded with another convincing victory over the Pakistanis, completed in three days. Tom Graveney was outstanding among the batsmen, scoring 153, while Fred Trueman and Len Coldwell captured 18 wickets.

Willie Watson only managed one game for Leicestershire in July, against Warwickshire at Edgbaston where they had the better of a drawn match. The long-awaited first victory of the season came in mid-July, courtesy of Sussex. The visitors to Grace Road declared both their innings, the second offering a sporting target of 274 runs in 200 minutes. Leicester needed nine runs off the final over, which they achieved with two wickets remaining. Later in the month Sussex gained their revenge at Hastings, winning by 106 runs.

Early in July, England and Pakistan met for the third time, on this occasion at Headingley. The selectors made three changes. Stratham was restored in place of the unfortunate Coldwell, John Murray returned for the accomplished Bedfordian keeper Geoff Millman and Fred Titmus came in for Tony Lock. The result was another easy victory for England by an innings and 117 runs. Peter Parfitt was the most successful batsman with 119 while captain Ted Dexter had his best Test bowling figures of 4-10 in Pakistan's first innings. The selectors and their captain could take satisfaction from a Test series certain to be won.

At the end of July, Willie Watson remained at the top of the Leicestershire batting averages but no one from the county made it into the national averages.

For the fourth Test at Trent Bridge, the selectors revealed that their priority had turned to the forthcoming Ashes tour to Australia. The main issue surrounded the captaincy of the tour party. Peter May had retired after 41 Tests as captain, winning 20, drawing 10 and losing 11, while Colin Cowdrey had taken a rest from the 1961–62 tour of India and Pakistan. Ted Dexter was the current captain. However, as early as the spring of 1962, EM Wellings writing in the London *Evening News* suggested that David Sheppard was the main man to restore vitality to English cricket. Sheppard, an ordained minister in the Church of England, had been retired for five years. Walter Robbins was impressed with the proposal and sought to persuade David Sheppard to take a sabbatical from his church duties to play cricket again and win a place in the Australia tour party. Sheppard was persuaded and began his comeback with Sussex on June 20 at Oxford. He got off to an impressive start by scoring 108 and 55, although this form was not maintained in July. Robbins convinced him to persevere until the Gentlemen v Players fixture at Lord's. Sheppard responded with a century against the Players and the press was convinced that the captaincy in Australia was a straight choice between Dexter and Sheppard. Most of the papers favoured Sheppard but the selectors chose Dexter, who it was felt was a better long-term prospect.

This decision meant the selectors needed a tour manager who would cope with Dexter, not always an easy man to deal with. Initially the selectors favoured Billy Griffith, but because he was about to take over as MCC secretary they were dissuaded. The Duke of Norfolk happened to be at Lord's for a meeting when the selectors were pondering the choice of manager. The Duke could not understand their worries because he never had any problems with Dexter at Sussex. 'I can manage him,' he claimed and from that time on the momentum for his appointment gathered pace. The announcement of his acceptance of the post astonished the press. The position of the Duke's assistant manager was given to Alec Bedser.

So when the selectors made their decisions for the England team for the fourth Test they decided to recall the Rev David Sheppard to Test cricket after six years. They also brought back Geoff Pullar, to create a new opening partnership with Sheppard. Tony Lock was restored to the team and Barry Knight, the Essex all-rounder, took over from Ken Barrington, who was going through a bad patch with the bat. Although England's batting was again impressive, there was not enough time to bowl out Pakistan twice so the match was drawn. As far as the tour to Australia was concerned the most important score was David Sheppard's 83.

Willie Watson returned to Leicestershire for the first game in August after a three-week absence in a match against Derbyshire at

Grace Road that had been chosen by Maurice Hallam for his benefit. In reply to Derbyshire's first innings total of 334-5 declared, the bank holiday crowd were entertained by an unbroken stand of 129 by Hallam and Watson. Batting at number three Watson produced some magnificent shots that meant he quickly caught up the more watchful Hallam. Unfortunately rain caused the abandonment of the match, which meant the benefit fund lost an estimated £400 (about £3,800 today). Willie Watson followed his 68 not out against Derbyshire with a classic 97 against Nottinghamshire. Both games were drawn but the third game in August against Northants at Wellingborough School brought Leicester their second victory of the season. This time the opposition were bowled out twice, thanks to John Savage's 5-70 in the first innings and Jack van Geloven's 6-28 in the second. Willie Watson's contribution to the victory was 35 and 91.

Around this time Watson would have noted the departure of his old England soccer manager Walter Winterbottom after 15 years in the job. He would have been pleased for his friend and England team-mate Trevor Bailey who completed the double of 1,000 runs and 100 wickets in a season for the eighth time, a post-war record. He would also have been aware that the great Welsh footballer John Charles was to lead the Leeds United attack in the pre-season friendly match against Leicester City.

Watson missed the next Leicester fixture against Yorkshire because it clashed with the final Test at The Oval. The Test selectors made a number of changes in order to finalise the tour party for Australia. Certainties like Brian Statham, Fred Trueman and Tom Graveney were rested while Len Coldwell and Ken Barrington were recalled. Most intriguing, the giant David Larter, the Northants fast bowler, was given his Test debut. For the fourth time in the series the England first innings easily passed the four hundred mark and the visitors were beaten by nine wickets. Larter took nine wickets and guaranteed his place in the tour party.

Willie Watson left The Oval as soon as he could in order to join his county team-mates at New Road, Worcester. At this point he headed the Leicestershire batting average on 46. Against the home attack he scored exactly 100 and during the course of his innings he passed 1,000 runs for the season and 25,000 in his career. The teams met again in the following fixture at Grace Road, which was also drawn, but before Leicestershire players could leave for Cardiff to play Glamorgan, the *Leicester Mercury* ran the headline 'Willie Watson Sacked'. The shock announcement from the management committee was on the grounds of economy as five other players, along with Watson, would be released at the end of the 1962 season. The newspaper recalled that it was only on April 30 that he had been appointed player-coach. Watson had confirmed that he intended to retire as a player at the end of the season. He hoped to continue as a Test selector but was also keen to develop his coaching role. He was anxious to organise and run the coaching in his own way. Mike Turner had had negotiations with Willie Watson about his future at the club. He recalls discussing the possibility of Watson taking on the role of the county's cricket manager. This was a role ahead of its time in cricket in the early 60s but Turner was not able to deflect Willie Watson from his coaching ambitions and therefore the Leicester committee were unable to offer him a post. Willie Watson was not prepared to comment but the *Mercury* announced that supporters were angry and predicted that the annual general meeting would be lively.

Only a few weeks before this controversial decision was announced, Willie Watson was the subject of a special article in *Playfair Cricket Monthly*. John Arlott, the writer and broadcaster, paid tribute to him and called Watson one of cricket's great players and gentlemen. He went on to state that in his opinion Watson had been the best county captain in the previous season, 1961. The *Leicester Mercury* recalled that the captain of the recent tour of New Zealand, Dennis Silk, had publicly acknowledged what a tower of strength his vice-captain Willie Watson had been.

Also Watson's recent appointment as a Test selector made the county's committee's decision all the more incomprehensible to the newspaper. A keen supporter of the club wrote to the *Mercury* to say how much Willie Watson would be missed. He also rated him with Neil Harvey and Frank Worrell as one of the finest left-hand batsmen in the world. Praise indeed! Meanwhile members of the cricket club continued to demand an explanation for Watson's departure. The man himself, however, did not encourage any agitation because he did not wish to leave the county 'under a cloud'. He preferred to be involved in the final game of the season against his old county, Yorkshire. Despite Leicestershire's position at the bottom of the table, they pushed Yorkshire to the limit. Maurice Hallam produced a fine 129 and Rodney Pratt took 11-121 in a match which was drawn.

Against Yorkshire, Willie Watson completed his last full season with Leicestershire. He once again headed the county's batting averages on 42.18, having scored 1,139 runs and three centuries. Unfortunately the county finished bottom while the title went to Vic Wilson's Yorkshire. The season's success story was Jack van Geloven, who took exactly 100 first-class wickets and scored 1,055 runs, which was his first and only 'double' and the first for Leicester since 1955. The disappointment of the season was the decision of David Kirby to resign from the captaincy after one season in order to take up a teaching post in York.

Early in September the Leicestershire members were granted an extraordinary meeting and, whatever the arguments used by each side, Willie Watson thought it best for him to keep out of it. He believed it would be embarrassing for him to be asked back now. In any case he had been approached by Ron Roberts about a cricket tour in the close season. While the Duke of Norfolk, Alec Bedser, Ted Dexter and David Sheppard were packing their bags for the Ashes tour of Australia, Willie Watson was contemplating an International World Tour which would include East Africa, the then Rhodesia (Zimbabwe), Malaya and Hong Kong. Ron Roberts was still in his thirties but had already shown considerable organisational flair. For a short period in the early sixties his tours were well known, large crowds watched his teams and many of the leading players of the day were pleased to join his exotic trips.

Willie Watson was invited to captain this tour party, supported by the Hampshire skipper Colin Ingleby-Mackenzie, while the rest of the party were a talented and cosmopolitan collection of cricketers. From the West Indies came Everton Weekes, Wes Hall, Sonny Ramadhin and Roy Marshall. South Africa was represented by Roy McLean and Neil Adcock, from India came Chandra Borde and from Pakistan, Hanif Mohammed. Perhaps the surprise invitee was Basil D'Oliveira, a 'coloured' (mixed race) South African who was playing in the Lancashire League and had only recently played in a first-class match. He would take his opportunity on this tour to show his potential to reach the top levels of the game.

The first leg of the journey was a flight to Athens. When the party disembarked at the airport they found that Ron Roberts had left all the passports in the bus which had taken them from the terminal at Heathrow to the plane. So arrangements had to be made for the passports to be sent on. A fixture had been organised in Corfu (Kerkira) on a piece of ground right in the middle of town. The tourists had a very strong side but they had no idea how good the opposition would be. So when Willie Watson won the toss he decided to put the locals in to bat. The match was won by an innings in two days. On the third day Watson asked their skipper what he wanted to do but he did not speak much English. So the tourists batted and reached about 200 when suddenly the local team walked off the field. In Watson's words, 'They thought we had batted long enough but we hadn't declared – they had declared for us!'

Passports safely arrived, the tour moved from the Mediterranean to Zimbabwe and East Africa. In order to reach Kuala Lumpur (Malaysia) from East Africa it was necessary at that time to stay overnight in Karachi, Pakistan). When Willie Watson handed the tickets and passports over in Karachi, the authorities said 'you have a South African national in your party – Basil D'Oliveria.' Although it was 6pm and they were leaving at 7am, they required £300 to let him in. Further problems arose when it was found that Colin Ingleby-Mackenzie had lost his yellow fever certificate, essential when you travelled from East Africa. So the Pakistan authorities put him in a house on the far side of the airport and would not allow him to enter the country. When the tour management tried to get evidence of the certificate from the British embassy but they could not find any proof, Ingleby-Mackenzie, who was very well connected, tried to contact his doctor back in England without any success. In the end the tour party left for Kuala Lumpar without him and when he did arrive he was met by an ambulance and again placed in an airport room where he remained for seven days. He eventually emerged just in time to leave for Singapore.

Ron Roberts, organiser and manager of the tour, reported that the tour had generally been a success. Roberts, who had been a regular cricket correspondent of the *Daily Telegraph* for ten years, died at the age of 38.

For professional cricketers like Willie Watson these short eight-week tours were a welcome supplement to their earnings. When Barbara Watson arrived at the airport to pick up her husband after the tour, she found herself persuaded by Colin Ingleby-Mackenzie to give him a lift to a hotel in the Edgware Road. Barbara Watson described the journey across the London traffic as a nightmare, as she recalled it 45 years later. However, the saga continued the next day when Ingleby-Mackenzie insisted that the Watsons accompany him to Newmarket for the races. Eventually, it was back to Huddersfield and the poultry farm.

Soon after his return home Willie Watson would have taken a keen interest in the results from the tour party he had helped to select. The series finished 1-1 and from the point of view of a selector, Willie would have been pleased with the batting of Ken Barrington, who topped the England averages on 72.75, and with Ted Dexter and Colin Cowdrey, who both averaged more than 40 runs. The contentious selection of the Rev David Sheppard was justified as he opened the batting in all five Tests and averaged 37.80 on the tour, while less successful were Geoff Pullar and Peter Parfitt. The selectors would have admired the bowling contributions of Fred Trueman and Fred Titmus, well supported by captain Ted Dexter. The highlight for Brian Statham was to overtake Alec Bedser's record of 236 Test wickets. Only seven weeks later on the New Zealand leg of the tour, Fred Trueman passed his partner's total and left for home on 250 Test wickets. England comfortably won all three tests against New Zealand with Cowdrey and Barrington in particularly fine form.

When cricket returned to England in 1963 it was the first summer since the war that Willie Watson was not playing the game at first-class level. He was able therefore to concentrate on Test selector duties and on his poultry farming. The selectoring task was a daunting one this time as the tourists were a powerful West Indies party captained by Frank Worrell. As England had managed to level the series in Australia a hard fought contest with the West Indies was anticipated. With the Rev Sheppard returned to his London parishioners, the selectors' first task was to find a reliable opening partnership. They chose the Surrey openers Micky Stewart and John Edrich, who was making his Test debut. However, the most controversial selection was the recall of the Yorkshire all-rounder Brian Close.

The first Test at Old Trafford showed Willie Watson and his fellow selectors just what they were up against as England crashed to a ten-wicket defeat. The combination of Lance Gibbs's spin bowling with 11 wickets, and Conrad Hunte's batting with 82, reinforced the West Indies' reputation. For the Lord's Test the selectors made two changes: Keith Andrew of Northants, widely regarded as England's best wicketkeeper, was dropped after the first Test in favour of Jim Parks in order to strengthen England's batting. The tireless and very accurate Derek Shackleton came in for Statham.

This second Test proved to be the most thrilling and heroic of the series. The West Indies led by four runs on the first innings and were then bowled out for 229. England needed 234 to win, but once again had to face the most feared pair of fast bowlers in the world, Wes Hall and Charlie Griffith. Colin Cowdrey's left forearm was broken but England were well served by Ken Barrington, who added 60 to his first innings 80, and by Brian Close, whose brave confrontation with the hostile bowling almost won the game. Cowdrey returned, his arm in plaster, at number 11 to join David Allen and secure a draw, six runs short of victory. Next day, back in Yorkshire, the press photographers pictured Close covered in bruises. Fred Trueman showed that great fast bowling was not confined to one team by taking 11 wickets in the match.

For the third Test at Edgbaston Watson and his co-selectors made three changes, recalling opener Peter Richardson, now playing for Kent, and Tony Lock, who returned to the bowling attack. They also introduced a newcomer, Phil Sharpe, the Yorkshire batsman, to replace the injured Cowdrey. This was a surprise selection because his batting form for Yorkshire was inconsistent. Some observers maintained that Sharpe must have been the only player to win a cap on the strength of his slip fielding. However, in this case the selectors were proved right when Sharpe topped the batting averages in the series. Willie Watson, as the only selector from north of London, was especially pleased with Phil Sharpe's success.

The Edgbaston Test was a low-scoring match in which the West Indies were bowled out for 91 in their second innings and beaten by 217 runs. Once again Fred Trueman bowled magnificently and had the impressive match figures of 12-119. However, it was now that Garfield Sobers made his first impact on the series by taking 5-60 in England's first innings. As a result the series was now all square, so when the selectors came to choose the England team for the fourth Test at Headingley they were not likely to make many changes. In fact the only change was the selection of another newcomer, Brian Bolus, a Yorkshire opening batsman, now playing for Nottinghamshire.

But England's third Test win proved a false dawn as the West Indies swept to victory in the remaining two matches, with Charlie Griffith proving particularly lethal by taking 18 wickets in the two matches.

With the 3-1 defeat in the West Indian series in mind, the selectors met to choose a tour party for a shortened series against India. In an eight-week tour the MCC would play ten fixtures, five of them Tests. Before selecting a tour party, 36 players were asked if they were available. The selectors eventually chose Colin Cowdrey to be captain with Mike Smith as his deputy. Also included were Ken Barrington, John Edrich, Phil Sharpe, Jim Parks and Fred Titmus, but it lacked Ted Dexter, Fred Trueman and Brian Close. A few weeks after the party was announced Colin Cowdrey had to withdraw with an arm injury so Mike Smith was promoted to captain. The tour was marred by sickness and injury in the England camp and slow batting by the Indian team. Consequently all five Tests were drawn. Colin Cowdrey and Peter Parfitt, who had both responded to an emergency call from Mike Smith for reinforcements, topped the England Test batting averages, and Fred Titmus, with 27 Test wickets, was easily England's most successful bowler.

Before the tour party for India left at the beginning of January 1964 and the end of the English cricket season in September 1963, Willie Watson had time to fit in a four-and-a-half week tour of East Africa. The party was led by Mike Smith and Willie Watson was player-manager. There were 12 good first-class county cricketers including Test players Parfitt, Micky Stewart, John Mortimore and David Larter for a tour which covered Tanganyika, Kenya and Uganda; in all eleven matches were played. The tourists were unbeaten, winning seven games and drawing four. The only match which was at all close was a two-day game with Kenya Kongonis where Mike Smith set the locals 298 to win. A last-wicket stand of 83 brought the home team within 11 runs of victory. One of the MCC party, Tom Cartwright in *Tom Cartwright – the Flame Still Burns* by Stephen Chalke, described it as a magical tour. He said, 'It was like exploring with your school atlas.' All the players fitted in and it was a happy tour. Cartwright went on, 'Willie Watson was such a good manager, very calm and good at receptions. He was a real father figure – and still a wonderful player.'

On tour Watson scored three half centuries. Cartwright added that Watson was 'so stylish, so elegant in everything he did. Young Richard Longridge, a member of the tour party, had to bat with Willie Watson in one game. He was a left hander as well, and you couldn't help but see the difference. It was very hard on Richard.'

One anecdote about Willie Watson's time as a selector concerned a selection meeting at Walter Robbins' flat at 10am on a Sunday morning. It was a long haul for Watson, who had once again travelled down from Huddersfield. All selectors were assembled on time except for Dexter. At 10.15 the phone rang and Dexter explained that he had overslept but in any case he did not advocate any changes. Watson, who'd had to organise someone to supervise his battery hens, was understandably not amused but was only heard to say 'a funny old game'. However, Doug Insole reports that 35 years later Willie Watson was able to smile about it.

CHAPTER 28

BACK TO THE BASEMENT

WILLIE WATSON'S RENEWED involvement with football began in 1961 when a friend, a director of Halifax Town FC, asked him to help out when their manager, Harry Hooper, left at the start of the season. As he did not live far away, Watson agreed but only till the start of the cricket season. When he finished playing the club asked Watson to become manager. His appointment as successor to Don McEvoy was announced early in August 1964 while Watson was still a Test selector. Eight years earlier, when he had finished as Halifax's player-manager, they were members of the Third Division North, but that division and the Third Division South were amalgamated in 1958 and by 1964 they were struggling in Division Four. The contrast between Watson's role in selecting the England cricket team and his responsibility in choosing the Halifax Town football team could not have been starker. Watson could not have returned to The Shay at a tougher time as attendances were low and there was little money. In fact one of his first jobs was to interview the transfer-listed Willie Carlin and Eric Harrison. To ensure the club's survival the board decided to become part-time for the season 1964–65 and Carlin was appointed team captain even though he remained on the transfer list.

Halifax Town were dismissed from the League Cup at the first hurdle by Darlington and as this competition was a likely source of income defeat meant that the departure of star player Carlin was more likely. Willie Watson was coping with a squad of 15, and in September was faced with two goalkeeper crises. The solution was to sign an amateur, John Wray, from Stainland Athletic. In October Halifax's form, especially away from home, was impressive, with Carlin outstanding.

At this point Halifax played a special part in the general election of 1964. The Conservatives had been in office for 13 years and the Labour opposition was sensing victory. The election result was very close with Harold Wilson, the Labour leader, having an overall majority of just five seats. The Halifax constituency provided one of the Labour gains by electing its first woman member of parliament, Dr Shirley Summerskill. She was the daughter of former MP and minister Dr Edith Summerskill, while her opponent was Maurice Macmillan, the son of former prime minister Harold Macmillan.

Meanwhile the football club won its third consecutive fixture, with representatives from eight clubs in the crowd to watch Carlin. Within days Carlisle put in an offer of almost £10,000 for him and the club issued a detailed explanation of why they had to accept the bid. In brief, the transfer money was needed to finance the club's survival, and consequently manager Watson would not receive any extra cash for new players.

In November league form declined steadily while the FA Cup was a disaster when non-league South Liverpool beat Halifax after a replay. December brought no escape from the poor results so Halifax dropped into the re-election zone. The only diversion for the players from regular defeats was a Boxing Day flight to Brighton. It was the first time the club had travelled by air and waiting to greet them were 19,300 Brighton supporters. Halifax also faced the former Tottenham and England striker Bobby Smith, but were unfortunate to lose a close contest.

The year of 1965 brought snow, postponements and further struggles against re-election. However the world was mourning the death of Sir Winston Churchill, Britain's World War II leader, with The Queen leading the nation's tributes to a respected elder statesman.

Willie Watson spent some time in February trying to secure the services of his former Yorkshire colleague Ken Taylor. Halifax were able to raise the transfer fee but negotiations with Huddersfield Town broke down over the length of the contract and Taylor moved to Bradford Park Avenue. By the end of the month Halifax were fifth from the bottom of the table with the four lowest clubs faced with re-election. The results in March showed little improvement while Willie Watson's tactics proved controversial. He experimented with a four-two-four formation which was regarded as a radical break. The battle against re-election continued into April with six clubs in the fight and five points covering them, with four games each still to be played.

Despite the poor results and re-election struggle, the Halifax board of directors were prepared to extend Willie Watson's term as manager beyond the current arrangement, which was due to finish at the end of April 1966. Walter Robbins, the chair of the Test selectors, had not sought re-election and neither had Willie Watson. So the Halifax board knew that Watson had no cricket commitments, except a few charity games in the summer, and would be able to concentrate on his duties with them.

Halifax Town's re-election fate was decided in the three fixtures over Easter. Defeats against Stockport County and Notts County confirmed that Halifax would have to seek re-election along with Barrow, Lincoln City and Stockport County, who finished bottom. At the end of April Willie Watson announced that the club would retain 13 of the playing staff and give free transfers to another eight. He was anxious to sign new players but was unable to approach anyone until re-election was secured. There were 17 non-league clubs seeking election to the Football League. Among the applicants were Cambridge United, Wigan and Wimbledon. The League meeting was held on May 28 1965 and Halifax Town were represented by their chairman, vice-chairman and manager. As was the custom at that time, all four applicants from Division Four were re-elected. It was the seventh time Halifax Town had been re-elected and they received 45 votes while the best of the non-leaguers, Bedford Town, received only four. Much more importantly for the rest of the leagues, the meeting decided to permit one substitute per team at any time in the game. This was a surprise; nevertheless, the vote was decisive, 39 to 10. It was a first step towards the much wider use of substitutes which is a feature of the modern game.

There had been disappointment caused by Willie Watson's decision to release stalwart centre half Alex South, who had made 301 league appearances, but the acquisition of a free-scoring forward, Bill Atkins, and the signing of midfielder Jim Smith were both welcome. Smith would later become a well-respected Premiership manager. The club turned out in their annual charity cricket match against Sowerby Bridge CC, a village just south of the town, in early August. The game attracted the biggest crowd of the season to the Walton Street ground and was noteworthy because when Sowerby reached 80 runs without losing a wicket, Willie Watson came on to bowl and took 5-64 runs. However, he scored only three runs and the footballers lost by 66. This was a very rare example of Watson's bowling making an impact on a cricket match.

The new football season got under way on August 21 1965, with a home fixture against Tranmere Rovers. The new-look Halifax Town team showed nine changes from the team which had contested the final game of the previous season. Keith Bambridge was the first substitute to be selected by the club but was not used. The game finished 2-2. Ten days later Halifax made an abrupt departure from the League Cup, losing by a single goal to local rivals Bradford City. In mid-September Halifax gained their first away point at Lincoln, which ended a sequence of 12 away defeats.

The *Halifax Courier* headlines on September 25 announced that the campaign for 'the World Cup starts now'. Alf Ramsey, the England manager 'has ten months to get a winning team'. At the start of October, Halifax Town recorded their first win of the season against Bradford Park Avenue and this was immediately followed by a second win, this time against the other Bradford club, City. There was further news from Bradford a few days later because a wealthy local businessman, Stafford Heginbotham, aged 32, was elected chairman of Bradford City. He was a man with big plans and a larger-than-life personality. He would shortly make a significant impact on Willie Watson's career in football management.

By the end of October, Alf Ramsey had managed to settle on the defensive permutation which would serve England so well in 1966: Gordon Banks, George Cohen, Ray Wilson, Nobby Stiles, Jack Charlton and Bobby Moore. Willie Watson was also making progress as Halifax Town produced an outstanding display in beating Rochdale 4-1. November brought the first round of the FA Cup and a football reunion for Watson. The draw was tough, away to Southport, whose coach was Watson's old team-mate at Sunderland, Billy Bingham. The Northern Ireland international commented, 'It will be nice to meet Willie again but we shall be out to hammer his team.' It was more a case of Halifax blunders which resulted in a 2-0 win for Southport.

The early exit from the FA Cup exposed again Halifax Town's financial vulnerability. They were already the least well-supported of the Football Leagues 92 clubs, averaging just 2,797. Some consolation could be drawn when they beat Hartlepool, their first away win in 13 months. At the other extreme of the English game, Alf Ramsey was in Madrid with his England squad. He was hoping to finalise his midfield and attack. The victory over Spain was achieved with a four-three-three formation which meant an attack without conventional wingers. Alan Ball, Roger Hunt and Bobby Charlton all strengthened their claims for a World Cup place.

Back at The Shay, on December 11, Halifax's fine 4-0 win over Wrexham was watched by the smallest crowd, 1,750 at any League venue that season. The rest of the month was encouraging as nine points were gained from six games (only two points were awarded for a victory in those days). On New Year's Day 1966 Halifax shared eight goals in a thrilling match against Newport County but the attendance of 2,444 was the lowest of all the 46 matches that day. The club had climbed from 22nd to 17th in the league and the *Courier* correspondent wrote, 'I think Mr Watson is doing a good job. So come on the Halifax public, let's have some support.' But in January and February the crowds remained disappointing.

The crisis came to a head on February 22 when the football club became the front-page headline in the *Courier*: 'Shay Directors Ultimatum'. Unless the club received more support, the directors would resign from the League at the end of the season. The club's overdraft had soared by £5,000 since Christmas and now stood at £48,000. The five postponements in the previous two months had precipitated the crisis as the club were losing between £150 and £200 per week. The next home game, a draw with Lincoln City, was watched by 2,853 fans, double the previous home gate. Early in March, Halifax Town moved up to 15th, their highest position so far that season. The Mayor launched a £25,000 appeal to save the club and hoped that 5,000 supporters would turn up for the next home fixture against Doncaster Rovers. In fact there was an encouraging attendance of 6,718, although the thrilling and keenly contested match was won by the visitors 3-2. Further success came with the completion of the first double of the season over local rivals Bradford City.

Halifax Town produced their best display of the season in mid-March by beating promotion-chasing Chester 2-0. Ominously, it was Stafford Heginbotham, chairman of Bradford City, who was quoted in the press as saying, 'It was the best game I've seen in division four this season.' Despite another good attendance at the match, Halifax's cash crisis remained acute. The headline in the *Courier* on March 30 read 'Bradford City want Halifax Town Manager'.

Heginbotham revealed that 'We have approached Mr Watson to be our team manager and he wants a couple of days to think it over.' The Halifax chairman, Sid Hitchen, explained, 'I think this approach underlines the gravity of our situation. Willie Watson knows our financial position and has to look after his own interests. These jobs don't come round every day and Bradford is convenient for him.'

As Willie Watson had no contract with Halifax he could leave as soon as he liked and this was part of his appeal to Bradford City, who wanted him to take over as soon as possible. However, Watson was aware of Bradford City's problems at the bottom of the league so it was not an easy decision.

On April 2 1966 it was announced that Watson would take over as Bradford City manager in two days. Chairman Heginbotham predicted that 'time will prove this appointment is one of the best moves we have made.' So Willie Watson bade farewell to Halifax and The Shay for the second time in his career. The *Bradford Telegraph and Argus* pictured the new manager with chairman Heginbotham and two of the players. Halifax Town decided not to appoint a replacement manager but instead promoted Vic Metcalfe to be adviser to the directors. The decision proved a success as the club finished a creditable 15th.

As Willie Watson settled into his new post, Alf Ramsey's World Cup preparations were given a boost by a 4-3 victory over Scotland at Hampden Park, watched by 123,000. Therefore, on April 6, Ramsey was able to announce a squad of 40 for the World Cup finals. By contrast Watson was immediately thrust into a battle to avoid re-election, but at Valley Parade he had only eight games left with which to save the day. In the event two wins and three draws were not sufficient and Bradford City finished in 23rd place. However, re-election to the Fourth Division of the Football League did not cause Bradford City any difficulties. Some years later Willie Watson recalled that the new board at Bradford had spent large sums on transfer fees for older players who were past their prime. When he took over at the club the policy changed and youngsters were given a chance.

As Willie Watson drew up his plans in the close season 1966–67, he heard the news at the end of May that the Test selectors had included Basil D'Oliveira in the England 12 to face the West Indies at Old Trafford. This was a decision which would eventually have serious repercussions for Test cricket in South Africa. D'Oliveira was a refugee from the apartheid laws in South Africa where 'Cape-Coloureds' were excluded from Test cricket. Thanks to his remarkable determination he had established himself in England through the Lancashire League and Worcestershire.

Also in the news at the end of June and the start of July were Alf Ramsey's final preparations for the World Cup. In ten days England played four friendly matches, all of which they won. The team which played the fourth game included ten of the players who would eventually play in the World Cup final; only Geoff Hurst was missing.

On June 20 Willie Watson joined his Bradford City players in a cricket team to play the Press. The footballers fielded first and soon needed the bowling skills of their manager. Willie responded with 6-12 runs off seven overs. The Press were dismissed for 91 but revenge was secured when John Helm took Willie Watson's wicket for nought. However, the footballers won by four wickets. Meanwhile, the manager was strengthening the squad with close-season signings including two players from Swindon Town, Wilf Shergold and Tom Hallett, the latter going on to become captain.

In July the World Cup finals got under way and while England triumphed against West Germany at Wembley, the priorities at Valley Parade were much more mundane – to get the ground ready for the start of the new season 1966–67. Chairman Heginbotham led by example in the push to complete improvements. He had cut short his holidays to lend a hand and had lost a lot of weight concreting where required. Some people regarded him as a breath of fresh air at the club; others had their reservations. For example, Willie Watson became embarrassed by Heginbotham always introducing him as 'the man who saved England'. The deadline for the completion of work was the first home game, a League Cup fixture against Doncaster on August 24. The ground was ready and the match was drawn. This promising start was halted in the replay that Doncaster won in extra time.

Willie Watson had decided that his Bradford City team would adopt the progressive four-two-four formation, even though the programme printer used the orthodox line-up. Early results in September were moderate but in October Bradford City won five successive home games. The recruitment of the experienced Jim McAnearney from Watford contributed to the improved results. However, the whole country was shocked and saddened by the Aberfan coal-tip slide which buried the local school and killed 144 people, including 116 children. There was an immediate demand for an enquiry into the National Coal Board's responsibility for the tragedy.

November brought the first round of the FA Cup and a home tie against Port Vale. The visitors' general manager was Stanley Matthews and the team manager was Jackie Mudie. They had played together for Blackpool in two FA Cup finals, including the dramatic 4-3 victory over Bolton in 1953. Port Vale must have captured some of their FA Cup experience because they overcame Bradford City 2-1. This defeat joined Willie Watson's long run, both as a player and as a manger, of modest achievement in the FA Cup. Fortunately it did not have a detrimental effect on league form because early in December 1966 the *Bradford Telegraph and Argus*, commenting on two successive away wins, suggested a promotion challenge.

However, success on the pitch was not matched by soundness in the club's finances. Heginbotham announced 'The most serious financial position in the club's history' although he outlined the progress being made on the playing side under the management of Willie Watson. While he believed that Bradford City could challenge for promotion he also forecast record deficits and as a consequence the club introduced an economy drive that was especially necessary as the December weather caused fixtures to be postponed. However, the situation did not improve and the *Telegraph and Argus* headline on December 21 reported that 'City send out an SOS'. The chairman warned that the club were deep in the red and called for a public 'survival' meeting. It was arranged that it would be held at St George's Hall on January 4.

The Christmas holiday produced two draws against Barnsley and significantly the home match attracted a bumper crowd of 6,813, giving Heginbotham the opportunity to explain to a large audience how the club's finances could be turned around. The next big audience was in St George's Hall, where 2,000 supporters were accommodated. This meeting has been described as Stafford Heginbotham's finest hour. The full house listened to their chairman outline a seven-point survival plan in a 100-minute speech. It was a one-man show – no one else spoke.

By February 1967 Willie Watson had been working for Bradford City for nearly a year without a contract. Negotiations then took place between the directors and the manager, resulting in the offer of a two-year contract from April 1. The team celebrated the deal with the biggest away win of the season – 3-0 at Aldershot. Into March the team maintained its best form with three wins and two draws. This successful run moved them up to ninth, eleven points behind the top place. One sad note at this time for Willie Watson and all cricket lovers was the death of the former West Indian captain Sir Frank Worrell at the age of 43. He had been a great cricketer, a great captain and a wonderful ambassador for West Indies cricket.

The headline in the *Bradford Telegraph and Argus* on April 2 was, 'Watson's MCC Honour'. The newspaper reported that Willie Watson had been elected an honorary life member of the MCC for his outstanding contribution to county and England cricket. Back in the Fourth Division April was another successful month for Bradford City, including successive 4-1 victories over Rochdale and Lincoln City. The final game was played on May 7 and the club finished in 11th place on 48 points. They had scored 74 goals, the third highest total in the league and five more than champions Stockport County. All that was left for the season was the West Riding Senior Cup in which Bradford City faced Huddersfield in the semi-final. Bradford reached the final by winning 1-0 at Leeds Road, Huddersfield, but in the final were well beaten by old rivals Halifax.

There was little to report from Valley Parade during the close season. In May Willie Watson and two of the Bradford City players set to work to improve the ground's playing surface. The Yorkshire cricket captain Brian Close was chosen to lead England against the Indian and Pakistani touring teams and Celtic became the first British football club to win the European Cup by defeating Inter Milan 2-1. The only summer news from Bradford City was the signing of Tony Lee from Leicester City and a cricket match against Allerton Cricket Club in July. For this game the local paper pointed out that the Bradford manager would be aged 47 but still worth his place.

Near the end of July chairman Stafford Heginbotham spoke to the Basildon branch of Bradford City supporters club and his comments gave an early indication that relations between himself and his manager were strained. He complained that he had no information about new players and hoped, ironically, that the Basildon branch might let him know what was happening. He told them there was no one 'closer' than Willie Watson, who did not inform directors about new players until 'he wants a cheque or till he has rung the local paper'.

The 1967–68 season began with a sparkling display to beat Exeter 2-1. Despite the early exit from the League Cup at Hartlepool, Bradford City started the season well, two shrewd signings greatly strengthening the push for promotion. Pat Liney, a goalkeeper, was recruited from near neighbours Bradford Park Avenue and then Willie Watson strengthened his attack by pursuing Paul Aimson, whom Bury had bought for £10,000 when they were in the Second Division. Since they were relegated Bury were prepared to accept £8,000 for the young striker. However, the Bradford City Board said they only had £2,000 so Willie Watson went back to Bury, but they said they would not accept a penny under £6,000. So the resourceful Watson suggested a £2,000 down payment and the balance paid in instalments, to which Bury agreed. Aimson was soon on his way, although he did score 11 times in the 23 games he played.

During the Autumn of 1967 Bradford City's form was very encouraging and they were seldom out of the league's promotion places. However, it seemed that the more successful the team the more the bumptious Heginbotham had to interfere. Willie Watson had to make it clear to his chairman that he was only prepared to manage if he picked the side. When Bradford City reached top place, the Huddersfield manager, Tom Johnson, wanted to buy Paul Aimson but Watson rejected the offer of older reserve team players as payment. In November Willie Watson had a major row with his opinionated chairman. As he was on a three-month-notice contract, the manager said he would finish at the end of the season and would give his notice in February 1968.

Bradford City had a great first half to the season, winning 15 out of 25 games, losing only six. In January they were well placed for a promotion position, producing some thrilling attacking play, especially at Valley Parade. In February, Willie Watson sought to hand over his letter of resignation but the chairman was now anxious to retain him and offered a pay rise. Watson could not be persuaded to withdraw his notice so Heginbotham retaliated by insisting that he would bring in a new manager immediately. Consequently Watson picked up his belongings and walked out, secure in the knowledge that the club would have to pay him for the next three months.

The remainder of the season for Bradford City was a mixture of tragedy and foolishness. The man appointed to replace Watson was 36-year-old former Leeds United full back Grenville Hair, who had made 474 appearances for Leeds United. But sadly he died after only 46 days at Valley Parade. Once Watson was out of the way the club directors decided to sell Paul Aimson and a promising defender. This move weakened the squad and results in the spring of 1968 declined so that the club finished fifth, just out of the promotion places. Few supporters doubted that had Willie Watson remained at the club Bradford City would have moved up to Division Three. The experience of working with Stafford Heginbotham convinced Watson that football management was not for him and he needed to look elsewhere to make a living.

CHAPTER 29

A PLACE IN THE SUN

WILLIE WATSON'S CHANGE of direction was instigated after he'd attended an evening match at Oldham as part of his managerial duties. After the game he got talking to reporters, who suggested that the best prospects for him might lie in South Africa. In particular there were opportunities for coaching cricket, a welcome alternative to Fourth Division football at that stage in Watson's career. As soon as he was free to do so, Willie Watson decided to fly out to South Africa to see for himself. His destination was Johannesburg and the contact was the former South African Test cricketer Athol Rowan, who was involved in the cricket coaching at the public schools in the area. Willie Watson's first impressions were favourable, so he phoned his wife Barbara to ask her to join him and have a look for herself. However, the initial offer was for a coaching post in the summer and something 'suitable', but undisclosed, in the winter. This proposal was not acceptable to the Watsons, but while he was there Willie went to the Wanderers club in Johannesburg on a Sunday morning to give a talk.

The Watsons returned to England. but within days they received a letter from Douglas Roberts, the Wanderers chairman, asking if Willie Watson was interested in becoming their sports manager. This was a newly created post at the Wanderers Sports Club, which was a magnificent facility catering for 16 sports. In 1956 the Wanderers Stadium had replaced the Old Wanderers Stadium and it quickly became a favourite with cricket lovers thanks to its beauty and facilities. When South Africa were re-admitted into Test cricket in 1991 it was completely overhauled.

It proved a happy venue for its first Test visitors in 1956, Peter May's England, who won by 131 runs. Willie Watson accepted Roberts' job offer. From his family's point of view the move could not have been better timed; son Graham was 18 and had just finished school at St Peter's in York, and daughter Val was 11 and had recently completed junior school in Huddersfield.

Despite these advantages the move was a big step for the Watsons. First their house, called Laund Heath, was sold but the chicken farm of two-and-a-half acres had to be disposed of separately. The Watson's farm manager was willing to take over but did not have sufficient funds. Eventually a long period of repayment was agreed so that the manager could acquire the business. There was also the contents of the house, collected over more than 20 years of marriage, to be transported to the port and then loaded aboard a ship. They even took their car.

Next Willie Watson had to approach the Yorkshire cricket committee who had invested the proceeds of his benefit year in 1956. The policy had been adopted by the paternally minded committee to prevent cricketers from squandering the proceeds of their biggest source of income from cricket. However, in Willie Watson's circumstances the committee were prepared to release his money. At The Oval Test of 1968, the Watsons said their goodbyes to all their cricket friends and looked forward to seeing some of them in the winter when the MCC toured South Africa. That Test was to prove significant for South Africa. England beat Australia by 226 runs to share the series 1-1, with the recalled Basil D'Oliveira scoring a first innings 158.

Despite this D'Oliveira was left out of the original MCC party to tour South Africa – a decision seen by many as politically expedient. Then on September 16 1968 Tom Cartwright withdrew from the tour party because of injury, despite strenuous efforts to get him to change his mind. Doug Insole, the chairman of the selectors, had little choice but to name Basil D'Oliveira as Cartwright's replacement. The South African government saw the whole affair as a political plot to interfere with the internal laws of their country. The prime minister, John Vorster, made it clear that his government would not receive a team which included a 'Cape-Coloured' cricketer. On September 24 the MCC cancelled the tour which led to an international ban on tours of South Africa for more than 20 years. For the Watsons, settling into their new life, there would be no reunion with their cricket friends in 1968 after all.

The position at the Wanderers Club had been especially created for Willie Watson and involved both administration and coaching. Unfortunately there was already a general manager in post, Eric Reid, who maintained that he had not been informed of Willie Watson's appointment. Reid was not interested in sport, only catering, and certainly was not prepared to cooperate in any way with the newcomer. He also appeared to Willie Watson be two-faced because when Watson made suggestions or requests he was met with hostility, but when the same points were made by committee members Reid readily acceded.

However, there was a great deal to do at the Wanderers Club. The new sports manager introduced himself as Bill Watson and never mentioned his earlier career as a double international in England. He was in charge of all the grounds and all the groundstaff for a variety of sports from squash to bowls as well as cricket, tennis and hockey. There was a great deal of preparation and organisation to be done during the week and at the weekends all the fixtures and competitions took place. At this time the Wanderers Club was in its prime, with more than 20,000 members, and they were able to field 13 cricket teams. So for Willie Watson it was an exhausting schedule, especially as at 48 he had not stopped playing cricket. The Wanderers used to run two second XIs in the same league, one of which was a team of promising cricketers from schools in the Johannesburg area, and for two or three years Willie Watson captained and coached these talented youngsters.

Although official MCC tours to South Africa had come to a halt, there were still a lot of contacts from England. For example, in early 1969 RJ McAlpine captained a party from England for a three-and-a-half-week tour. It was not a very strong group; apart from Alan Moss and Bob Gale, they consisted of university blues and minor counties stalwarts. They played two games in Salisbury, now Harare, before reaching Johannesburg where they played five matches, including one against the Wanderers which they lost.

In 1972–73 Derrick Robins, a former Warwickshire player and wealthy businessman who was also chairman of Coventry City, organised a much stronger party – the DH Robins XI – to tour South Africa. It included several Test cricketers: Clive Radley, John Murray, Bob Willis, Jackie Hampshire and Peter Willey. They were captained by David Brown of Warwickshire and the manager was Jack Bannister. The tour lasted five-and-a-half weeks and culminated in a 'virtual' test and 'virtual' one-day international against an invitation section A XI. The South Africans, inspired by Barry Richards and Mike Procter, won both matches which were played in Johannesburg. Bannister had the chance to meet with Willie Watson again in Johannesburg and over the next 19 years Jack Bannister went back to South Africa 14 or 15 times and always found time to catch up with Willie Watson.

While Jackie Hampshire was touring in South Africa, he was going through a bad spell with the bat, so he approached Willie Watson to ask him to watch him batting in the nets. Watson readily agreed and at the end of the session Jackie asked what was wrong. Watson replied, 'Nothing, you are just having an unlucky patch but you will be OK.' In fact he was soon back to top form.

Another early visitor for the Watsons was Dickie Bird. He had retired from playing first-class cricket in 1964, something Watson had advised him to do. Dickie had made rapid progress as a coach, and in January 1966 was presented with the advanced coaching certificate. Only about 350 coaches in the world had this qualification, and it gave Dickie the chance to work in South Africa. Before the Watsons emigrated, Bird had already joined Don Wilson and Phil Sharpe coaching in Johannesburg during the English winter. Over the next ten years Dickie returned regularly to South Africa to coach in Johannesburg and also in the black township of Soweto. All this, of course, before he took up his more famous career as a Test match umpire.

In 1973–74 Derrick Robins returned for a second tour. This time he recruited a stronger party. Captained by Brian Close, it included John Edrich, Bob Woolmer and John Snow. More significantly the visitors included Younis Ahmed, of Pakistan and Surrey, and John Shepherd, of the West Indies and Kent. The inclusion of these two was seen as a major breakthrough in sporting relationships in South Africa. Further history was created when Derrick Robins' team played against an African XI in Soweto. The tour party played three times in Johannesburg, first against Transvaal, a victory by eight wickets, and a second against a South African Invitation 'Test' XI, defeat by an innings and 83 runs. The third match was the final one of the tour, a limited overs game, again against the Invitation XI, whom they beat by three runs. So Willie and Barbara had the chance to catch up with the news from England. By this time Willie had retired from the Wanderers second XI and moved into social cricket on Sundays with some of the older players like John Waite, one of South Africa's greatest wicketkeeper/batsmen.

Derrick Robins returned for a third tour of South Africa in 1974–75. Close was again the captain, but in spite of including Clive Radley, Jackie Hampshire and Frank Hayes, they did not win a single first-class match. Again the party included West Indians, a Pakistani and a Sri Lankan to test the South African authorities' attitude to sport between white and non-white players. Only one of the eight games was played in Johannesburg, against Transvaal, which was drawn.

By 1975 Willie Watson was exhausted by his seven days a week commitment to the Wanderers Club. The chance to change careers came from a Hull-based engineering company, Fenners. They had been established in the East Riding by Joseph Henry Fenner in 1861. Willie Watson had first come across the firm when he played for Yorkshire and Fenners sponsored the Scarborough cricket festival. The chairman of the company was Sydney Wainsworth, an enthusiastic member of the Yorkshire committee. It was not a surprise when Fenners offered Len Hutton a directorship. Willie Watson knew Wainsworth quite well and of course Len and Dorothy Hutton were long-term friends.

When the Watsons moved to Johannesburg they found that Fenners had established a company in the area. It was this branch of the company, run by managing director Tony Clegg, which offered Willie Watson the chance of employment as an alternative to the Wanderers club. From time to time Len Hutton's responsibilities brought him to South Africa, accompanied by his wife. They were often entertained by the Watsons.

Willie Watson once again introduced himself to his colleagues as Bill, and his achievements as a sportsman in England were unknown at Fenners in Johannesburg. He began on the shop floor and was involved in time study, stores, transport and eventually managed the manufacture of conveyor belts. However, he retained his cricket links by coaching after work and sometimes watching at weekends. In 1976, at the age of 56, he played for one of the Wanderers' teams and his 20-year-old team-mates could not believe how rapidly he covered the ground from cover-point.

A regular visitor from England was former Leicestershire colleague and fellow Yorkshireman, Jack Birkenshaw. He had first toured South Africa in the early seventies with an amateur club and took the opportunity to meet up again with Willie Watson. It was a highlight of Jack Birkenshaw's visits, because he believed he could learn more from Watson than from any coaching manual. He said that when Willie spoke you listened because he was able to simplify and clarify cricket coaching, especially for batsmen. They might also enjoy a gin and tonic together, and when the Watsons returned to England every two or three years, one place they stopped at was the home of Jack and Gloria Birkenshaw in Leicester.

A couple of years after Willie Watson started work at Fenners, he was walking round the factory during one of the break times. As he walked past one group of workers he noticed that one of them was reading a pink sports paper, which made him stop because he had recognised the *Sunderland Echo* sports edition. He turned to the man and began to recount the Sunderland team of his day: 'Mapson, Stelling, Hudgell, Watson... Hall!'

'You bugger!' the man exclaimed. 'I've known you all this time and you never said you were Willie Watson. One of my heroes.'

Another regular contact in the early years was Ken Taylor, another old Yorkshire team-mate and former Huddersfield Town footballer. Taylor had retired from first-class cricket at the end of the 1968 season, and in January 1969 moved with his wife to Cape Town to take up a coaching and teaching post. After a year, the Taylors moved to a new teaching post in Pretoria, much closer to Johannesburg, so there were a lot more opportunities to meet up with Willie and Barbara Watson. However, after a few years, Ken Taylor was offered a teaching appointment in Norfolk, so he and his family returned to England.

In 1975–76 Derrick Robins made his fourth visit to South Africa in successive years. The tour was overshadowed by the Angolan War and by the internal politics of South African cricket. The three bodies governing white, black and coloured cricket in the county merged into one, but teething troubles prevented a selected 'mixed' team from playing against the tourists. The tourists were captained by former England manager David Lloyd, of Lancashire, and managed by Ken Barrington, of England and Surrey. The party included Derek Randall, David Steele, Phil Carrick and the least well-known of Australia's Chappell brothers, Trevor. They played two matches in Johannesburg, including a victory over Transvaal. However, this proved to be the last of Derrick Robins' tours because the Commonwealth Heads of Government were moving to challenge South Africa's apartheid regime. In 1977 they met for their bi-annual meeting at Gleneagles in Scotland, where the members of the Commonwealth unanimously agreed to isolate South Africa from international sport by discouraging any contacts or competitions with that regime. It was known as the Gleneagles Agreement, and its timing was influenced by the need to prevent a boycott of the forthcoming Commonwealth Games in Canada.

Prior to these developments, the Watsons continued to host visitors from England. While they were overwhelmingly cricketing colleagues, there was also a representative from soccer. The second Knight of the Realm to call was Sir Stanley Matthews. Willie Watson had played against Stan Matthews several times and they had both been part of the England squad for the World Cup finals in Rio in 1950. Sir Stan had been coaching young boys and girls in various townships including Soweto, and from 1956 he returned almost every year to South Africa for a period of 25 years.

Every two or three years Willie and Barbara Watson returned to England for a holiday, usually to coincide with the Lord's and Headingley Tests. Their old friend Alec Bedser sometimes met them at Heathrow Airport. Twenty years earlier the twins, Alec and Eric Bedser, had stayed the night in Sunderland with the Watsons after attending a function in Newcastle. Young Graham Watson could not understand how two people could look so alike. From London the visitors headed north; usually the first stopover was at Tarporley, Cheshire, where Barbara had a cousin. The next move was to Yorkshire to visit Huddersfield and Bradford, and then north east to Sunderland to visit brother Albert and niece Shirley. The 1980 visit to England was organised to coincide with the centenary Test between England and Australia at Lord's. The game was marred by heavy rain and crowd trouble. Umpires Dickie Bird and David Constant were unfairly targeted because of long delays before play could be resumed.

However, because the fixture was such a historic occasion, the MCC invited all the great cricketers who had played in the Tests between the two countries to attend the match at Lord's. They accommodated all those who had to travel from abroad in a hotel, and hired a coach to take them to and from the game. This meant that the Watsons were staying mainly with Australians, although once at Lord's they had the chance to meet up with many of Willie's old English team-mates.

Once the early controversy and frustration had subsided, the centenary Test produced some fine cricket, including centuries by Kim Hughes and Graeme Wood for Australia, and Geoff Boycott for England. Both teams contained a number of outstanding cricketers. As well as Boycott, England fielded Graham Gooch, David Gower, Mike Gatting, Ian Botham and John Emburey, while the Australian team included Greg Chappell, Alan Border, Rodney Marsh and Dennis Lillee. At the close of the final day the match was drawn.

In the winter of 1981–82 the MCC toured India and Sri Lanka. On their return home the England party landed at Gatwick in February 1982. A few days later 12 of the England cricketers arrived in Johannesburg and the news of an unofficial tour of South Africa hit the headlines. The party, led by Graham Gooch, was very strong, including Geoff Boycott, Derek Underwood, Denis Amiss and Bob Woolmer. The tourists played an unofficial 'Test' against South Africa at Johannesburg, which they lost, but the cricket was overshadowed by the hostile reaction to the tour back in England. Prior to the third unofficial 'Test', the TCCB (Test and County Cricket Board) announced that the touring English players would be banned from Test cricket for three years. So South Africa's sporting isolation was reinforced despite attempts by the cricketing authorities in the country to break down the rigid divisions of the government's apartheid policy. Thus the Watsons' visitors from England would be mainly confined to individuals who coached or played in South Africa, like Woolmer and Arnie Sidebottom, of Yorkshire. Willie Watson did play his last game of cricket, at the age of 61, just before these events, against a team led by Geoff Pullar, the Lancashire and England opener.

In 1985 the Northern Transvaal cricket team playing in Pretoria were coached by John Reid, the former New Zealand captain. Willie Watson and John Reid were long-standing friends since they first met at Leicester in the late 1950s. Halfway through the South African season Willie Watson received a call to let him know that Reid had been offered an important post in New Zealand cricket. The proposal that came out of Reid's dilemma was that Watson should step into Reid's role and complete the season with Northern Transvaal for him. By this time Watson had taken on a part-time post at Fenners so that he was free in the afternoons. He therefore agreed to take over the coaching job at Pretoria and successfully completed the season. In 1986 the Northern Transvaal club were just completing a new stadium just outside Pretoria. The Centurion ground replaced Berea Park to become South Africa's latest Test-standard venue. Willie Watson carried on with Northern Transvaal for another season before retiring to make way for a younger man.

Although cricketing contacts with South Africa had become increasingly restricted, Willie Watson knew he had not been forgotten, because in 1986 the Yorkshire County Cricket Committee announced that he would be made an honorary life member. It would be another five years before South Africa's sporting isolation was ended but during that time momentous change was taking place in South Africa. On February 11 1990, Nelson Mandela was released from his prison on Robben Island and negotiations to abandon apartheid began.

At a meeting of the ICC (International Cricket Council) at Lord's in July 1991, South Africa were re-admitted to Test cricket, and in November they played their first international in Calcutta. Much of the credit for this return to the ICC is due to Dr Ali Bacher and his dedicated cricket administrators in South Africa.

This meant that the traditional contacts with English cricketers could resume, which meant the Watsons were able to meet up with Fred Trueman, Peter Richardson and Micky Stewart in Johannesburg. They were also in touch with Tom and Jackie Graveney, whom they had first met in Scarborough in the late 1940s at the cricket festival where they were spending their honeymoon. In 1993–94 the Australians toured South Africa again, which gave Willie Watson the opportunity to meet one of his opponents from the famous Lord's Test of 1953, Richie Benaud. Ten years later, 50 years after the Ashes struggle of 1953, they met again when South Africa hosted the World Cup.

In 2000 Willie Watson celebrated his 80th birthday on March 7, and with Barbara he attended the fifth Test against England at the Super Sport Park in Centurion. They were guests of Richard Harrison, the President of the Northern Cricket Union. The weather ruined three days' cricket, so there was plenty of time to reminisce about the game from an earlier age. Tom Graveney recalled his partnership with Willie Watson against Guyana in 1953–54 when they put on 401 together. The score was 51-3 when they came together, but both went on to make double centuries. Mickey and Shelia Stewart were also at the Centurion, and Mickey recalled fielding at short leg when Watson was batting and hearing him say to himself 'Wait, wait, wait' as the bowler ran up. Willie explained that Maurice Leyland had advised him to wait and not to reach for the ball. Also among the President's guests was former Essex captain and England Test selector Doug Insole. He had been top of the England batting averages when they toured South Africa in 1956–57.

It was around this time that another reunion took place, because the Tests now being regularly played in South Africa needed a match referee. Twice the man appointed for the Johannesburg Test was Raman Subba Row, the former Northants skipper and England Test cricketer. Watson and Subba Row had toured Australia and New Zealand in the MCC party of 1958-59, where they were teammates for five months. When he visited the Watsons' home on the edge of Johannesburg he was perturbed by the level of security the houses needed. Clearly crime could be a problem.

During the summer of 2003, Willie and Barbara Watson, together with Trevor Bailey and his wife, were entertained by the President of the MCC during the Lord's Test against South Africa. The host was Sir Tim Rice, the highly successful lyricist and former musical partner of Andrew Lloyd Webber. Sir Tim was a long-standing cricket enthusiast who had formed his own cricket club, Heartaches CC in 1973. The inspiration for this reunion was the 50th anniversary of the legendary match-saving stand by Watson and Bailey against the Australians at Lord's. Sir Tim presented both players with a copy of his brother Jonathan's book *One Hundred Lord's Tests*. Trevor Bailey has described it as a delightful occasion. Unfortunately it proved to be the last time the two old friends would meet, because Willie Watson did not return again to England.

But with Barbara he did complete his customary tour of the old country. When they reached Huddersfield they stayed with an old friend of Barbara's whose home was in the district of Almondbury. Here it was arranged that they would meet up with another, Ken Taylor and his wife. The photographs taken by Ken have become important mementos in Barbara's Johannesburg home. After their visit the Taylors left for a holiday in Scotland, while the Watsons headed for the north east. This was to prove the last reunion with

Willie Watson's family in Sunderland. It was also a chance to see the new Stadium of Light, which had recently replaced the more familiar Roker Park.

The Watsons returned home to South Africa, but it was not long before Willie Watson's health declined. He died in Johannesburg, on April 24 2004. Willie and Barbara had been married for 59-and-a-half years. As well as his widow, Willie Watson left a son, Graham, and a daughter, Val, both of whom have done very well in South Africa.

CHAPTER 30

SILENT WILL

THERE IS COMPLETE agreement among Willie Watson's cricket friends and colleagues that he was a quiet man, a shy man and a modest man. Both Peter Richardson and Jack Birkenshaw drew attention to his nickname 'Silent Will'. At the same time, many people described him as a lovely man and charming once the shyness had been overcome. Trevor Bailey thought him delightful and a great companion, a view that was entirely supported by Dickie Bird and Ken Taylor. Several former players like Jack Bannister and Raman Subba Row recalled a dry sense of humour, while Bob Appleyard remembered a private man who was highly respected throughout the game. Fred Trueman described him as a smart and handsome professional, while Mike Brearley recalled film star good looks.

Commentators and journalists wondered if this unassuming and undemonstrative personality had limited Watson's ambition and consequently his achievements. But there were other factors which may have been equally influential on his career, such as the six critical years lost to the war, seeking to play professionally two major sports during the year, and not being given a regular top four place in the Yorkshire batting order. In any case, it could be argued that his 23 Tests and four football caps make him the greatest of England's 'double internationals'. Not a bad career really!

In addition to the tributes and accolades from his contemporaries, it is possible to describe three sporting incidents which illustrate the qualities of Willie Watson. Each event is described by a player who was involved.

PETER WALKER (Glamorgan and England all-rounder and specialist short-leg fieldsman)

'We were playing at Grace Road in the late 1950s and Leicestershire were captained by Willie Watson. I was fielding at short square in a match we looked like winning, when Willie clipped a ball off his legs low to me in my position. I scooped it up and, as was the custom in those days, Willie asked me if I'd caught. When I said yes, without reference to the umpire or taking into account the state of the game he turned and made off towards the pavilion.

'He'd gone a short distance back when several of my team-mates fielding on the off side in the slip area called out 'Peter, you caught that ball on the half volley, it never carried.' I was absolutely mortified at this – although I came to realise as my career continued that very often the last person to know if the ball had carried on the full is the catcher!

'Willie had heard this and stopped for a moment and looked back. I put my hands up in the air by way of an apology, but he said in his quiet way "if you think you caught it young man, that's good enough for me", and continued his walk to the pavilion.

'A good man was Willie Watson – I'm afraid there are fewer of his kind in today's game.'

ROY BOOTH (kept wicket for Yorkshire in the early 1950s before enjoying a successful career with Worcestershire from 1956)

'I remember a game against Lancashire at Old Trafford. It was a Roses match and Willie Watson was acting captain of Yorkshire because Norman Yardley was not available. It was Lancashire's innings and the England batsman, John Ikin, was at the wicket. He played a shot which gave a chance to a Yorkshire fielder. John Ikin asked the fielder if he had caught it, who replied that he had caught the ball. So John Ikin started to walk back to the pavilion. But before he had gone far Willie Watson called him back saying, "I had a good view of that and the ball did not carry."

'So Ikin returned to the crease to continue his innings. This was a very sporting intervention by Willie which many would not have dared to do, especially in the context of a Roses match.'

BRYAN STOTT (left-handed opening batsman for Yorkshire between 1952 and 1963, but he did not establish a regular place until 1957)

'I had found Willie Watson to be a beautifully balanced and elegant batsman, and as nice a chap as you could wish to meet. I was always having to bat for Yorkshire with Freddie Trueman's roughed-up follow through outside my off stump. One day at Sheffield Willie took Ken Taylor and I to the nets. "Come on Brian, I'll show you what to do," he said. He roughed up the patch and got Ken to bowl me leg spinners. He showed me how he used to sweep the ball from an upright position, with his bat almost vertical. Here was I, a new player, threatening to take his position in the team and he was prepared to show me how to play. There were others in the Yorkshire team who wouldn't have done that.'

There is a similar picture to be found in the comments made about Willie Watson the footballer. His Sunderland team-mate Ivor Broadis referred to 'that delightfully elegant player Willie Watson'. Trevor Bailey said that Willie was 'a superb natural athlete and ball player who glided over the football pitch with grace and pace'. Brian Glanville, who wrote Watson's obituary in the *Guardian*, said that Willie was elegant and effective enough to win back an England place in his new position of wing half. He was also well regarded enough to displace the legendary Billy Wright from the England team for two games. Ted Lester, Willie Watson's Yorkshire team-mate, was once at Roker Park to watch the international against Wales. He remembers Willie's ball skills and passing ability, but emphasises that he never became involved in rough or foul play. The Sunderland AFC. (Archive Photo Services) noted that Willie Watson 'was a stylish footballer who could play in a variety of positions and who was one of the game's gentleman'.

Dickie Bird summed up the man by recalling that in 274 peacetime matches and more than 130 wartime matches, Willie Watson was never spoken to, cautioned or sent off by the referee.

STATISTICS

A brief overview of Willie Watson's playing career

Test Career Batting and Fielding (1951–1958/59)

	M	I	NO	Runs	HS	Ave	100	50	Ct
Engl	23	37	3	879	116	25.85	2	3	8

First-Class Career Batting and Fielding (1939-64)

	M	I	NO	Runs	HS	Ave	100	50	Ct
Overall	468	753	109	25,670	257	39.86	55	132	295

Bowling

	M	I	NO	Runs	HS	Ave
Overall	194	4	127	0		0-1

Football
Internationals
v Northern Ireland won 9-2 at Maine Road Nov 16 1949
v Italy 2-0 at White Hart Lane Nov 30 1949
v Wales won 4-2 at Roker Park Oct 7 1950
v Yugoslavia drew 2-2 Highbury Nov 22 1950

Club
11 games no goals for Huddersfield Town 1938–39
223 games 17 goals for Sunderland 1946–54
33 games 1 goal Halifax Town player manager 1954-56

Index

Index

Index

Index

Index

Parkhouse, Gilbert 77, 170
Parks, Jim 118, 176, 177, 179, 180, 182, 199-200
Pearson, Stan 48, 53, 58
Platt, Bob 145
Port of Spain 115
Portsmuth (cricket ground) 67, 186
Portsmouth FC 16, 42, 45, 52, 54-55, 57-58, 85, 90-91, 108
Portugal 60
Port Vale 211
Potter, Cecil 9
Pratt, Rodney 172, 196
Preston North End 7, 16, 52, 68, 90, 92, 109
Prideaux, Roger 176, 177, 179
Pritchard, Tom 74
Procter, Mike 218
Pullar, Geoff 191, 193, 198, 223
Purdon, Ted 117-18
Pye, Jesse 25, 55

Queensland 158
Queens Park Rangers 50
Quigley, Eddie 68

Racing Club de Paris 109
Radley, Clive 218-19
Rae, Allan 141
Ramadhin, Sonny 112, 113-15, 135, 197
Ramsey, Alf (Sir) 55, 57, 69, 85, 206-07, 209
Randall, Derek 221
Red Star Belgrade 76, 77
Reid, John 178-79, 223
Reid, Eric 217
Reynolds, Tommy 43, 52
Rhodesia 196
Rhodes, Wilfred 110
Richards, Barry 218
Richardson, Peter 134, 153, 159-63, 168-69, 200, 224, 227
Ring, Doug 97, 99
Robbins, Walter 188, 190-93, 205, 221
Robertson, Jack 75
Roberts, Ron 196-98
Roberts, Douglas 215, 216
Robins, Derrick (DH Robins XI) 201, 218-19, 221
Robinson, Ellis 31
Robinson, Jackie 41, 44-45, 51
Rochdale 207, 212
Roker Park 34, 40-42, 44, 45-46, 48, 52-53, 55, 57, 67-69, 71-72, 77, 80, 82, 84-85, 89-91, 107-09, 117-18, 124, 226, 229, 230
Rorke, Gordon 161
Rous, Stanley (Sir) 55
Rowan, Athol 80, 215

Index